Economy, Gender and Academy

Economy, Gender and Academy: A Pending Conversation

EDITED BY

MARIO ENRIQUE VARGAS SÁENZ
Eafit University, Colombia

LAURA ANDREA CRISTANCHO GIRALDO
Institución Universitaria Politécnico Grancolombiano, Colombia

MARISOL SALAMANCA OLMOS
Institución Universitaria Politécnico Grancolombiano, Colombia

AND

GLORIA NANCY RIOS YEPES
Institución Universitaria Politécnico Grancolombiano, Colombia

United Kingdom – North America – Japan – India – Malaysia – China

Emerald Publishing Limited
Howard House, Wagon Lane, Bingley BD16 1WA, UK

First edition 2023

Reprints and permissions service
Contact: www.copyright.com

British Library Cataloguing in Publication Data
A catalogue record for this book is available from the British Library

ISBN: 978-1-80455-999-4 (Print)
ISBN: 978-1-80455-998-7 (Online)
ISBN: 978-1-83753-000-7 (Epub)

Printed and bound by CPI Group (UK) Ltd, Croydon, CR0 4YY

INVESTOR IN PEOPLE

This book is dedicated to all women who play different roles, from academia, research, science, housewives, professionals, entrepreneurs and in the workplace, who every day seek for their work to be visible and recognized, in order to achieve better opportunities, greater equity and general well-being. We hope this is a call to all stakeholders to continue promoting the development of policies and guidelines that can make it possible to achieve these initiatives to achieve more just and egalitarian societies.

Contents

List of Figures and Tables

Figures

Tables

List of Abbreviations

Chapter 1

INEGI	National Institute of Statistics, Geography and Informatics (Mexico)
SEP	Ministry of Public Education (Mexico)

Chapter 2

ECLAC	The Economic Commission for Latin America and the Caribbean
OAS	Organization of American States
UN	United Nations
UNODC	The United Nations Office on Drugs and Crime

Chapter 3

ACEGI	Inclusive Management Educational Civil Association of Argentina
ACNUR	United Nations Refugee Agency
BM	World Bank
ENPOVE	Survey of the Venezuelan population
EPA	Self-Managed Public Schools
ESIAL	Higher Education and Indigenous and Afro-descendant Peoples of Latin America
GRANMAV	Great Woman love and value yourself
GrET	Work Studies Group
IFAD	Distance Learning Institute
INEI	National Institute of Statistics and Informatics
NNA	Children, Girls, and Adolescents
ODS	Sustainable Development Goals
OIT	International Labor Organization
ONG	Non-Governmental Organization
UNESCO	United Nations Organization for Education, Science, and Culture
UNICEF	United Nations Children's Fund
UNFPA	United Nations Population Fund

Chapter 4

SIES   Servicio de Información de Educación Superior
CONFECH Confederación de Estudiantes de Chile

Chapter 5

CAN   Andean Community of Nations
SAI   Andean Integration System
WHO   World Health Organization
CONPES   National Economic and Social Policy Council
INEC   Ecuadorian Institute of Statistics and Census
SNIG   National System of Gender Indicators
CEDAW   Convention on the Elimination of All Forms of Discrimination
          against Women
SDGs   Sustainable Development Goals
ILO   International Labor Organization

Chapter 6

IDH   Human Development Index
ONU   United Nations Organization
UNICEF   United Nations International Children's Emergency Fund
PIB   Producto Interno Bruto
BM   World Bank

Chapter 7

CDMX   Ciudad de México
IMCO   Instituto Mexicano para la Competitividad
ECLAC   Economic Commission for Latin America and the Caribbean
COVID-19 Coronavirus-19
D.W.   Deutsche Welle
IMCO   Mexican Institute for Competitiveness
MYT   Museum Memory and Tolerance

Chapter 8

UNESCO   United Nations Educational, Scientific and Cultural Organization
ITC   Information Technology and Communications
IES   Higher Education Institutions
WEF   World Economic Forum
SITEAL   Latin American Education Trends Informations System
STEM   Science, Technology, Engineering and Mathematics

ODS	Sustainable Development Objectives
UNAD	University Nacional Abierta y a Distancia
EAFIT	Escuela de Administración y Finanzas e Instituto Tecnológico
UNAB	University Autónoma de Bucaramanga
ONU	United Nations Organization
OXFAM	Oxford Committee of Aid Against Hunger (Oxford Committee for Famine Relief)
EAN	University EAN – Escuela de Administración de Negocios
IPG	Gender Empowerment Index
CIDESCO	Corporación para la Integración y Desarrollo de La Educación Superior en el Suroccidente Colombiano
IESALC	UNESCO International Institute for Higher Education in Latin America

Chapter 9

SDG	Sustainable Development Goals
DANE	Departamento Nacional de Estadística
IMF	International Monetary Fund
CEDAW	Convention on the Elimination of all Forms of Discrimination against Women
GEIH	Gran Encuesta Integrada de Hogares
ILO	International Labor Organization
ECLAC	Economic Commission for Latin America and the Caribbean
IBD	Inter-American Development Bank
PET	Población en Edad de Trabajar
UDCW	Unpaid Domestic and Care Work
ONU	Organización de Naciones Unidas
TDCNR	Trabajo Doméstico y de Cuidados No Remunerado
TDCNR	Unpaid Domestic and Care Work
GDP	Gross Domestic Product
NTUS	National Survey of Time Use
SCN	Sistema de Cuentas Nacionales
PNUD	Programa de las Naciones Unidad para el Desarrollo
IMF	International Monetary Fund

About the Authors

Marcela Mandiola Cotroneo She holds a degree in Psychology from Diego Portales University Chile, also M.A. and Ph.D. in Management Learning from Lancaster University England. She is part of HechoenGénero collective devoted to research, teaching and consulting in critical gender studies on education and organizations. Currently she leads the Critical Management & Organizational Thought Area at 17, Instituto de Estudios Críticos México. She is also Associate Researcher of the Program of Studies in Gender and Sexual Diversity, GEDIS Universidad Alberto Hurtado, Chile. Her research interests articulate Gender and Organizational Studies from a critical and decolonial understanding. She actively participates in academic networks, the MINGA Chile Organizational Studies Network, the Latin American Organizational Studies Network, Reol and Decolonial Alliance.

Nolbis Espinosa Cruz holds a degree in English as a Foreign Language Education from the José de la Luz y Caballero Holguín Pedagogical Sciences University in Cuba. Currently, he is a Teacher at the International St. George's College and a Collaborator with the International School Partnership (ISP). He is a Specialist in Educational Psychology with a focus on special educational needs and a Specialist in Project-Based Learning. He has participated in research on learning, resulting in publications in journals such as Antesala, Peru, and contributions to books.

Olga Adriana Domínguez is President of the Civil Educational Association for Inclusive Management. She obtained bachelor's degree in Educational Technologies; Specialist in Management and Administration in Educational Centers; and Specialist in Editorial Design for the Development of Didactic Materials.

Aleosha Eridani He holds a degree in Psychology and a M.A. in Philosophy from Catholic University of Valparaíso, Chile, and a Doctorate (c) in Interdisciplinary Studies on Thought, Culture and Society from University of Valparaíso, Chile. He is part of HechoenGénero, collective devoted to research, teaching and consulting in critical gender studies on education and organizations. Also, he facilitates socio-educational workshops from a gender perspective, around issues such as gender, men and masculinities; and he works with the theatre of the oppressed, performing in forum-theatre plays in various social and educational contexts.

Laura Andrea Cristancho Giraldo is an Economist from the Pontifical Javeriana University, Colombia. He has a Master's degree in Economics and a PhD in Analysis of Social Problems from UNED in Madrid, Spain. She is currently a University Professor at the Business, Management and Sustainability School of the Grancolombiano Polytechnic in Bogotá, where she is currently the Coordinator of the Economics Program. Her research interests include gender policies, the care economy, the labor market, and working conditions in decent work conditions. She has experience in the public sector in entities such as the National Administrative Department of Statistics of Colombia DANE and the Secretary of Education in the city of Bogotá. He has published/edited five books, participated in some book chapters, and has published articles in refereed journals.

Nicola Rios González (he/him) is a gender and sexuality studies scholar from Chile. He holds a Doctorate (c) in Education and Society from University of Barcelona, an M.A. in Educational Research from the same University, and a degree in Psychology from Catholic University of Valparaíso (Chile). Since 2010 he has worked as an advocate for critical sex education and erotic justice for several institutions and organizations. He is part of HechoenGénero, a collective devoted to research, teaching and consulting in critical gender studies on education and organizations. As an activist and promiscuous researcher, his areas of interest includes gender and sexuality education, cultural pedagogies, higher education, and critical sexuality studies.

Magdaloys Peña Gutiérrez obtained Bachelor's degree in Sociology. Currently serving as a UN Volunteer at IOM Peru with experience in humanitarian work, particularly with refugees and migrants. In the past five years, focused on the study and work of the Venezuelan migrant population in Peru. He is the Founder of the "Se hace camino al Andar" Association in Lima, Peru. Has been published in national and international journals.

Marybexy Calcerrada Gutiérrez is a Professor at the Center for Cultural and Identity Studies at the University of Holguín and holds a degree in Psychology, a Master's degree in Gender Studies, and a PhD in Philosophy. She has been involved in research that studies the composition of higher education in Cuba from an intersectional perspective. She is a Social Sciences Advisor in her area and for the government in the area of social care. She is the Coordinator of the Cuba Team in the Second and Third Campaign against Racism in Higher Education in Latin America at the UNESCO Chair on Higher Education and Indigenous and Afro-Descendant Peoples in Latin America at the National University of Tres de Febrero. She has participated in and directed psychosocial and cultural projects, which have led to publications in international journals and book chapters in national and international publishers.

José Baltazar García Horta has a first degree in Psychology from the National Autonomous University (UNAM), Mexico. He has a Master's degree in International Education Management (MEd) and a PhD in Education, both from the

University of Leeds, UK. He is currently a University Professor at the Faculty of Social Work and Human Development, Autonomous University of Nuevo Leon (Mex). His research interests have to do with educational policies, implementation of governmental initiatives, teachers' working conditions, gender, and equity in education. He is a Member of the National System of Researchers Level 1. He has carried out an Academic Visit to the University of Salamanca in Spain and has been a Visiting Scholar at the University of British Columbia in Canada. He has graduated students from master's programs as well as PhD students. He has published/edited five books, has participated in some book chapters, and has published articles in peer-reviewed journals.

Rafael Lorenzo Martín is a Teacher–Researcher with a Bachelor's degree in Education, specializing in Mathematics-Computing (1997), a Diploma in Science Didactics (2001), a PhD in Pedagogical Sciences (2009), a postdoctoral in Education Sciences (2010), and a Full Professor of Higher Education in the Republic of Cuba (2012). He is an Arbitrator for various scientific journals in Colombia and Argentina. He is a Member of the Consulting Staff of the GT-CLACSO: Territories, Spiritualities, and Bodies, based at the Doctorate in Social Studies at the Francisco José de Caldas University District of Colombia (www.udistrital. edu.co). He is a Member of the Latin American and Caribbean Teacher Network RedDOLAC. He is also a Member of projects at the UNESCO Chair on Higher Education and Indigenous and Afro-Descendant Peoples in Latin America at the National University of Tres de Febrero (UNTREF-Argentina https://www. untref.edu.ar/). He is the Vice President of the Inclusive Educational Management Civil Association based in San Luis-Argentina (https://acegi.guiadidactica. net/) and a Member of the Sustainable Educational Civil Association based in San Luis-Argentina.

Diana Mercedes Valdés Mosquera is Professional in International Business, Specialist in Virtual Tools for Education, Master in Public Administration Management, Master in Business Administration (MBA), Master in Commercial and Marketing Management, and Research Professor at the School of Business and International Development of the Politécnico Grancolombiano focused on the study of Business Internationalization.

Marisol Salamanca Olmos obtained Master in Business Management and Administration from UNIR Spain. She is Specialist in Financial Management and Administration from Universidad Piloto de Colombia, Economist from Universidad Pedagógica y Tecnológica de Colombia, and Professor at the Faculty of Business, Management and Sustainability, Institución Universitaria Politécnico Grancolombiano. Her research interests include gender and labor market policies.

Daniela Rivera Ortega obtained Master's student in Interdisciplinary Social Research at the Francisco José de Caldas District University and Professional in Business and International Relations at La Salle University. She worked as a Teacher at the San José Higher Education Foundation and as an Academic

Assistant at Semillero In-Vestigium. She is currently a Researcher in the Representation, Discourse and Power research group at the Francisco José de Caldas District University.

María Teresa Guerra Ramos is a researcher in Science Education at Centro de Investigación y de Estudios Avanzados, Unidad Monterrey, México (CIN-VESTAV). She studied Psychology at the National Autonomous University of Mexico (UNAM), an MEd in Science Education and a PhD at the University of Leeds, UK. She worked at the Ministry of Education in Mexico for several years and was involved in the elaboration and classroom trials of textbooks and teacher manuals for primary science education. Her research interests are focused on teachers' representations of scientists and scientific activity, the development of science teaching competencies, features of discourse in science teaching–learning interactions and collaboration among teachers and researchers for pedagogical innovation. She is a Member of the National System of Researchers Level 1. She is currently a Visiting Scholar at the University of British Columbia, Vancouver, Canada.

July Alexandra Villalba Rodriguez is Professional in International Business, Master in Innovation Management, and PhD student in Complex Thinking. She is a Director and Researcher of the Finance and International Business program at the Fundación Universitaria del Area Andina, and also a Business Consultant focused on promoting the development of agricultural productive projects.

Mario Enrique Vargas Saénz is Philosopher and Industrial Relations Specialist. He obtained Master in Administration from EAFIT University; Advanced the International Senior Management program with the Universities EAFIT – ESADE –ICESI; and Doctor in Philosophy – Magna cum laude – from the UPS of Rome. He is Director of EAFIT University for more than 14 years. Currently in charge of EAFIT Social and is also in charge of the GUIE, Research Group on Innovation and Entrepreneurship. He also Coordinates the Master in Management of Social Enterprises for Social Innovation and Local Development. With more than 25 years of experience in university teaching at national and international level, he has been a Consultant to companies and has provided his services to international organizations such as UN Habitat and the OECD.

Alejandra Elizabeth Urbiola Solís is Researcher specialized in Economic Anthropology, Gender Studies and Migrations. Member of the Autonomous University of Querétaro since August 2007, Faculty of Accounting and Administration as a Professor–Researcher. She is a Member of the National System of Researchers (SNI) Level 1. Her professional objective with the institution of membership is to collaborate as a professor–researcher in the areas of education, research, tutoring, and community outreach.

Jaime Andrés Wilches Tinjacá is Doctor Cum Laude in Communication from the Pompeu Fabra University of Barcelona, Master's in Political Studies from the National University of Colombia, Social Communicator and Journalist from the Central University. Political Scientist Degree of Honor from the National University of Colombia. Research Coordinator and Professor of the Faculty of Business, Management and Sustainability, Institución Universitaria Politécnico Grancolombiano, and Professor of the Master's Degree in Interdisciplinary Social Research at the Francisco José de Caldas District University, Colciencias Junior Researcher.

Laura Velez, Human Rights Campaign Awardee, obtained degree in Communication Sciences specialized in audiovisual production and PhD in Political and Social Sciences. She is Deputy Director of Interinstitutional Liaison in the Ministry of Culture of Mexico, Funds raiser, and currently Research Coordinator in temporary exhibitions of the Museum Memory and Tolerance.

Gloria Nancy Ríos Yepes, Economist from the University of Manizales, Colombia and Management Specialist, obtained Master in Human Resources Management. She is Professor of Economics Program, School of Business and International Development, Gran Colombian Polytechnic, Medellin Colombia. Her research interests include gender equity issues and alternatives to combat poverty within the framework of the Sustainable Development Goals.

Foreword

Presentation
Our organizations, reproducers of a normalized inequity

Angel Wilhelm Vázquez García
Economic Production Department,
Universidad Autónoma Metropolitana, Unidad Xochimilco
Ciudad de México, México

Money, its a crime. share it fairly but dont take,
a slice of my pie. Money, so they say,
is the root of all evil today.
but if you ask for a raise its no surprise
that they are giving none away"
Money, Roger Waters

Understanding the behavior of modern organizations from the perspective of gender and economics acquires different nuances depending on their geospatial location. This is due to the importance of the place where its members travel. Traditional definitions of the concept of organization conceive it as a collectivity with relatively identifiable boundaries (Hall, 1996). Contemporary meanings emphasize that this collectivity does not exist as an abstraction; the collective action manifested within it is oriented by its gender composition, that is, modern organizations are composed of men and women, bearers of customs, learned interactions reproducing ways of seeing the world (Montaño, 2020).

In the 1960s, organizations in industrialized countries were reluctant to recognize the contribution of women. Discussions focused on the predominance of men in the development of strategic tasks. This implied that the management of organizations implicitly carries a patriarchal vision. Burin (2009) indicates that the gender mandate that points to the male as the possessor of economic rationality is perpetuated, attributing to him an untouchable strategic capacity. Women, on the other hand, are associated with remaining isolated in decisions involving public space. This mandate promotes a society based on levers that inhibit the possibilities of building equitable and inclusive organizations. In terms of the contributions of men and women, there is a latent questioning of universalist and naturalistic biases that point to the white, heterosexual male with an aggressive attitude as the profile best suited to hold power (Acker, 1998). On this basis, a web of meanings and conditioning practices is woven to develop an economic activity anchored in business organizations.

Therefore, the transformation of women's economic role is associated with the functioning of the capitalist economic system, which places them in the background. At the world level, the Great Depression of 1929 exposed the male predominance in decision-making in large corporations. The strategic leadership was occupied by men. Decades later, there were other challenging moments that challenged the functioning of financial systems in different latitudes. Capital, as its engine, does not contemplate women in this game. Various restrictions have been eased as a result of different social movements. The struggles of the first feminists who demanded, through collective resistance, legislative reforms to recognize women as an important part of the economic engine of Western society.

It is enough to go back to the nineteenth century, with the hard work of women and girls at the height of industrialization. The Scientific Labor Administration laid the ideological foundations, based on the predominance of men, to weave nodes that operate and reproduce labor practices, under the pretext of the efficiency of time and movements dictated by the machine (Billing, 2011). In the development of operational activities, historically there has been an absence of regulations to improve their precarious conditions. Undoubtedly, the perception of the contribution that exists between men and women in an organization crosses the patriarchal paradigmatic model. The organization affects the appropriation of masculinized conventions and routines, developed from susceptible practices where violence against women is made invisible and normalized (Alvesson & Due, 2009).

In modern organizations, those who are not within the masculinized control of rational economic logic are considered vulnerable groups. In other words, women, Indigenous women, and members of LGBTQ groups are excluded (Alvesson & Due, 2009; Billing, 2011). As an example, an Indigenous lesbian woman, originally from a rural community, with barriers to accessing middle and higher levels of education will have more difficulties in achieving social mobility. In countries such as Mexico and Colombia, with great economic instability, insecurity, and vulnerability to guarantee the recognition of labor and human rights, the basis for strengthening structural violence that does not contribute to equity in every sense is laid.

By combining gendered economic perspectives, they contribute to the dimension of labor precariousness. Yancey (2003) and Acker (2004, 2006) point out that women's participation in the workplace presents different disadvantages. The first is the possibility of accessing, developing, and ascending to higher hierarchical levels. If other variables, such as ethnicity, are crossed, more inequalities appear that are linked to their access to health services, education, housing, and decent food. The notion of economic independence, to generate autonomy in the maintenance of women, is crossed by different conditioning factors. In the words of Acker (2012), each one is a product of the combination of representations associated with the region where the organization is located. This directly generates a gender structure designed to establish both explicit and implicit rules for behavior at work.

In Latin American countries, the arrival of industrialization was late, due to the colonization processes. Processes of resistance to Eurocentric capitalist visions were favored, patriarchal domination has a face of individualism, maximization of resources tinged by machismo (Acker, 2004). The distribution of tasks within our organizations also reproduces internal household dynamics. Women's work outside formalized spaces is often devalued. Unpaid activities, including health care for members, are part of the increased domestic burden that goes unrecognized.

Women's work in organizations tends to omit its importance, which Alvesson and Due (2009) agree in calling gender blindness. In other words, it would seem that organizations are places free of any inequity generated by the gender dimension. This bias has an affective and symbolic charge, which gives it a series of experiences and aspirations that exclude and inhibit feminization to exalt its opposite. This blindness leaves its blindfold when crises make visible the hidden inequalities between men and women. For example, this book in front of you develops an interesting reflection on the economic crisis derived from COVID-19 confinement. How a health crisis placed marginalized women who did not have sufficient economic resources to cope with it in greater vulnerability. In this regard, the female presence in Hispanic American organizations, as already mentioned, is associated with a pattern oriented by a labor market that punishes them for their age, roles of care in the home, and the imposition of beauty stereotypes. A pattern that fades when the concept of professional success exalts the male more than the female. Female achievement is a line of analysis addressed in this book under the pretext of opening up possibilities to explain the gender gap. Consequently, economic growth is not only found in statistical coldness and indicators.

There are different cultural and institutional barriers that conceal a parallel structure that limits employment opportunities. From this perspective, patriarchy imposes different devices that differentiate who has access to better-paying jobs (Goldin & Sokoloff, 1982). According to Yancey (2003), women are historically exposed to greater economic vulnerability reflected in salary differences. In business organizations in our region, there are wage gaps in economic activities associated with the tertiary sector and senior management.

In this regard, academic research (Acker, 1998; Billing, 2011) attributes the lack of representation of women at higher hierarchical levels to the persistence of stereotypes based on the legitimacy of a violent social order, where the white heterosexual male stands out in a logic of "rational" knowledge production. This is due to the persistence of stereotypes based on the legitimacy of a violent social order, where the white heterosexual male stands out in a logic of "rational" knowledge production. In this regard, Burin (2009) recalls the existence of a glass ceiling, to refer to the invisible and discriminatory barriers to climbing to certain positions that raise gender-based stereotypes.

With the above, the authors of this book *Economics, Gender, and Academia: A Pending Conversation*, combine a collective effort for you, the reader, to broaden your view of our region around economics and gender. The critical and updated perspective, based on academic rigor, characterizes each of the chapters that comprise it. This text is led by the Politécnico Grancolombiano and the Universidad

EAFIT and is the result of two international symposiums related to gender equity during the years 2021 and 2022. The topics discussed here are part of a polyphonic conversation that emphasizes inequality between men and women. The gathering of these conversations seeks to ally on the front of the denunciation against violence by giving the floor to those who have not taken it. The university imprint sets the tone for influencing the closing of gender gaps.

Each page of this book challenges the status quo, anchored in an interest in probing beyond the concept of equity. When theory is not removed from day-to-day action, context is relevant. It is possible that there will be those who only see a book integrated with thematic chapters. Just as there will surely be those who discover, in rigorous research and the written word, that no resistance is exhausted, which opens the infinite possibility of imagining a world built on respect for difference. Let us begin the conversation.

References

Acker, J. (1998). The future of 'gender and organizations': Connections and boundaries. *Gender, Work & Organization*, 5(4), 195–206.

Acker, J. (2004). Hierarchies, jobs bodies: A theory of gendered organizations. In R. Ely et al. (Comps.), *Reader in gender, work and organization* (pp. 49–61). Blackwell Publishing.

Acker, J. (2006). Inequality regimes: Gender, class, and race in organizations. *Gender & Society*, 20(4), 441–464.

Acker, J. (2012). Gendered organizations and intersectionality: Problems and possibilities. *Equality, Diversity and Inclusion*. 31(3), 214-224. https://doi.org/10.1108/02610151211209072

Alvesson, M., & Due Y. (2009). *Understanding gender and organizations* (2nd ed.). Sage Publications.

Billing, Y. (2011). Are women in management victims of the phantom of the male norm? *Gender, Work and Organization*, 18(3), 298–317.

Burin, M. (2009). Construcción de la subjetividad masculina. In M. En Burin & I. Meler (Coords.), *Hombres. Género y subjetividad masculina* (2nd ed., pp. 127–154). Librería de Mujeres Editoras.

Goldin, C., & Sokoloff, K. (1982). Women, children, and industrialization in the early republic: Evidence from the manufacturing censuses. *The Journal of Economic History*, 42(4), 741–774.

Hall, R. (1996). *Organizaciones: Estructuras, procesos y resultados*. Editorial Pearson Educación.

Montaño, L. (2020). Encrucijadas y desafíos de los Estudios Organizacionales Una reflexión desde las perspectivas institucionales. *Innovar*, 30(78), 19–34. https://doi.org/10.15446/innovar.v30n78.90304

Yancey, P. (2003). Said and done versus saying and doing. Gendering practices, practicing gender at work. *Gender & Society*, 17(3), 342–366.

Preface

Research on equity and the gender gap has led each of the authors to find different perspectives that are relevant when it comes to identifying the advances that have been made in this matter, and invites reflection from areas such as the economy, the education, culture, organizations, academia, in order to validate and recognize the achievements and existing gaps in terms of gender equality. In this tour it is possible to collect the vision of different Latin American researchers, who present relevant positions and arguments while inviting them to continue reflecting on the importance of continuing the discussion and promotion of gender issues.

With this book, we want to contribute once again that reading on issues of gender equity continues to generate awareness of the importance of strengthening the results achieved for both women and men, recognizing the role played by the people and their willingness to advance in policies that become a mandate. The value of education when training in different knowledge and how from there it must also be promoted for this equality, in addition to exercising a facilitating role, so that it is there where it can advance in policies aimed at reducing gender gaps, including organizations and society in general.

There is a conversation and pending actions, although progress is recognized, the challenges must become a real commitment on the part of society, the gender problem crosses borders and takes on a global character, in this way, it is invited to recognize those elements that have been advancing in the region and continue with their reflection and actions that in compliance with the Sustainable Development Goals (SDGs) can increase the opportunities for equity, freedom, and dignity, for men and women on equal terms.

This tour begins with an analysis that is presented from Mexico in relation to the contents of gender equity in texts and official educational documents in Mexico, with the idea of being able to identify if they are promoting equity, or maintaining stereotypes, superiority, and authority.

It is evident the inequality of rights, wage gaps, and gender stereotypes, it is the context in which women live in Latin America, which aggravates their situation of poverty. Under this scenario, a reflection is presented in relation to how drug trafficking is presented as a legitimate job offer and a response to the economic needs of women.

The analysis continues, in the post-pandemic context in the education sector, referring to Cuba, Peru, and Argentina, particularly in education, which is conceived as a platform for social integration in the workplace, the authors then raise from their experience and the vision of sources, the proposal of political theoretical criteria that facilitate inclusive public policies in the field of education and the productive sector that lead to overcoming gender and racial gaps in the post-pandemic context.

In this context, an analysis is presented between academia, organization, and gender in Chile, the authors make an analysis based on gender and organizational studies, which leads them to find that the practice of management in institutions acquires a central and hegemonic status.

The study of the gender perspective must be done from the pillars of human rights, which when considered universal do not suggest political ideologies, cultural differences, and economic systems, in this context the authors present a reflection on gender policies in Latin America for the case of the Andean Community of Nations CAN (Colombia, Bolivia, Peru, Ecuador).

From the practice in organizations, an analysis is presented regarding the alternatives of change that they must have in the light of a gender perspective, the author presents macroeconomic indicators of development and gender gap, where she shows their relationship and multiple variables, which lead to propose and recognize conditions around what should be the intervention within organizations.

Finally, it considers what are the difficulties and challenges that a woman in Mexico must face to generate a company in the education sector, and what COVID-19 meant, exploring the different strategies that guaranteed her to maintain the organization, which can be an example of all those women in Latin America who wish to undertake.

The importance of progressing in the dialogues between academia and economics on gender gaps in organizations is reviewed, identifying the advances that have been made in this area in Latin America, with emphasis on the Colombian case, evidencing the challenges that persist in accordance with the provisions of the Sustainable Development Agenda and the role played in this scenario by the Institutions of Higher Education the progress achieved and the challenges that are proposed.

There is a lack of conversation about economics and gender because the analysis is from a macroeconomic perspective by writing that, regardless of who does the care work or domestic work, one can also question the assumptions of economic science that, by convention, in national accounts ignores the value of domestic work and almost deals with scarcity, selfishness and competition and rarely abundance, altruism, and cooperation.

The text presented is a compendium of experiences and a tour of Latin America, so that it interpels, motivates, and invites to continue working to achieve true inclusion and gender equity, its reading will lead to enrich the discussion and to continue developing spaces, which allow advancing and answer the following questions:

What are the challenges and opportunities in gender equity presented by economic analyses in Colombia in a Latin American context?

Why, despite the fact that most large companies and organizations have protocols and complaint management instances to address gender-based violence, in many cases asymmetrical relationships persist and structural changes are not observed in most of them?

Can environmental culture determine resistance to change within organizations, or are new processes part of an isomorphic organizational response to environmental pressures?

To answer these questions, it is shown that there is still a pending conversation between academia, organizations, and actors that make change possible, the distinctive features of the book are themes that encompass critical pedagogy, gender equality and equity, gender stereotypes, equality in education, capital, public policies, racism, organization, management, masculinity, hegemony, human rights, social relations, invisible costs, Latin American women leaders, anti-semitism and female performance, Holocaust education, economics, higher education institutions, and leadership, among others, so this conversation has to keep moving forward.

Acknowledgments

Research opens doors and motivates us to continue advancing, for which we are grateful for the support of Grancolombiano Polytechnic and Eafit University and each of the authors who participated in the construction of the book with their contributions, based on their realities and experiences that they gather from their countries of origin. More than thanking, we want to leave open the dialogues and the interest to add new knowledge that is reflected in a more prosperous and equitable society in Latin America and the Caribbean.

With appreciation,
Mario, Laura, Marisol y Gloria Nancy

Part I

Gender Equity, The Impact of Gender Equality on the Development of Latin American Territories

Chapter 1

Educational Materials in Elementary Education in Mexico: A Missed Opportunity to Promote Gender Equity

José Baltazar García Horta and María Teresa Guerra Ramos

Abstract

This chapter presents an analysis of gender equity messages in textbooks and official educational documents in Mexico. For that purpose, critical pedagogy, understood as a framework to dissect power dynamics and gender relations in educational settings, is employed. From the point of view of critical pedagogy, stereotypes and imbalances of power are learned through everyday discourses and narratives and have been shaped by a long history of dominance and suppression; they are part of a system erected precisely to exercise control and limit possibilities particularly of those groups in the margins of society: poor, women, addicts, indigenous peoples, etc. Schools are regarded as spaces where inclusiveness is encouraged but also places where the reproduction of the status quo also occurs; in that sense, schools reflect whatever occurs in society at large, not only the positive cases but the bleak instances as well. Our main intention was to identify and examine books and documents on educational policy, guidelines, contents, or learning outcomes, which have been expressed to promote gender equity and respect for diversity. The idea is to identify whether the content that promotes equity is being communicated or if, on the contrary, gender stereotypes continue to be reinforced, the theme is avoided, or it is not considered relevant. We identified texts (activities and instructions) and images embodying messages connected to gender equity, or inequities, and even discourses that, proactively or by omission, perpetuate the transmission of gender stereotypes. The textbooks of *Civic and Ethical Education* of the final three grades of primary education are analyzed. A perusal of legal documents and official textbooks suggests that mixed messages that include both explicit statements

Economy, Gender and Academy: A Pending Conversation, 3–26
Copyright © 2023 by José Baltazar García Horta and María Teresa Guerra Ramos
Published under exclusive licence by Emerald Publishing Limited
doi:10.1108/978-1-80455-998-720231007

of equity between binary gender options and implicit messages of superiority and authority attributed to men are somehow transmitted. In particular, the iconography let through implicit messages, probably unintentional but nonetheless powerful, in conveying stereotypes and imbalances of power.

Keywords: Critical pedagogy; gender equity; gender equality; gender stereotypes; textbooks; equality in education

Introduction

This section examines a topic that has the potential to exercise a meaningful and unpostponable social change that, however, has consistently been postponed either explicitly or unconsciously: gender equity. This idea is quite often referred to from a variety of perspectives and is frequently attached to an extensive set of practices and policies as well. However, despite its undeniable importance, it seems clear that not enough has really changed other than some instances of political discourse, with certainly good meanings, but not much more.

In our view, one major concern is that gender inequalities are not perceived as a structural or systemic issue but are regularly regarded as a private matter, or maybe something that is wrongfully happening at the workplace or in a particular family. Considering gender inequalities as a problem that imperfect individuals have is a poor diagnostic but, more importantly, misses the opportunity to set real social change in motion (Arnot, 2013). Gender inequalities need to be addressed as a systemic issue that involves power dynamics, subjugation, and awareness, or else whatever is proposed will be hopeless.

Gender education is difficult to define, and it is hard to identify a set of unified practices other than an undisputed foundation of unequal gender relations; "gender continues to be an important organizing and disempowering principle in the school system" (Klein et al., 2007, p. 1). Generally, it has been identified that male domination is at the core of an uneven distribution of power; however, without denying this blunt truth, it has also been suggested that gender education capable of generating social transformation and autonomy must transcend this notion.

Despite its importance, gender education has proven to be an extremely difficult and challenging subject to deal with teachers' education programs and in classrooms with students, and it is regularly lost among the countless concepts and notions that public education seeks to communicate.

Gender Equity and the Critical Perspective

Schools are places where day-to-day practices and discourses are guided by particular ideologies. The notion of schools as places of unbiased views and neutral activities is, to say the least, mistaken: "proponents of critical pedagogy understand that every dimension of schooling and every form of educational practice are politically contested spaces" (Kincheloe, 2008, p. 2). Rather, it has been recognized that quite often violence and gender inequities are part of school practices that normalize male domination patterns and gender stereotypes, as well as other forms of discrimination and marginalization (Kanpol, 1999).

We use the term equity instead of equality since the latter is appropriate when discussing about rights, opportunities, or payment for performing the same activities in equal circumstances. However, equity is considered

> to be more comprehensive and flexible than equality because it implies the concept of fairness or some differences in education processes rather than the concept of sameness when dealing with a diverse student population. (Klein et al., 2007, p. 3)

Disparities in gender relations in education have a long history; therefore, any effort to disrupt this system that has given primacy to a white-middle-class-male view must be under a critical perspective: critical educational policies, critical textbooks, and critical syllabuses (Arnot, 2013). If we summarize these tasks under a single question that would probably be: Are we preserving the status quo? In other words: Are we still giving primacy to a male-driven view of the world?

Critical pedagogy addresses these issues, questioning those structures of power and oppression, inviting students to become active participants in this process, and caring particularly for those that are segregated. "Critical pedagogy is interested in the margins of society, the experiences and needs of individual faced with oppression and marginalization" (Kincheloe, 2008, p. 23).

Critical pedagogy, Kincheloe (2008) says, "explores the cosmos of power and its efforts to regulate human beings" (p. 97); he also puts forward essential questions for the work that is described in this document: "What is the relation between [the sociocultural role of schooling] and dominant power blocs? How does this relationship affect the construction of the curriculum?" (Kincheloe, 2008).

Gender education must be directed, among other things, to the identification of day-to-day instances where power relations are exercised and acknowledge that those instances are part of a structure where individuals must conform to a rigid system of socially constructed hierarchies. Stereotypes and imbalances of power are learned through everyday discourses and narratives and have been shaped by a long history of dominance and suppression; they are by no means accidents, or minor misfortunes that we can disregard, they are fundamental blocks of a system built precisely to exercise control and limit possibilities of certain groups: poor, women, black and indigenous peoples to name some.

Gender Equity: Schools, Teachers, and Teaching in Mexico

It is fair to say that in Mexican public schools, discussions about gender and gender inequities are rare. One possible reason for this is a misguided conception of schools as neutral spaces free from undesirable interests, and teachers as unbiased individuals that can put their own preconceptions aside. This idealistic way of seeing schools may be a deterrent to dissect gender issues regularly; perhaps, it would be a more productive path to consider schools as places that reflect whatever occurs in society at large, not only the luminous side of the real world but the gray areas as well.

> [...] sexism in schools is not only related to sexual harassment and/or sexual abuse but becomes a national pastime, amplified in many areas of curriculum, teacher–student relationships, and home relationships with mothers, fathers, grandparents, and brothers and sisters. I would go as far as to argue that sexism varies for different cultures, depending on the culture-minority or not! (Kanpol, 1999, p. 20)

In this sense, it is possible to say that schools are spaces where inclusiveness is encouraged but also places where the reproduction of the status quo also occurs. It may be worth keeping in mind that "gender is a major organizing principle, applied to uniforms, curricular subjects, administrative practices, classroom activities and even the use of space within and around the school" (Acker, 1994, p. 93).

It may also be that the way the teaching profession is characterized may influence on the perception of teachers' abilities to deal with gender inequity issues. We have mentioned that one feature is to do with the notion of teachers as unbiased and objective individuals, but there is also the belief that teachers are mainly committed to the academic side of teaching; other areas such as appreciation of arts, equity, and equality, and social justice may be perceived as outside their area of expertise. Regarding teaching as a political activity, among many other things, it may be considered by many as going against what "respectable" teaching should be about.

Recent history of teachers participating in several social movements and protests has unjustly pictured teachers as social misfits as opposed to professionals that conform to the norm: it is fine to have different views, so long as they are "the correct views." In this context, teaching about social injustices, discrimination, poverty, respect for sexual orientations and gender identity may be seen, by some layers of society, as a transgression and a threat. It might be acceptable to talk in schools about the more palpable instances of discrimination and inequities, which are quite often discussed in a rather superficial way while leaving ingrained power dynamics intact.

The essence of critical pedagogy is to build awareness of the uneven society in which we live and teach students about the economic and political truths, with a view on collective efforts and socially responsible initiatives, with respect for the environment. This is opposed to individualistic notions that are the norm in liberal societies, where individual achievements are celebrated and considered to be a triumph of a self-made person.

> The way individualism and individuality appear in schools is quite often simple. Conceptually, individualism is intrinsically related to a modernistic view of Western civilization. Values such

as hard labor, self-discipline, and self-motivation carry overtones of a general quest for human individual supremacy, critical-mindedness, and self-achievement. These values are reinforced by self-gratification, instant gratification, and narcissism within the culture-striving for one's own in the guise of community welfare. (Kanpol, 1999, p. 43)

The idea of an autonomous individual is appealing, since self-determination is one of the foundations of capitalism and, to tell the truth, we all like to think we are in control of our own life and choices.

One of the downfalls of this mode of thinking is that disadvantages and inequities are seen as a product of individuals that have taken bad decisions or, at the very least, as a misfortune. On the other hand, success is seen as gifted individuals making the right choices. Under such model, male supremacy is justified, and inequities are attributed to individuals' poor choices, overlooking the systemic nature of male-dominant discourse, that has given shape to identities and disparities.

The danger of not transmitting to students a critical view about gender issues is that they may develop the notion that whatever happens in terms of disparities among individuals, discrimination, and oppression may appear as disassociated from their lives, creating the impression that those inadequacies occur to someone else, and that they have nothing to do with them. However, a word of caution is necessary, we are not saying that this is going to be easy; adopting a critical stance in gender education means contradicting assumptions about the man–woman relationships that have been learned from the cradle and that questioning them is likely to get messy and will require patience and persistence.

Gender in Article 3 of the Mexican Constitution

The Mexican Constitution, officially the Political Constitution of the United Mexican States, in its current form, is the legacy of the Mexican Revolution of 1910, written shortly after the major armed conflicts had settled down; although some of its aspirations can be traced down to the Constitution of 1857 (Barba, 2019). It is said to be one of the first constitutional documents to have included social rights, followed by the Soviet Constitution of 1918.

Article 3 is the one that deals with education and has traditionally included the high aspirations assigned to the educational task; among the customary topics included, we can mention the idea that the education provided by the State is to be free, will be secular, and available for all (Barba, 2019). Like many other segments of the Constitution, Article 3 has had some reforms with different intentions (Cámara de Diputados, 2000); interestingly, the word *gender* has appeared only recently in the Constitutional text of Article 3; however, its meaning is unclear and is mentioned only, in general, an imprecise way.

The current text of Article 3 includes the expression of gender in three different paragraphs; in one of these, the word gender is used to establish that the

Technical Council of Education will be conformed considering gender equality. The other two instances are included here:

> Plans and programs of study will have a *gender* perspective and will have a comprehensive orientation therefore knowledge of science and humanities will be included .... (Secretaría de Gobernación, 2020, p. 2)

> [the criteria that will lead the educational task will...] (e) Be equitable, the State shall implement measures that will favor the full exercise of the right to education of individuals and will fight socioeconomic, regional, and *gender* inequalities in access, transit, and permanence in educational services. (Secretaría de Gobernación, 2020, p. 3)

Although it is to be recognized that the inclusion of the term is an important step, its meaning is general and vague, with a certain shallowness; only in the second paragraph, it may seem that the idea of fighting against inequalities is a move in the right direction, but its connotation is somehow restricted to access to the educational services.

It is also fair to say that a Constitutional text is general in nature and that there are other instruments and regulations of the State where many initiatives and aspirations take a real shape and are operationalized. However, it is not a minor aspect that it is only until recently that the term has been included in the Constitutional Article devoted to education, and even then, it is only treated in a rather superficial way.

Educational Context

In México, compulsory government-funded schools provide elementary education to 90% of children and young people. Over past decades, state schooling has faced the challenges of meeting the needs of a large population with high growth rates, linguistic and ethnic diversity, difficult geographical accessibility, and a limited budget. Nowadays, official data show that the education service involves 13.67 million primary school students and employs 568,857 teachers in 95,699 schools (INEGI, 2022). Besides progress in education provision, several efforts have been made to reinforce the development of the national educational system and to improve the quality of elementary education. A strand of such efforts has been curriculum development. The last reform in 2017 introduced the current curriculum for primary education, for children aged six to 12 years. The Ministry of Education was responsible for defining the new plan of studies and the curriculum for primary education, which has a national character and must be followed by all schools, both state and public.

Generally, the approach, principles and stated aims of the curricular document could be regarded as forward-looking and well-intentioned. However, it makes use of a pedagogical official rhetoric that describes an idealized view of schools as places where diversity naturally occurs. We use the term *official rhetoric* to refer to the body of ideas and language used in current official educational documents in Mexico, concerning teaching and learning in primary education. Such persuasive written language has been elaborated through time, and several agents have been involved in its development: policy-makers, technical-pedagogical specialists, authors of textbooks, external consultants, and, although not significantly, some teachers. All of them have contributed to the pedagogical rhetoric with their own background and views in a process of document and material generation. The official rhetoric contained in curriculum documents then results from a complex process where individual voices cannot be identified.

Gender issues were incorporated into the curriculum document and were regarded as a priority aligned with international trends. This work intends to provide information and reflections that serve in the current process of curricular renewal that started in 2021 but is still incomplete. We also would like to contribute to a broader discussion that stimulates the reflection of the main actors and relevant policy-makers.

In the context of Mexico, since the creation of the National Commission of Free Textbooks in 1959, the policy was established that the Ministry of Public Education would be the entity responsible for generating and supervising the preparation of national textbooks for all subjects of the primary education curriculum. Official free textbooks have played a decisive role as the most important educational materials, and sometimes the only ones available in Mexican schools. In our view, Mexican textbooks constitute the de *facto* curriculum; that is, the interpretation of the official *curriculum* closest to teaching practice. It is because of this that analyzing textbooks become relevant.

Methodological Perspective

Our main intention was to identify and examine in the curricular documents those guidelines, contents, or learning outcomes, which have been expressed to promote gender equity and respect for diversity. This type of analysis places special emphasis on some forms of expression of written and iconographic language, with the idea of prefiguring whether the content that promotes equity is being communicated or if, on the contrary, gender stereotypes continue to be reinforced, the theme is avoided, or it is not given relevance in the official curriculum.

On the other hand, the textbooks of *Civic and Ethical Education* of the final three grades are taken up to investigate whether, as proposed in the official discourse, gender equity is promoted in a transversal way. The choice of these books is due to their textual density and the appearance of curricular themes related to gender inequity. The aim was to identify the texts (activities and instructions) and images embodying messages connected to gender equity, or inequities, explicit or subtle discrimination, and even discourses that, proactively or by omission, perpetuate the transmission of gender stereotypes. The different components of the textbooks like segments of texts and images were reviewed, and relevant items were identified, pointing out those instances that exemplify equity and inequities. The units of analysis are identified from a detailed reading of the curricular pages and textbooks. The two authors of this work were engaged in the selection of units of analysis, discussing extensively their meaning and relevance for the aims of the analysis.

Findings: Gender in the National Curriculum Document

The analysis of the curricular document (SEP, 2017) sets out to identify the presence of gender declarations in the general pedagogical discourse and specific contents. The initial analysis of the National Curriculum document consisted of a systematic search of paragraphs where the word *gender* is explicitly mentioned, including sections on policy aims, teaching purposes, or specific subject themes and learning outcomes.

Paragraphs were preferred as unit analysis, over sentences, or isolated phrases, since they provide more comprehensive and contextualized illustrations, that may validate our interpretation and analysis. When the word gender appeared twice in the same paragraph, it counted as a single unit.

A total of 32 paragraphs with the word *gender* were found, associated with gender issues (Table 1.1). When the word *gender* appeared in a different connotation (musical style, literary genre), the paragraph was not considered. Only 16 paragraphs were connected to be expected learning outcomes in curricular subjects, featuring mainly *Civic and Ethical Education, Arts, and Socioemotional Education*.

Table 1.1.   Frequencies of Gender-related Paragraphs in the National Curriculum Document.

Document Section	Frequency	Frequency in Specific Subjects	
Legal page	1		
I. Introduction	1		
II. The aims of education in the 21st century	1		
III. Elementary education	4		
IV. The curriculum for Elementary education	2		
V. Study programs for Elementary education (subject contents)	19	Introduction	1
		Knowledge of environment	2
		Civic and ethical education	**11**
		Art	1
		Socioemotional education	3
		Curricular autonomy	1
VI. Bibliography, glossary, acronyms and credits	4		
Total 32			

Source: Created by authors.

These findings suggest an infrequent appearance of gender issues in an official curricular document of 678 pages. They were useful to determine that *Civic and Ethical Education* textbooks were worth reviewing in search of more specific data for this analysis. Before the description of what we found in textbooks, the ideas exposed in the identified paragraphs deserve a closer look to grasp the nature of their messages.

After a careful review of the salient features of the paragraphs and drawing upon our general gender perspective framework, some broad themes emerged in the analysis (see Table 1.2).

The theme of *equality in access to educational services* can be illustrated with a paragraph in the introductory section of the curriculum document pointing out the reiterative idea of inclusion and universal access to state education:

> The main objective of this Educational Reform is that public education, both elementary and high school, not only are to be secular and free, but of good quality as well, equitable and inclusive. This means that the State must guarantee access to schools to all children and youngsters, and make sure that the education they receive will give them learnings and meaningful knowledge, relevant and useful throughout their lives, independently of their socioeconomic milieu, ethnic origin, and *gender*. (p. 19)

This broad intention of providing access to educational services without distinction of gender and other conditions appears several times in the curriculum document as a statement connected with a desirable socially expected value of inclusiveness. A second instance is found in the section describing the general framework and intentions of elementary education at the national level, it reads:

> Beyond the differences among schools, it is desirable students with different backgrounds interact within every establishment to constitute a plural and complex community. Schools must be inclusive spaces in which appreciation for diversity must be fostered and discrimination connected to ethnic origin, *gender*, disability, religion, sexual orientation, or any other issue is eliminated. Inclusion

Table 1.2.   Broad Themes Emerging From the Documentary Analysis.

Broad Themes	Frequency
• Equality in access to educational services	7
• Equality to engage in the learning process	3
• Equality in learning outcomes	2
• Equity in society	20
Total	32

Source: Created by authors.

must be understood as a benefit for vulnerable persons and those groups frequently excluded, but also for all actors participating in the educational process. (p. 79)

Discrimination due to gender is acknowledged as a form of discrimination and is to be eliminated in school communities, but it also remarks on the idealized idea that diverse school communities are desirable and unproblematic.

Regarding equality to engage in the learning process can be exemplified by the following purpose of collaborative work in the introduction to the subject Knowledge of the environment:

Collaborative work. Value attitudes for working together and manifestations of respect for other persons, promoting the elimination of gender stereotypes and valuing peaceful coexistence with others. (p. 338)

It refers to students engaging in collaborative tasks in the class, although how to eliminate gender stereotypes is not stated. Interestingly, the theme of equality to engage in the learning process could not be identified more than twice occasions.

Equality in learning outcomes was connected to the educational divides among male and female students:

Another foundation for equity and inclusion in the curriculum is the impulse of actions aiming to equality between males and females. Although Mexican educational system has practically reached gender equality access in all educational levels, there are still achievement divides in some subject disciplines. Particularly, girls and female adolescents obtain lower results than male pairs in exact and natural sciences. Anxiety associated to math learning and gender stereotypes affect girls from early stages and impact in math learning development at all levels. (p. 82–83)

In this case, the recognition of achievement differences is associated with gender stereotypes and learning anxiety without any further discussion of the cultural or systemic aspects of them, nor any description of the nature of the actions to promote equality.

Equality in society as a broad theme came from the inclusion of learning outcomes referring to situations that may take place in other settings:

Equality and gender perspective (Transversal curricular theme)
Secondary, 2o. grade, Learning outcome
– Analyze the implications of gender equality in situations associated
   to teenage:
friendship, romantic relationship, study (p. 451)

This text implies that some learning activities must be developed by teachers and the textbook's author to meet such learning outcome. This is a teaching demand that requires some level of understanding and awareness of the social situations in which students may face gender issues and how to help them to analyze the implications of gender equality in such context.

This initial documentary analysis suggests that attention to gender in elementary policy documents has been partial, sporadic, and unsystematic. Unfortunately, attention to gender has proceeded somewhat unevenly across different curriculum subjects, with more attention given to Civics and Ethical Education. This last finding directed our attention to find out how gender issues were aborded in the national textbooks of this specific subject. Given that there are 45 textbooks in total for the six grades of primary education (6–9 per grade), looking at those of *Civic and Ethical Education* for 4–6th grades because of their text density provided the highest probability to find gender issues in either text or images.

Findings: Gender in Textbooks

In this section, we present the findings of our search in the selected textbooks that were in use during the last completed school year (2021–2022) and aligned to the still-in-use official curriculum document (SEP, 2017). Given they are free textbooks, nationally distributed in state and private schools, they are vehicles of information and teaching-learning activities that are suggested as proposals but that most teachers adopt to guide the classroom dynamic. We intentionally wanted to look at information, activities or images in which gender issues were considered.

In the book of *Civic and Ethical Education* for 4th grade (SEP, 2019a) for students aged 9 to 10 years, the first unit called *Boys and girls take care of the health and personal integrity*, associated with the learning outcome of recognizing similarities and differences (physical, cultural, and social) among persons and appreciate and respect their qualities and capacities; it reads:

> A difference that divides humanity is that of sex. If we talk about biological differences between men and women, we refer to sex; if they are cultural differences or expectations, we refer to gender.//As more educational opportunities are presented for women and men, social roles and jobs are now performed by both. Both woman and man study and work and, when they form a couple and establish a family, they share household duties. This has created greater equity in our country. Today, Mexico's laws establish the same rights for men and women. (SEP, 2019a, pp. 13–14)

This explicit recognition of cultural gender differences is mentioned just in this instance, and it is followed by the assertion that gender equality is improving given the provision of more educational opportunities. It is remarkable that it is assumed that a couple is formed by a man and a woman, leaving aside other family configurations and non-binary options in modern society. Additionally, the term equity seems to have been imperfectly used here, since given the idea specified in the next line, the word more suitable would be equitable, because when we refer to rights established by the law, the expression has to do with equality and not equity. No further consideration of gender issues was found in 4th grade textbooks, apart from the citation of the First Constitutional Article that prohibits any form of discrimination including gender discrimination (SEP, 2019a, p. 97).

Figs. 1.1–1.3 provide examples of the theme of *equality in society* featured in the 4th grade textbook.

Fig. 1.1.   Equality in Society: A Policewoman Illustrating a Text on Legality and Law-abiding Behaviour and a Prototypical Family Illustrating the Right to Have a Family (*Civic and Ethical Education, 4*, p. 40). *Source*: SEP (2019a).

Para aprender más
60

Héroes y heroínas: guías de valor

Aquí recordaremos algunas de las principales figuras que lucharon para que nuestro México gozara de libertad y soberanía.

De esta lucha surgieron hombres y mujeres que, de distintos modos, han sido capaces de orientar la acción colectiva hacia la libertad y la justicia. Entre esas personas están héroes patrios como Hidalgo, Allende, Morelos, entre otros; pero también están aquellas mujeres como Juana de Asbaje, que en el periodo del Virreinato lucharon por el derecho a la igualdad.

Los héroes, su memoria y su ejemplo son necesarios para ti, para tu pueblo y para tu misma patria porque orientan la vida en común.

Juana de Asbaje

A quien tú conoces con el nombre de sor Juana Inés de la Cruz es, por las obras que escribió, una notable fundadora de nuestra patria. La literatura mexicana encuentra en ella el principio de su gloria. En primer lugar, conquistó la lengua y la cultura de España, y al mismo tiempo se empeñó en mantener vivo el idioma náhuatl, que es la lengua que hablaban las personas entre las cuales ella pasó su niñez y juventud. Como mujer, es la primera de las mexicanas que combatió por obtener la libertad y la capacidad intelectual que da el estudio, y que en aquel tiempo se negaba a las integrantes de su género.

La Corregidora

La Independencia de México no hubiera podido iniciarse en el momento que se hizo, de no haber sido por el heroísmo de Josefa Ortiz de Domínguez, personaje a quien tú conoces como la Corregidora de Querétaro. En efecto, ella sabía cómo se preparaba el despertar de nuestra independencia y para cuándo se había determinado que ese evento ocurriera. Enterada de que los planes habían sido descubiertos por los enemigos de la libertad, pudo anticiparse y comunicárselo a nuestros héroes para evitar que fueran sorprendidos y capturados; les avisó del peligro que corrían e hizo posible que se iniciara el movimiento de Independencia antes de lo que se tenía planeado.

Miguel Hidalgo

Llamado Padre de la Patria por tener la gloria de ser el que dio inicio al movimiento de Independencia. Sus estudios de filosofía y política lo llevaron a creer firmemente en la libertad esencial del ser humano y en la soberanía del pueblo.

José María Morelos

Recorriendo los caminos de su patria como arriero, comprendió la necesidad de cambiar la situación de injusticia que se vivía. Estudió para superar su pobreza. Su lucha para impulsar nuestra independencia fue militar y cívico-política.

Fig. 1.2.   Equality in Society: Images of Important Persons in Mexican History Depicting Two Women and One Man (*Civic and Ethical Education*, 4, p. 60). *Source*: SEP (2019a).

In the book of *Civic and Ethical Education* for 5th grade (SEP, 2019b) for students aged 10–11 years, an explicit paragraph with a definition of gender stereotypes appears as follows:

Stereotypes are characteristics that society attributes to a certain group of people. From them, generalizations are made and may lead to prejudices or misconceptions about their abilities, values and attitudes. Prejudice breeds discrimination and limits equal

Fig. 1.3.   Equality in Society: Images of Persons in Diverse Jobs: Men as Building Workers, a Woman Selling Traditional Clothes, Men and Women in a Science Lab, Men as Farmers, a Woman Using a Computer and a Man Repairing Shoes (*Civic and Ethical Education*, 4, p. 111). *Source*: SEP (2019a).

opportunities. Nothing justifies discrimination, because it damages self-esteem, violates rights and prevents the realization of justice. (SEP, 2019b, p. 36)

The former text offers a rather formal and abstract definition that students must make sense of and eventually apply. Additionally, other images complement these ideas (Fig. 1.4).

Para aprender

Observar el camino que ha seguido tu vida te ayuda a conocerte y a valorar tu desarrollo.

Las personas se transforman a lo largo de su vida; y los cambios que más se notan son los del cuerpo. En éstos influyen la alimentación, la herencia familiar, el lugar de residencia y otros factores. Por eso, cada persona crece y se desarrolla de manera distinta, con su propio ritmo. Pero también ocurren cambios emocionales, ya que con el crecimiento físico se incrementan las capacidades, surgen nuevas responsabilidades y se experimentan emociones distintas. Cada persona va aprendiendo a expresarlas, a convivir y a construir una identidad propia, resultado de la visión que tiene de sí misma y de la manera como se presenta ante las demás personas.

Fig. 1.4.   Equality in Society: Images of Change in Body and Appearance for a Woman and a Man Depicting Gender Stereotypes (*Civic and Ethical Education*, 5, p. 15).   *Source*: SEP. (2019b).

These images illustrate observable changes in life and, probably unintentionally, gender stereotypes in connection with colors in the clothing, toys associated with boys and girls, emotional expressions, and active/passive attitudes (Figs. 1.5 and 1.6).

Escribe en tu Anecdotario alguna situación que, a partir de la participación democrática, haya contribuido a mejorar la convivencia en tu casa, en la escuela o en el lugar donde vives.

Lo que aprendí

En equipos, retomen el caso presentado al inicio de la lección y elaboren en su cuaderno una propuesta para solucionar el problema considerando que:

- La ciudadanía y el gobierno trabajan juntos para resolverlo.
- La solución se encuentra en el diálogo.
- Se respetan las leyes y los acuerdos establecidos.
- Se aplican los derechos establecidos en la Constitución que están relacionados con el problema.
- Las autoridades toman en cuenta la opinión de la ciudadanía.

B IV LECCIÓN 15

153

En la escuela, como en el gobierno municipal, estatal o federal, la autoridad debe aplicar los principios democráticos.

Fig. 1.5.   Equality in Society: Image of a School Meeting With a Female Teacher in a Protagonist Role (*Civic and Ethical Education*, 5, p. 153). *Source*: SEP (2019b).

BLOQUE V   LECCIÓN 18

3. Dibujen en una cartulina el croquis del conflicto, como en la ilustración del inicio de la lección.

Palabras claras

En la vida diaria es habitual que existan conflictos que no se reconocen, a veces porque se ocultan y otras porque se piensa que es natural; por ejemplo, que las mujeres sean las únicas responsables de la limpieza de la casa o del cuidado de los hijos.

La costumbre ha llevado a las personas a no afrontar el conflicto hasta que la situación se pone tan tensa que explota y es más difícil de manejar. A esto se le llama *crisis del conflicto*.

186

Algunos conflictos se pueden resolver al dialogar
y tomar acuerdos en los que ambas partes
puedan lograr lo que se proponen.

Fig. 1.6.   Equity in Society: Image of a Situation of Conflict to be Solved With Dialogue and Agreement Depicting Stereotypical Male and Female Roles (*Civic and Ethical Education*, 5, p. 186). *Source*: SEP (2019b).

In the book of *Civic and Ethical Education* for 6th grade (for students aged 11–12 years), a definition of gender stereotypes is provided (Figs. 1.7–1.10):

A stereotype is an immutable image, shared by many people, about how someone should be or what the characteristics and behaviors of a certain group of people are. An example is believing that girls

Palabras claras

Un *estereotipo* es la imagen inmutable, compartida por muchas personas, acerca de cómo debe ser alguien o cuáles son las características y comportamientos de cierto grupo de personas. Un ejemplo es creer que las niñas deben vestir de color rosa, jugar sólo con muñecas, y ser delicadas, sumisas y frágiles. Estos estereotipos de género se basan en prejuicios, es decir, en ideas falsas; por ejemplo, que la mujer es más débil que el hombre, que llora con facilidad o que es menos inteligente y, por lo tanto, sólo puede trabajar en cosas sencillas. Los prejuicios y los estereotipos llevan a la discriminación y limitan el desarrollo pleno de las personas. Las mujeres, como todas las personas, tienen fortaleza e inteligencia y los hombres sienten miedo y lloran, como cualquier persona.

LECCIÓN 4   B I   37

En los medios de comunicación suelen presentarse estereotipos de niñez, de belleza, de éxito y de género. Aprende a identificarlos y a cuestionarlos.

Fig. 1.7.   Equality in Society: Image of a Stereotype About Being a Man Inviting Students to Identify and Questioning Such Stereotype (*Civic and Ethical Education*, 6, p. 37). *Source*: SEP (2019c).

BLOQUE IV LECCIÓN 15

2. Describan qué problemas y desafíos enfrentó nuestro país durante esos momentos de la historia.
- ¿La población estaba conforme o había descontento social?
- ¿Se respetaban los derechos de la población?
- ¿Había paz social?

3. Consulten cómo se logró transformar estos rasgos antidemocráticos.
- ¿Cómo se derrotó la dictadura a principios del siglo xx?
- ¿Cuándo se logró el reconocimiento de los derechos sociales y políticos? ¿En qué documento se plasmaron estos derechos?
- ¿Qué instituciones han sido importantes para fortalecer el respeto al voto?

4. Expongan al grupo sus trabajos y, al terminar, comenten cuáles son las fortalezas de la democracia en México y cuáles son sus desafíos. Consideren los rasgos de la democracia incluidos en el mapa conceptual.

144

En 1953, se reconoció en México el derecho de las mujeres a votar. Las mujeres y los hombres que lucharon por el reconocimiento de este derecho contribuyeron a fortalecer la democracia mexicana.

Fig. 1.8.   Equity in Society: Image of the Recognition of Women's Right to Vote (*Civic and Ethical Education*, 6, p. 144). *Source*: SEP (2019c).

should wear pink, play only with dolls, and be delicate, submissive and fragile. These gender stereotypes are based on prejudice, i.e. misconceptions; For example, that the woman is weaker than the man, that she cries easily or that she is less intelligent and, therefore, can only work on simple things. Prejudices and stereotypes lead to discrimination and limit people's full development. Women, like all people, have strength and intelligence and men feel fear and cry, like any other person. (p. 37)

BLOQUE IV LECCIÓN 16

Palabras claras

Los datos personales de las autoridades y de la población deben protegerse porque son propiedad de cada individuo. Cada persona debe decidir qué datos dar a conocer y a quiénes; por ejemplo, sobre sus creencias religiosas, las enfermedades que ha padecido, su vida amorosa, entre otros datos.

152

El trabajo de los servidores públicos debe ser transparente porque su función es servir a la población, pero su vida personal no es asunto de interés público.

1. En equipos, analicen una obra de beneficio colectivo realizada recientemente en su municipio o en el estado. Pueden consultar en periódicos locales impresos o digitales, o preguntar a sus familiares.
   - Anoten las características de la obra, la manera como se tomó la decisión y si la población fue consultada. También indaguen cómo y cuándo se informó a la población sobre el costo, el origen de los recursos y los beneficios esperados.
   - Expliquen qué opina la población sobre la obra, si está informada, si ha sido escuchada por las autoridades cuando tiene quejas o dudas y si considera que la obra le traerá beneficios.
   - Identifiquen qué tan transparente es esta obra: ¿existe suficiente información? ¿Los servidores públicos encargados de la obra han rendido cuentas sobre las decisiones que tomaron, el costo y los resultados?

Fig. 1.9.   Equity in Society: Image of a Public Servant Depicted as a Man in Formal Dressing Depicting a Stereotype of Authority and Efficiency Associated to a Male Figure (*Civic and Ethical Education, 6*, p. 152). *Source*: SEP (2019c).

In the description of the results, we were interested in verifying whether previous findings that highlight gender inequities could be found in the selected textbooks. It was confirmed that the presentation of professions and jobs with traditional roles, the existence of a prevalence of male images, and the persistence in the presentation of "male" professions or trades, more than "female" roles. We could not find evidence that politics, science, and work are systematically shown as diverse and inclusive worlds. It seems that there is a continuity in the task of

BLOQUE V LECCIÓN 20

Para aprender

Para que una persona pueda crecer, aprender y desarrollarse, necesita recibir educación, tener acceso a medidas y servicios que le ayuden a mantener su salud y contar con lo necesario para su bienestar físico, emocional y social. Pero también requiere vivir y convivir en un ambiente sano y sin violencia, en el que la cultura de paz y el buen trato estén presentes.

Según la Organización de las Naciones Unidas, "la cultura de paz consiste en una serie de valores, actitudes y comportamientos que rechazan la violencia y previenen los conflictos tratando de atacar sus causas, con el fin de solucionar los problemas mediante el diálogo y la negociación entre las personas, los grupos y las naciones". Estos valores, actitudes y comportamientos que requiere la cultura de paz deben basarse en el reconocimiento y respeto de los derechos humanos y también en el rechazo a la violencia y el seguimiento de principios y valores como la libertad, la justicia, la solidaridad, la tolerancia y la comprensión mutua entre personas, grupos y pueblos.

El logro de un ambiente de paz en la relación cotidiana con otras personas necesita del compromiso y la participación de todos, y el buen trato es el mejor punto de partida. El buen trato es un modo de convivir basado en la aplicación de valores como la solidaridad y el respeto en las relaciones humanas, así como en la prevención de toda forma de violencia. Está presente cuando se ofrece y recibe afecto, cuando se pueden expresar las ideas libremente y se respeta a las personas en su forma de ser, pensar y vestir, en sus creencias y en sus opiniones. De manera especial, el buen trato exige que se respete tu cuerpo, que no te agredan, ofendan ni maltraten de forma alguna.

190

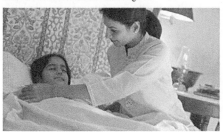

Los adultos tienen la obligación de proteger a los niños de todo tipo de riesgo, abuso, descuido, maltrato o explotación. Ésta es una condición más de la cultura de paz y buen trato.

Fig. 1.10.   Equality in Society: Image of Health Care at Home Depicting Stereotype of Kindness and Child Care to a Woman (*Civic and Ethical Education*, *6*, p. 190). *Source*: SEP (2019c).

elevating men to the pedestal of the protagonists of the story, making women invisible, pigeonholing them in activities that are an extension of work at home.

The information processing and analysis carried out so far suggest that both the curricula and the textbooks analyzed present a picture of mixed messages that include both explicit statements of equity between binary gender options and implicit messages of superiority and authority attributed to men in images. Special attention was given to images that let through implicit messages, probably unintentional but nonetheless powerful, in the iconography of educational materials.

Final Remarks: Gender Education and Inequities

Adopting a gender perspective to improve curricular documents and educational materials represents a substantial but urgent challenge. Any educational document of this nature implicitly or explicitly reflects a stance on the social reality of gender diversity. The coherence and solidity of such a position lie in the presence and absence of the messages that are postulated.

As we have commented earlier, quite frequently, gender education and topics regarding inequities, sexism, or feminism are included and dealt with in schools' curriculum and textbooks in a shallow way. A critical view is quite often absent and, in general, questioning the status quo is not an objective; to a certain extent, activities and policies regarding these issues are basically to give the appearance that schools are doing something about it.

Several initiatives to promote equity are turned into ends in themselves; for instance, the use of inclusive language, but they do not lead to lasting solutions, nor do they tackle the core of the problem. Instead, for example, feminists' demonstrations are deemed violent, stigmatizing dissents, and condemning being vocal about male dominance.

The use of 'easy' solutions, such as teaching about tolerance, being thoughtful regarding other people's preferences, and treating everyone equally does not constitute, in essence, a radical solution that encourages social change;

> we now see more clearly that attempts to integrate and treat women and men equally do not achieve the restructuring necessary for gender equity. "Gender blindness" is not a prime virtue or goal in the education setting today. (Kramarae, 2007, p. 231)

By contrast, perhaps we ought to remember that neutrality quite often favors the oppressor. In the current context, being 'the same' may conceal the notion of a certain model in social terms that frequently is the one approved by the status quo: white-male-straight-middle class-young.

Nowadays, the Mexican educational system is undergoing yet another process of reform that will modify the basic education's curriculum, books, and educational materials. It is an old favorite of Mexican authorities, regardless of political parties and ideologies, to undertake processes of change that this time, it is promised, will solve old and neglected educational issues, gender education, and other sensitive areas included. Nevertheless, this may indeed present another opportunity to include gender equity not just as part of the official, well-intentioned discourse, but clearly introduce a critical stance toward gender and the pervasive nature of a male-dominated power structure among individuals, within families, and in society at large. In that sense, we are once again facing an invaluable opportunity to consolidate the gender vision in primary education, planting the seed to build relationships that are based on equity, respect, and solidarity.

Perhaps it is about time to recognize that schools and the educational system have been compliant with oppression, that teachers require intensive training regarding this matter, and that we should be dealing with the "why" instead of only considering the "how." "Critical pedagogy is about consciousness raising, is moral in intent, ethical in nature and seeks justice as an end" (Kanpol, 1999, p. 186). Teachers will require to develop a sense of lucidity, in political terms, and acknowledge their own complicity in preserving the status quo, accepting that their work is not impartial, but located within a male-dominated structure. "Personal confession involves each individual first becoming aware of how they are implicated in oppressive social structures ... Awareness, it must be reiterated, is but a part of the 'battle plan' " (Kanpol, 1999, p. 187). This will require risk-taking qualities as well, identifying and criticizing inequities, going quite often against the school culture of normalizing disparities.

The challenge is to question the notion of neutral and unbiased schooling, to be alert and ready to respond to a male-dominated culture; surely there are many Mexican teachers cultivating instances of more progressive gender education, but widespread action is needed.

References

Acker, S. (1994). *Gendered education: Sociological reflections on women, teaching, and feminism.* Open University Press.

Arnot, M. (2013). Male hegemony, social class, and women's education [Online]. In B. J. Thayer-Bacon, L. Stone, & K. M. Sprecher (Eds.), *Education feminism: Classic and contemporary readings* (pp. 19–40). State University of New York Press.

Barba, J. B. (2019, February 28). Artículo tercero Constitucional. Génesis, transformación y axiología. *Revista Mexicana de Investigación Educativa, 24*(80), 287–316. https://dialnet.unirioja.es/descarga/articulo/6987389.pdf

Cámara de Diputados. Servicio de Investigación y Análisis. (2000). V. Evolución jurídica del Artículo 3o Constitucional en relación a la gratuidad de la educación superior. In *Cámara De Diputados. Servicio De Investigación Y Análisis.* Retrieved October 15, 2022, from http://www.diputados.gob.mx/bibliot/publica/inveyana/polint/cua2/evolucion.htm

INEGI (2022). Maestros y escuelas por entidad federativa según nivel educativo, ciclos escolares seleccionados de 2000/2001 a 2021/2022. https://www.inegi.org.mx/app/tabulados/interactivos/?pxq=8c29ddc6-eeca-4dcc-8def-6c3254029f19

Kanpol, B. (1999, April 30). *Critical pedagogy: An introduction* (2nd ed.). Praeger.

Kincheloe, J. L. (2008). *Critical pedagogy primer.* Peter Lang.

Klein, S., Kramarae, C., & Richardson, B. (2007). Examining the achievement of gender equity in and through education. In S. Klein et al. (Eds.), *Handbook for achieving gender equity through education* (2nd ed.). Routledge.

Kramarae, C. (2007). Overview: Gender equity strategies in the content areas. In S. Klein et al. (Eds.), Handbook for achieving gender equity throuhg education (2nd Ed). Routledge. *Handbook for achieving gender equity through education* (2nd ed., pp. 231–234). State University of New York Press.

Secretaría de Gobernación Unidad de Asuntos Jurídicos. (2020). Artículo 3o Constitucional. In *Secretaría De Goberación. Unidad General De Asuntos Jurídicos. Secretaría de Gobernación.* Retrieved October 15, 2022, from http://www.ordenjuridico.gob.mx/Constitucion/articulos/3.pdf

SEP. (2017). *Aprendizajes clave para la educación integral. Plan y Programas de Estudio para la educación básica (Key learnings for integral education. Plan and Programs Of Study For Basic Education)* (1st ed.). Secretaría de Educación Pública (Ministry of Education).

SEP. (2019a). *Formación cívica y ética, Cuarto grado (Civic and Ethical Education, Fourth Year)* (5th ed.). Secretaría de Educación Pública (Ministry of Education). https://historico.conaliteg.gob.mx/H2019P4FCA.htm#page/1

SEP. (2019b). *Formación cívica y ética, Quinto grado (Civic and Ethical Education, Fifth Year)* (2nd ed.). Secretaría de Educación Pública (Ministry of Education). https://historico.conaliteg.gob.mx/H2019P5FCA.htm#page/1

SEP. (2019c). *Formación cívica y ética, Sexto grado (Civic and Ethical Education, Sixth Year)* (2nd ed.). Secretaría de Educación Pública (Ministry of Education). https://historico.conaliteg.gob.mx/H2019P6FCA.htm#page/1

Chapter 2

Roles and Stereotypes of Latin American Women in the Drug Trafficking Economy

Jaime Andrés Wilches Tinjacá and Daniela Rivera Ortega

Abstract

Inequality of rights, wage gaps, and gender stereotypes are the context in which women in Latin America live, aggravating their situation of poverty. Under this scenario, drug trafficking is presented as a legitimate job offer as an answer to women's economic needs. Currently, drug trafficking not only categorizes women as merchandise for sexual services but also integrates professional, technical, and logistical services within the criminal structures.

This research follows a qualitative methodology, making a documentary review to identify the role of women in drug trafficking. As partial results, it is evident that women recognize that gender gaps are not solved by their insertion in the drug trafficking economy, because they must perform jobs that put them at greater risk with the authorities, but they do solve an economic need.

Keywords: Capital; participation; gender; prejudice; consensus; coercion; public policies

Introduction

The situation of inequality and poverty in Latin America has led men, young people, and women to seek new opportunities for wellbeing and progress in drug trafficking. The participation of women in the production and trade of illicit drugs has increased significantly; however, this participation is made invisible by the stereotypes and assumptions about women in this industry (sexual services). For this reason, this paper seeks to show that although in general there is a social

Economy, Gender and Academy: A Pending Conversation, 27–36
Copyright © 2023 by Jaime Andrés Wilches Tinjacá and Daniela Rivera Ortega
Published under exclusive licence by Emerald Publishing Limited
doi:10.1108/978-1-80455-998-720231008

stigmatization of the role of women in drug trafficking, the reality is that little by little it has been demonstrated that there is greater female involvement in this business and that their role is not only focused on covering sexual or sentimental needs.

Although drug trafficking does not guarantee equal rights, reduction of salary gaps, or gender stereotyping as a guideline for secondary functions and tasks, it is presented as a legitimate offer to solve the absence of institutional responses to women's economic needs, with special emphasis on areas where their rights are violated or inefficiently addressed by the State.

The drug trafficking industry is constituted today as a sector that allows the economic development of women, providing them with welfare, without them performing tasks that denigrate them, which shows once again that drug trafficking is able to cover the duties that the States have failed to achieve after so long.

The effects of drug trafficking on human and economic development are felt with greater intensity over time; for example, it has become involved in everyday aspects such as tourism, as there is an increasing interest in knowing and visiting places that allow people to experience up close the life of a drug trafficker and his challenges (narcotourism). Likewise, in critical contexts such as the COVID-19 pandemic, it proved to be an industry that is constantly evolving, unlike other economic activities and state institutions, showing that it has an adaptive capacity that allows it to handle any eventuality, be it economic, social, or political.

Drug trafficking showed that despite the fact that governments around the world took drastic measures to restrict travel and mobility of people, thus damaging their supply chains of most drugs, the illegal drug trade was not affected in the long term, drug trafficking operations managed to open new routes of operation, in addition to gaining the trust and support of the populations that for years have felt the abandonment of the State and more at that time of crisis, offering them food, loans, medical services, etc. Drug trafficking became the only agent and opportunity for many who live in poverty and want to have better welfare.

The fragility of the Latin American States for years has not been able to guarantee a decent quality of life to a large part of its population. Several fundamental rights are constantly violated, leading people to live in poverty and misery by not having certain opportunities, such as quality education, decent job, clean water, housing, food, medical care, among others. In this situation, drug trafficking becomes one of the few opportunities to progress; it is the door to get some money.

For this reason, although both at the international and national levels, more effective and humane alternatives have been sought to address the global drug problem, these measures have so far been ineffective in the face of drug production and consumption. Drug trafficking has established itself as a possibility of progress for many, thus gaining the social support of different populations, especially the most vulnerable (Organization of American States (OAS), 2006).

For example, young people find support and opportunity within illegal organizations, a situation that increased during the pandemic when schools were closed, so they had more free time, and also families began to live in a situation of economic crisis because there was nothing to eat. The Economic Commission for Latin America and the Caribbean (ECLAC) (2021) noted that poverty and extreme poverty reached previously unseen levels in Latin America in 2020. So that the economic need led more young people to enter the productive or commercial chain of drug trafficking (Infobae, 2021; Niño, 2021).

The fact that people living in poverty do not have a stable form of income leads them down the path of drug trafficking, thanks to the quick and huge amounts of money that can be made from the sale and production of drugs. Hence, the admiration for drug lords like Pablo Escobar and El Chapo Guzman, men from poor families who found cocaine the only way for their families to survive. In addition, their businesses offered many more people job opportunities they did not have before, giving families a sense of stability even though their economic activity was within the framework of illegality, a paradox that highlights the complexity behind the relationship between poverty and drug trafficking.

In the same sense, drug trafficking puts each person in a position where they have to choose between life and death. And in this case, to choose life is to remain in a situation of poverty full of needs, while death is to enter a life where illegal activity is one of the few opportunities to get ahead.

Economic needs affect an entire family, which is why this work focuses on an essential member of the family, the woman. Labor inequality, unpaid work and the devalued contribution of women maintain the conditions of poverty for women. Organizations such as the United Nations (UN) (2014) point out that a poor woman tends to live with multiple forms of discrimination, so she has a higher risk of violence, and not having any income or economic resources, she has no way to escape from this situation.

However, the participation of women in drug trafficking processes has been increasing (ECLAC, 2021), and their role has also changed, as they are no longer purely the partner or prostitute of the drug trafficker. Women have gradually become involved in the drug trafficking industry, often becoming the head of the organization. Doing business with the illegal drug trade has become an opportunity for women to progress and obtain economic benefits, leaving aside the idea that it is a business only for men.

Theoretical Framework

Women and Drug Trafficking

The role of women as the narco's wife, lover, or sexual partner was popularized and settled in society thanks to narcoseries and narcocorridos (Escobar-Arboleda & Velásquez-Upegui, 2019; León, 2022; Pavón et al., 2015). Women within the criminal structures were perceived as unimportant actors, their work was focused on satisfying the sexual needs of the narcos, in addition to fulfilling other tasks such as messengers, "mules."

In general, the plot of the stories spoke of women who attended parties or nightclubs, where they consumed drugs and sold themselves to the highest bidder, in addition, they are described as women who travel alone to another city or country all in search of improving their living conditions, even without having a stable place to live, with economic shortages and without a labor contract (Escobar-Arboleda & Velásquez-Upegui, 2019).

Something that stands out about these women was their beauty, drug trafficking reached the point of establishing the prototype of the ideal woman, it can be said that the drug trafficker was the one who had the money, so he was the one who wrote the rules and chose the women as he pleased (Jiménez, 2014).

The female image was highly sexualized and presented as a trophy, and the artificially curvaceous stereotype was a reflection of the ostentatious and luxurious attitude of the essentially macho mentality innate to the drug lords' lifestyle. The women's attributes were clearly their "beauty, sensuality and coquetry, possess voluptuous bodies, be charismatic and uninhibited" (Jiménez, 2014, p. 109) (translation by the author).

At this point, women could be categorized in two ways according to Mata (2012), on the one hand, there was the "narco woman," this category included wives, daughters, and other family members. They were the women who maintained a life of luxury, having access to different comforts, and although they were within the organization, they did not have a legitimate or important role within the network. On the other hand, there were prostitutes, women who entered the world thanks to their beauty and maintained a mainly sexual relationship with the drug traffickers. Both groups of women shared one thing in common, and that was that they had to remain under the command and control of the men.

However, in recent decades, the number of women involved in drug trafficking is increasing, and the presence of women in different areas of the drug trafficking universe is growing (Bernabéu, 2007). Women began to be part of the productive, commercial and logistical chains of drug trafficking. This is a sector that diversifies its roles within the spiral of adaptation and transformation strategies to maintain the income derived from the business. It is now not only stereotyped as a commodity of sexual services, but has also integrated professional, technical, and logistical services.

The United Nations Office on Drugs and Crime (UNODC) in its 2019 report noted that unemployment and poverty rates among women have significant implications for their role and place in trafficking networks. According to the 2018 World Drug Report, between 2012 and 2016, around 10% of the global prison population were women convicted of drug-related offense.

Rise of Women in the Narco-World

By the 1990s, the number of women in drug sales and production increased,

> the cocaine economy has provided new ways for women to escape their limited roles, statuses and incomes in previous eras. It also provides an outlet for women to achieve conventional goals for family through illegal work. (Fagan, 1994, p. 210)

There was a growing emancipation of women, and research no longer emphasized the powerlessness and vulnerability of women (Fleetwood & Leban, 2022; León, 2022). Women became an important piece for drug trafficking, and this thanks to the female stereotype established in organized crime. As Farfán (2021) points out, women became a human asset that can go unnoticed by the state and rival groups, the image of "innocence" and "weakness" of women allows them to collaborate with criminal groups in different areas directly or indirectly, opening up new economic opportunities at the same time, thanks to the paradox of invisibility.

Drug trafficking once again opened up new economic development opportunities for women. Women begin to occupy privileged social positions; the work that the narco-world offered them offers them the benefits of earning money, as well as a certain degree of independence and personal freedom. And although the majority of women are still mules, chemists or collectors, the new dynamics within the drug trade offer them a hope of "moving up" and out of poverty. The opportunity to earn "easy money" is not limited to men, and the narco-world now offers that possibility to women by changing their gender perspective.

Women's participation in drug trafficking and their rise within the criminal structures turned them into low-profile bosses (León, 2022). Different women have managed to implement strategies to maintain the leadership and power of the organizations, as is the case of the Black Widow or the Queen of the Pacific. The conceptions of femininity in the narco-world have begun to change, women are no longer seen only as victims, they have begun to be recognized as subjects who are also in search of power and money, although the media still does not show this image, and society keeps them in anonymity as Deborah Bonello, a Maltese-British journalist, points out (González, 2020).

The woman in the narco-world is generally presented as a female victim, but in reality, some women enter this business of their own free will, either because she is the narco's wife or has a relative; or because they live in a condition of poverty; or because the woman is attracted by the power and mysticism of drug trafficking (Acosta, 2012; Campbell, 2008) at the end of the day entering the narco-world allows them to access better levels of welfare, thanks to their various job opportunities as presented in Table 2.1, women not only perform operational but also administrative and logistic work.

Methodology

The research uses an exploratory qualitative methodology because its purpose is to study and analyze the current dynamics that women live within drug trafficking. The data collection procedure was carried out through documentary analysis of governmental and non-governmental reports on the relationship between women and drug trafficking. The method of analysis is approached from the scenarios in which the needs of women, the promises of rights and the offers for their labor occupation converge.

Results

Women within the drug trade began to acquire new responsibilities (cultivation, processing, transportation, logistics, drug sales, and control). Their work began

Table 2.1.   Women's Work in Drug Trafficking.

Illegal Economy	Definition	Roles
Drug trafficking	Drug trafficking means the criminal activity carried out by common or organized criminal networks, representing the illegal manufacture, trade and sale of any substance (or derivative thereof) contained in the international protocols developed within the framework of the United Nations and in national regulations	Hawks Drug dealers Narcomodels Logistics Day laborers Scrappers Farmers Cooks Chemists Mules Collaborators

Source: Tickner et al. (2020, p. 22).

to challenge the notion and stereotype of a submissive and sexualized woman. Within the drug trafficking industry women can now be traffickers or hitmen, or friends, wives or lovers, prostitutes or other employees paid by them. They may also occupy central and leading roles (Pavón et al., 2015).

In the narco-world, a revision of femininities within drug trafficking begins to take place, opening an idea of gender identity outside the sexualized stereotype, it

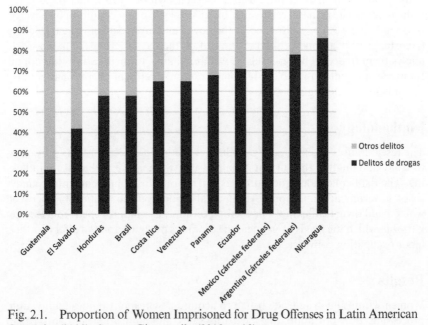

Fig. 2.1.   Proportion of Women Imprisoned for Drug Offenses in Latin American Countries (2013). *Source*: Giacomello (2013, p. 13).

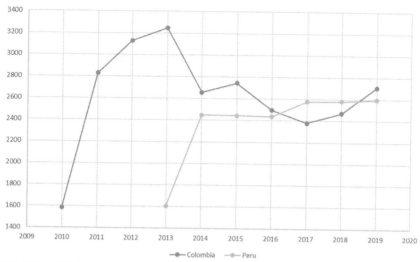

Fig. 2.2.   Number of Women for Drug Trafficking-related Crimes in Colombia and Peru (2010–2019). *Source*: Tickner et al. (2020, p. 42).

can be said that femininity as a sexual item is left aside, building new socio-cultural characteristics that hierarchize and make women visible.

As can be seen in Figs. 2.1 and 2.2, the increasing involvement of women in the narco-world is a reality, as evidenced by the number of women in prison who have been convicted of drug-related crimes. In most Latin American countries, more than half of the women deprived of liberty are charged with drug production, trafficking, or possession. In this case, although drug trafficking offers them an opportunity for work and progress, it also puts them in a vulnerable position, making them easy prey for the authorities because of their higher-risk roles.

In the specific case of Colombia, this is the main cause of imprisonment of women in the prison system in the country, the main conviction activities are for trafficking, manufacture, and possession of narcotics, for the year 2022 to May 31, one of four women is in prison for this crime; in total, there is a population of 2,703 women.

Several social science studies on the insertion of women into the narco-world coincide "in pointing out that drug trafficking activities imply a specific way of life, characterized by the cohesion offered by the fact of sharing an illegal and clandestine activity from which important economic gains are derived" (Ovalle & Giacomello, 2006, p. 299) (translated by the author), this income may not offer them great luxuries, but it is a help in the face of the economic precariousness in which most women who decide to enter the narco-world live (Kapin, 2016).

Despite being an economic opportunity that goes beyond offering only sexual services, in drug trafficking, as in the legal economic sector, there is a gender gap with respect to wages; the UNODC (2019) in its report "Characterization of socioeconomic conditions of women related to drug problems" points out that there is "unequal payment with respect to men in some jobs" (p. 40). But

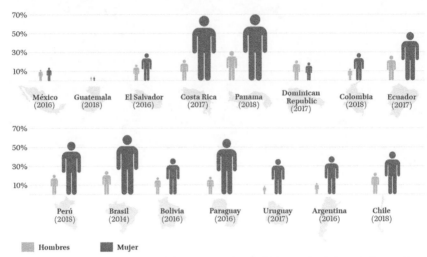

Fig. 2.3.   Persons Imprisoned for Drug-related Offenses in Selected Countries, By Gender. *Source*: Giacomello (2020).

this is not the only inequality that women experience within this business, they also receive greater "disproportionate affectations derived from the deprivation of liberty" (p. 40), as shown in Fig. 2.3 women become an easy target. In Latin America, the female population deprived of liberty for crimes related to drug trafficking is greater than the male population.

Women recognize that gender gaps are not solved by their insertion in the drug trafficking economy, but they do solve an economic need, drug trafficking allows to obtain substantial financial gains, no more than in the American continent drug trafficking earns between 80,000 and 90,000 million dollars a year (EFE, 2020). In addition, it is a sector that allows job climbing, becoming leaders in drug trafficking organizations.

Conclusion

The question of whether women are involved in the narco-world outside of sexual or affective activities is no longer a debate but a reality, whether in production, transportation, or negotiation, women are present. And although there is still a gender inequality regarding the income women receive compared to men, women's participation continues to grow, so their role in drug trafficking is far from inconsequential.

Women also participate in drug trafficking not because they are forced to do so by a man, but because economic and cultural factors influence their decision (Campbell, 2008). In this sense, it is necessary to associate gender analysis with other elements that account for the various factors that come into play in the decision to enter the narco-world.

The drug trafficking industry is nowadays a sector that allows the economic development of women, providing welfare by improving their income in places where the State has not been able to cover their basic needs. The impulse to act outside the law has allowed women to gain a certain degree of independence and freedom, which state institutions do not provide them, and they have a passive attitude in attacking illegal economies, especially in areas where they have limited control or where implicit alliances have been made, which allows them security, outside of the criminalization and prisionalization that is a consequence of being part of this business.

The participation of women in the growth of drug trafficking in Latin America should be studied from the perspective of drug trafficking economies due to their diversification with respect to the tasks and tasks they perform in the drug trafficking industry, as they have installed capabilities in money laundering, front man and investment in sectors that are not attacked or prosecuted by judicial bodies, resulting in a growing participation and increasing prominence of women in the narco-world.

References

Acosta, J. (2012). *Mujeres En El Tráfico Minoritario De Droga En La Frontera México-Estados Unidos: Exclusión, Poder Y Riqueza*. Master's thesis. El Colegio de la Frontera Norte. Institutional Repository. https://bit.ly/3PNWZAG

Bernabéu, S. (2017). La Saga de Camelia la Texana. La mujer en el narco y en el narcocorrido. *Conserveries Mémorielles*, (20). https://bit.ly/3JorKJZ

Campbell, H. (2008). Female drug smugglers on the U.S.–Mexico border: Gender, crime, and empowerment. *Anthropological Quarterly, 81*(1), 233–267. http://www.jstor.org/stable/30052745

Economic Commission for Latin America and the Caribbean (ECLAC). (2021). Pandemia provoca aumento en los niveles de pobreza sin precedentes en las últimas décadas e impacta fuertemente en la desigualdad y el empleo. ECLAC. https://bit.ly/3SeVFrU

EFE. (2020, September 9). Narcotráfico genera entre US$80.000 y US$90.000 millones en América. *El Tiempo*. https://bit.ly/3PVPw2s

Escobar-Arboleda, Y., & Velásquez-Upegui, E. (2019). Narcotráfico y prostitución: Estereotipos de la mujer colombiana en noticias digitales mexicanas. In L. Ayala y L. Rodríguez (Comps.), *Masculinidad, crimen organizado y violencia* (pp. 57–76). Colofón

Fagan, J. (1994). Women and drugs revisited: Female participation in the cocaine economy. *Journal of Drug Issues, 24*(2), 179–225. https://doi.org/10.1177/002204269402400202

Farfán, C. (2021). Women's Involvement in Organised Crime and Drug Trafficking: A Comparative Analysis of the Sinaloa and Yamaguchigumi Organisations. In J. Buxton, G. Margo y L. Burger (eds), *The impact of global drug policy on women: Shifting the needle*, (pp. 159–168). Emerald Publishing. doi:10.1108/978-1-83982-882-92020002

Fleetwood, J. y., & Leban, L. (2022). Women's involvement in the drug trade: Revisiting the emancipation thesis in global perspective. *Deviant Behavior*. https://doi.org/10.1080/01639625.2022.2033607

Giacomello, C. (2013) Mujeres, delitos de drogas y sistemas penitenciarios en América Latina. International Drug Policy Consortium. https://bit.ly/3cMhsqL

Giacomello, C. (2020). Los impactos de género de las políticas de drogas en las mujeres: Estudios de casos en México. *International Development Policy|Revue internationale de politique de développement [En ligne]*, (12). https://doi.org/10.4000/poldev.4426

González, M. (2022, June 7). Cuál es el verdadero papel de las mujeres en el narcotráfico y el crimen organizado en América Latina. *BBC News*. https://bbc.in/3cSedOJ

Infobae. (2021, March 23). Defensoría del Pueblo señala que la pandemia y los niveles de pobreza en Colombia han facilitado el reclutamiento de menores en el país. *Infobae*. https://bit.ly/3vqCp16

Jiménez, E. (2014). Mujeres, narco y violencia: Resultados de una guerra fallida. *Región y Sociedad, 26*(especial4), 101–128. https://bit.ly/2yxfUZW

Kapkin, S. (2016). Infografía: Narcotráfico y mujeres, una relación cada vez más estrecha. Pacifista. https://bit.ly/2EIv9T6

León, A. (2022). Jefas de perfil bajo en el narcomundo: Las mujeres "invisibles" de las organizaciones. *Cuadernos de Humanidades*, (35), 122–134. https://bit.ly/3zHShyz

Mata, I. (2012). *El imaginario social sobre el estilo de vida de las mujeres del narco*. Master's thesis. Instituto Tecnológico y de Estudios Superiores de Occidente (ITESO)]. Institutional Repository.

Navarrete, M. (2019, 13 de octubre). Women taking on more roles within Colombia's drug trade. *Insight Crime*. https://bit.ly/3vrrog5

Niño, C. (2021, February 8). La pandemia favoreció a los grupos armados ilegales. *Razón Pública*. https://bit.ly/3S6NQEV

Organization of American States (OAS). (2006). Mujeres y drogas en las Américas: Un diagnóstico de política en construcción. https://bit.ly/3vqqdxj

Ovalle, L. y., & Giacomello, C. (2006). La mujer en el "narcomundo". Construcciones tradicionales y alternativas del sujeto femenino. *Revista de Estudios de Género. La ventana*, (24), 297–318.

Pavón Cuéllar, D., Vargas Frutos, M., Orozco Guzmán, M., & Gamboa Solís, F. (2015). Las mujeres en los narcocorridos: idealización y devaluación, conversión trágica y desenmascaramiento cómico. *Alternativas en Psicología, 18*(31), 22–44. https://bit.ly/3cRWyqu

Tickner, A., Alonso, L., Loaiza, L., Suárez, N., Castellanos, D. y., & Cárdenas, J. (2020). *Mujeres y crimen organizado en América Latina: más que víctimas o victimarias*. Universidad del Rosario

United Nations (UN). (2014). Mujer y Pobreza. UN Women. https://bit.ly/3gphQxJ

United Nations Office on Drugs and Crime (UNODC). (2019). Workshop provides insight on role of women in illicit networks. https://bit.ly/3vrnovU

Val, V. (2020). La pobreza tiene género. Amnesty International. https://bit.ly/3Q2m5vi

Part II

Gender Policies and the Teaching of Gender Equity in the Context of the Countries Within the Latin American Territories

Chapter 3

Favoring Cultural Integration From an Education That Exceeds Sexism South–South Dialogue: Cuba, Argentina, and Peru in the Post-Pandemic Context

Marybexy Calcerrada Gutiérrez, Rafael Lorenzo Martín, Nolbis Espinosa Cruz, Magdaloys Peña Gutiérrez and Olga Adriana Domínguez

Abstract

The proposal takes as a reference of the post-pandemic context corresponding to Cuba, likewise, it includes experiences from Peru and Argentina, mainly in the field of education. In the epistemic order, enclaves of the theory of culture in its humanist aspect corresponding to cultural identity were adopted. Methodologically, we adhere to the critical interpretative paradigm, integrating results of the authors' social practice and critical review of sources, mainly contributions from critical theory. The exposed analyses contribute to base theoretical-methodological criteria aimed at reducing gender and racial gaps, and other inequalities determined by conditions that historically become inequities in access to development. Political theoretical criteria are proposed for the implementation of inclusive public policies in the area of education and productive activity, overcoming gender, and racial gaps in the post-pandemic context. As a result, it contributes to promoting the overcoming of the effects of racism and sexism in the pandemic context as well as enabling the development of cultural identity from actions aimed at the cultural integration of identity expressions neglected due to racial and gender conditions. As a result, it contributes to promote the overcoming of the effects of racism and sexism in the pandemic context; as well as to enable the

Economy, Gender and Academy: A Pending Conversation, 39–60
Copyright © 2023 by Marybexy Calcerrada Gutiérrez, Rafael Lorenzo Martín, Nolbis Espinosa Cruz, Magdaloys Peña Gutiérrez and Olga Adriana Domínguez
Published under exclusive licence by Emerald Publishing Limited
doi:10.1108/978-1-80455-998-720231009

development of cultural identity from actions aimed at the cultural integration of identity expressions neglected due to racial and gender conditions.

Keywords: Education; cultural integration; social policy; gender; racism; equality.

Introduction

The transnational experience that is exposed integrates processes of educational management that overcome exclusive binarisms, fundamentally, with respect to gender and racial condition. The proposal includes experiences from three Latin American countries: Cuba, Peru, and Argentina. These territories have partial differences in terms of ethnic-racial composition, socio-economic development conditions, cultural traditions, among other aspects. Despite the diversity, the analysis presented shows commonalities among them. New integrations that strengthen Latin American contributions to educational development management from their territorial practices are revealed.

The management of educational and labor development finds protection in international orders such as the 2030 Agenda, a global program that aspires to its contextualization by national territories according to their policies and structural conditions. It includes objectives aimed at promoting the progress of identity groups that have historically been neglected due to conditions of gender, race, generational, and territorial among others. The purpose finds situations of vulnerability from the pandemic event.

In the case of the behavior of school education, in this sense, there is systematicity regarding the criterion that the pandemic event produces a variation in the behavior of different educational dimensions, present, and future (Menéndez & Figares, 2020). In line with this idea, situations have been pointed out that lead to social inequalities for school children due to the inequitable distribution of technology that hinders the effectiveness of remote teaching based on the social distancing required by the health situation (Espada et al., 2020). In this same direction, the challenge and the complex effects that the emerging performance of teaching roles had on families are signified (García-Álvarez et al., 2020).

The pandemic event includes among its most severe marks, in addition, financial crises at the individual and family level due to variations in employability as one of the areas with the greatest weight in the quality of relational dynamics (Grupo Estudios del Trabajo (GrET), 2020). An issue that needs to be problematized in the relational, subjective order, both individually and collectively from the intersections that occur between territories, gender conditions, age, level of education, and employment.

Derived from the foregoing, an increase in development gaps in vulnerable groups (infants, subcontracted women, under schooled youth, students devoid of technological coverage, men employed in the informal economy, and older adults) regarding the standards of well-being and development of their contexts of life, in the face of the pandemic event that negatively impacts the fulfillment of the SDGs, in the case of:

Goal 1 is aimed at reducing poverty by gender and age groups, including building resilience to economic and social shocks.
Goal 5 and the corresponding Goal 17 with the elimination of all forms of violence against all women and girls in the public and private spheres as well as the valuation of care and domestic work and shared responsibility at home.
Objective 4 is aimed at an inclusive and equitable education.

Therefore, the problem to which this presentation responds is the need, in the current context, to base and guide criteria that contribute to reducing gender and racial gaps and those determined by other conditions that historically become development inequalities, particularly in the education, platform for social integration in the labor area. Consequently, its fundamental objective is to offer criteria that contribute to policies in the direction of equitable education.

From the identity and development conditions of the countries mentioned, in articulation with the objectives and policies oriented to human development in the post-pandemic context, this text includes the following axes of analysis:

School, professional, and occupational development, in the post-pandemic context in Cuba and areas of Peru and Argentina, fundamentally from a gender perspective, without neglecting the intersection with other axes such as racial. The presentations from Peru and Argentina correspond to experiences in areas of human development managed by civil associations based in those countries, co-directed and directed by Cubans with citizenship and residence in these territories, Argentina and Peru, respectively. In turn, they are part of the authors of this text. Thus, capacities formed in the Cuban context crosscut all the cases presented to a certain extent.

Likewise, political theoretical criteria are proposed for the implementation of inclusive public policies in the area of education and productive activity, overcoming gender, and racial gaps in the post-pandemic context.

As a result, it contributes to promote the overcoming of the effects of racism and sexism in the pandemic context, as well as to enable the development of cultural identity from actions aimed at the cultural integration of identity expressions neglected due to racial and gender conditions.

The paradigmatic contribution to which it aspires is the strengthening of cultural identity, at different contextual levels, from a conception of the recognition of diversity and the propitiation of cultural integration through an education that overcomes racism and sexism, which favors human development in the post-pandemic context.

In the epistemic order, enclaves of the theory of culture were adopted in its humanist aspect corresponding to cultural identity that presupposes identity in difference and cultural integration (Rojas, 2011). Likewise, it supports feminist thought and contributions from fundamentally intersectional politics. Methodologically, we adhere to the critical interpretative paradigm, integrating results of the authors' social practice and critical review of sources, fundamentally contributions from critical theory.

Theoretical Foundations and Regional Strategic Agreements: Conceptual Framework for the Understanding of Public Policies Regarding an Equitable Education

The foundations of this proposal are attached to a non-androcentric anthropological philosophy articulated with guidelines of distributive justice and human security. It supposes a decolonial vision regarding ethnocentric paradigms regarding the conception of bodies, subjectivities, and territories. Dimensions are integrated into the human condition and are affected in multiple ways by the pandemic event. Regarding the body, our theoretical support stems from subverting the schism between the body and spirituality, a characteristic dissociation of Western thought. The binary, opposed, and hierarchical character between the soul (psyche, mind) configured as rational and eternal; and the body: imperfect and mortal, place of experience and affections; corresponded in turn to a dissociation of the human race. In this sense, hegemonic masculinity was established as the eternal essential, the feminine, as devalued otherness. The hierarchy between the mind and body, as well as masculine and feminine traits, has been present in the philosophical tradition since Plato's time.

However, existentialist philosophies along with other analysis matrices that have emerged in contemporary times regarding the body have contributed to subverting traditional Western logic. The cultural conception of the body contributed by, among other matrices, anthropology of bodies, gender anthropology, feminist thought, and post-structuralist thought is a merit of the past century. Conception focused on critical understanding regarding the regulation and control of bodies from disciplinary societies, among which Michael Foucault (2005) stands out.

The sense of rupture with Western rational binary logic, as has been mentioned, appears between Feminism and post-structuralism, in which the performative conception of the American philosopher Judith Butler (2002) stands out. Expressions of this conception without defined margins of the bodies deserve an updated review in the pandemic context, in which alienation behaviors are reported, and integrations through the use of the screen should be reviewed in different groups in terms of advances and setbacks.

The blow dealt to Western rational logic by the theories of the twentieth century focused on the cultural construction of bodies, which prefigures their malleability. It also makes possible the interest and development of bodies neglected in history. The subversion of colonial knowledge, which essentializes identities, not only opens methodological paths with the subjects designated as subaltern but also revalues non-dominant dimensions in Western science such as experience and subjectivity, as personal meaning.

The pandemic event gains expression in different bodies according to age, gender, and other conditions that socially imply inequalities determined by racial, financial, technological factors, etc. For example, during the health emergency, affectations were reported in the body of women with greater domestic overload and in those who were confined to living with violent partners. Likewise, male subjects of different ages were alienated from the hegemonic gender identity, mainly due to the increase in the economic crisis that affects the expected performance of men with respect to dominant cultural demands.

Linked to the conception of the body emerges the sense of territory. The concept of territory is embedded in the perspective of Geography in its significance as a social science, it is in conjunction with the senses of space and territoriality; dynamic terms depending on epistemological trends (Trepat & Cómes, 2000). Substantive criteria in the conception of territory include legal delimitations, likewise, and with a progressive character, it implies appropriation and supposes the relationship between the human being, society, and terrestrial space (Brunet et al., 2005). From there emerges a cardinal property of the concept of territory, its relational character; it contains political, affective, and identity dimensions (Montañez, 2001). Each of these dimensions must be analyzed with respect to their mobility, greater roots, and integration.

Contemporary currents print the fate of their philosophies in the conception of territory; postmodern expressions highlight it as a process of identification and representation regardless of political and administrative delimitations (Claval, 1999). From the Marxist perspective, it supposes a space that integrates infrastructure (human component and economic activities), superstructure (the political and symbolic), and metastructure (relationship between subject and space) (Di Meo, 1993). In development management, it is essential to evaluate the relationship between these dimensions, corresponding to other nomenclatures. At the institutional level, there has been a lack of a deep understanding of culture and its incidence, even the most basic and most important expression that is the person. From a critical perspective of the territory, it is recognized that the spatial activity of the actors is differential, a difference that has become an unequal capacity to create, recreate, and appropriate territory (Montañez & Delgado, 1998, p. 123, as referred in Rodríguez, 2010). This idea is one of the most complex in the methodological order for its realization.

Fundamental in the conception of territory, which is assumed to be a dynamic relationship between subjects and their space, is the sense of the local situated. The determinations of particular contexts define the needs, expectations, and distinctive practices of the territory. Peculiarities as an expression of identity are also a central part of what is conceived as territory, which frames participatory work methodologies, convergent with the cultural identity of these collective subjects. The event of a pandemic has led to differentiated attitudes by territory both in relation to the infectious event and with respect to the systemic effects of the crisis. Hygiene policies were not received in the same way in all localities, likewise, integration and social discipline, required for the management of resources in health emergency conditions, have not been the same either. Cultural and identity conditions have emerged in some cases as resilience factors; in others, they have hindered or aggravated the effects of the crisis.

For its part, the understanding of subjectivities, from our proposal, we inscribe it in plural paradigms of knowledge unmarked from rational, androcentric, positivist logic, typical of the western world to modern thought. It supposes a phenomenological orientation that values the experience, from the perspective of the subjects, understood as actors. The humanist philosophy that sustains this vision supposes the subversion of any binary scheme that differs the identities designated as the subaltern other: boys, girls, women, non-white people, without scientific training, among others. We believe that it is necessary to analyze the dynamism of these subjectivities in the face of the pandemic event from the perspective of their experiences. The decolonial framework that sustains this conception implies the empowerment of these embodied subjectivities as project identities, which are reconstructed and reconfigured in their community settings. Therefore, they are strongly imbricated with the territory dimension.

The referential conception of action for the resilient management of the pandemic event is a phenomenon that has triggered disturbances at different levels of subjectivity. Both at the individual and collective levels, critical expressions regarding subjective well-being are recorded.

In understanding the intersection between subjective dynamics, the relationship with bodies and cartographic locations, and interrelated coordinates in the pandemic event, we assume the politics of difference, a fundamental thesis of contemporary feminism. Authors such as the aforementioned Butler (2002), without exception to other contributions, state that conditions such as gender are a point of convergence between specific cultural and historical relations, which include intersections with racial, age, and geographic conditions that vary contextually. Therefore, this plural determination cannot be dissociated from the way in which we understand ontological configurations.

The politics of difference and the thesis of equality – a principle that we also assume – in their intersection, imply a challenging relationship. The principle of equality, although it has not always been embodied with the same contents, invokes a sense of sameness that must be monitored to avoid homogenizations at various times in history have been producers of universal discourses. The inevitably growing plurality of the human condition and the need for consensus have also formed part of the political agenda of Marxist-oriented feminist thought and other aspects that integrate the logic of Marxist economic analysis or co-implicated principles such as democracy, a case of the Belgian philosopher Chantal Moufe (1999) in her work "The Return to the Political." In defense of that plurality, which expresses the concrete universal subject located, has also contributed to Latin American feminism, particularly oriented to the affirmation of the cultural identity of the indigenous and Afro-descendant population; in countries such as Mexico, Colombia, Brazil, and Argentina.

These theoretical-political referents face conceptions of universal-abstract identity, support a repertoire of exclusive attitudes that give rise to negative discrimination regarding, for example, certain knowledge, due to its origin, a form of production, that represents it, a case of epistemic racism.

The epistemic places from where we produce knowledge must be considered; while historically Cartesian dualism, heir to rational logic, has neglected affectivity, an important source of understanding; like the value of microstories. Cartographic coordinates guide the analyses that we expose here and we believe – together with Michael Focault and other thinkers in this direction – that it is the primary place of agency for change. From a subversion of the norm, materialized in a Northwestern culture, as Butler (2002) would say, recognizing the value of other identities that are not dominant in history as well.

These theoretical supports correspond to the criterion of identity in difference, a typology developed by Rojas (2011) in the conception that he develops regarding cultural identity, which we assume here. It supposes the recognition of different specific identity conditions without hierarchical distinctions that contribute to a collective identity through cultural integration. He implies a conception of equality that overcomes the abstract character that the excluding identity gave him based on the ideology of domination. Instead, equality is defined in relation to parameters inherent to the human condition, such as autonomy, as well as access to rights and opportunities that constitute the substratum on which recognition is given to the various expressions of identity.

On the contrary, the different centrisms that characterize the so-called cultures of domination materialize in a binary organization between essentialized identities and others that are ignored. Racism, sexism, and ethnocentrism, which subsidizes the latter. It is an obstacle to the authentic realization of minorities without historical power and become abject identities. Therefore, in these referents, we assume the intersectional perspective oriented in this case to overcoming racism and sexism in education in order to favor cultural integration as a condition for the development of authentic cultural identity, favoring horizontal relationships, without stimulated asymmetries in hegemonic power.

The cultural assumptions assumed in this proposal include criticism of traditional practices, questions about the idea of pseudo-culture (or hegemonic culture), instead, the adoption of authentic culture. Socio-anthropological conceptions that enable an understanding of inequities and their reverse: social inclusion, in this case through education. The critique of the culture of domination is articulated with the gender and racial condition, fundamentally, as excluding conditions from essentialized references that give rise to sexism, racism, and ethnocentrism.

We adopt the contributions of the so-called black feminism to the problematization of the racial component, understanding, as established by studies that integrate both perspectives, that the racial and gender condition are codependent (Collins, 1990).

In short, from historical-theoretical foundations, systematized in the theory of culture, feminist and intersectional thought, indicators were built for the understanding of inequities mainly due to gender and racial conditions; manifest among other contexts, in education. In the same way, a critique of epistemic racism is provided from the hermeneutics of the coloniality of power coarticulated with the intersection between gender, skin color, and other historical-social determinations that certain identity groups have neglected.

Theoretical-political criteria in the direction of equity policies:

- The equitable nature of relationships is configured in an alter-globalizing philosophy: multivalent recognition of concrete situated beings, unmarked from androcentrism, ethnocentrism, and other excluding essentialisms.
- Revaluation of the ontological condition from the de-biologization of parameters by sexual, racial, generational, or other physical conditions, whose cultural categorization becomes hierarchical relational systems.

• De-hierarchization of the territorial order configured binary and exclusively as center-periphery. Structuring of opposites, polarized as positive and negative on the basis of physical space, and culturally categorized. Based on a political economy of relationships, spaces of negative valence can concentrate on historically neglected identity groups. Case of black men in economically vulnerable neighborhoods, among other intersections between gender condition, territory, and other identity determinants. Instead of prioritizing the place of origin as a condition of identity confinement, stimulate a dialectical relationship based on the agency of territorial development and cultural identity that empowers people as the main subjects of their identity configuration.

These criteria are intertwined with regional strategic planning at different levels, ranging from international organizations to concrete ways in which the materialization by territories of the budgets contained at the world level are expressed.

Since the Universal Declaration of Human Rights, there are global agreements regarding, among others, education, which is a transversal development of identity and rights for opportunities for progress. Article 26 of the aforementioned text emphasizes the right to higher education without the exception of individuals, only determined by personal merits (Montañez, 2015). At the same time, this part of the corpus of principles of rights presupposes the admission to cultural diversity due to different identity conditions and their integration. The conditions of access for personal merits have become debatable since these are the results of the accumulation of cultural capital whose opportunities do not respond to a distributive economy. Overcoming meritocracy has progressively been embodied in international conventions, agreements, and agendas. Establishes the commitment to repeal all provisions (legislative and administrative) which justify discrimination in the field of education. Instead, formulate, where necessary, legislation favoring non-discrimination. Specify the implementation of these principles at the national level and favor the inclusion of identity minorities. Continuity of the vehicle of these rights is found in the International Covenant on Economic, Social, and Cultural Rights (1966), and also in The Convention on the Rights of the Child (1989), The New Delhi Declaration (1993). Equally, other international treaties aimed at the affirmation and educational development of subaltern identities such as the indigenous and rural population, and among others, included in the Declaration and Integrated Action Plan on Education for Peace, Human Rights and Democracy (1995), the Hamburg Declaration (1997), and the Beijing Declaration of the E-9 Group countries (2001) (Montañez, 2015).

Aligned with international conventions that specify general principles of Human Rights, the International Labor Organization established in 1958, the Convention on Discrimination (Employment and Occupation) (No. 111) that discards sex, race, color, religion, political ideas, origin, and social situation as conditions of labor exclusion. By virtue of the equity policy, the ILO also includes the Equal Remuneration Convention, 1951 (No. 100), which goes beyond the differentiation by sex. In addition, it incorporates the Workers with Family Responsibilities Convention, 1981 (No. 156), and the Maternity Protection Convention,

2000 (No. 183). All of these represent advances in gender equality and the core of the decent work agenda (International Labor Organization (ILO), 2012).

For its part, the 2030 Agenda, in several of the Sustainable Development Goals that it declares with its corresponding corpus of achievement, contributes to the improvement and scope of social equity. In terms of education and employment, it dedicates several objectives in a particular way. Case of Objective 4 aimed at promoting inclusive, equitable, and quality education throughout life, therefore, free of any type of discrimination. In the same way, Goal 5 aimed at gender equality, emphasizes the empowerment of girls and women, historically underdeveloped subjects. Likewise, Goal 8 dedicated to decent work for all, presupposes authentic opportunities for occupational training. Similarly, Goal 10 aimed at reducing inequities within and between countries. Goal 16, for its part, establishes peace and justice as the core aspiration and highlights the need for effective institutions in the management of inclusion, which is a guiding principle that guides the Agenda. Finally, Objective 17 expresses the Alliance for the achievement of the objectives, precisely a purpose aligned with the character of this text and volume in general that integrates the contribution of experiences at a transnational level.

In the field of education, a matrix of opportunities for occupational development, the role of UNESCO cannot be ignored. As part of its initiative for the development of Higher Education and within the framework of the Higher Education for Indigenous and Afro-descendant Peoples in Latin America (ESIAL), UNESCO Chairs are created with the purpose of promoting intercultural higher education in Latin America. The emphasis on historically neglected identity groups, which in general terms supposes the native population and Afro-descendants and the hierarchical structures by gender condition that are established in these groups, articulates the interest of laying the foundations for policy recommendations aimed at promoting their development.

Concretions of these legal frameworks are manifested, for example, in the Cuban case in the execution of the National Economic and Social Development Plan 2030. Structured work system on strategic axes co-aligned with the SDGs, expressed in various macro-programs, among which are "Human potential, Science, Technology and Innovation," and "Human Development, Equity and Social Justice." The macro-programs materialized through development programs and projects at different levels articulate with the Presidential Decree aimed at the advancement of women, complemented by the National Strategy against all forms of violence and discrimination.

Education and Job Occupation in Cuba: An Analysis in the Pandemic Context from the Perspective of Social Equity

The pandemic and post-pandemic scenario, as a trend, has coexisted with an increase in the virtualization of relationships in different areas. The situation that has partially favored or has been part of the management of solutions to problems such as psychological, educational, economic, and social in different orders. The necessary deployment of virtual resources interacts with social gaps.

Case of schoolchildren, due to the unequal distribution of technology, hinders the effectiveness of non-contact teaching, which is a requirement established in the health protocols during the course of COVID-19 in its epidemic phase. The possible increase in educational gaps and its impact on occupational development, observed in different international contexts, occupy our attention from racial and gender perspectives. Given the pandemic event, it is necessary to reflect on the behavior of development differences from an understanding of capital accumulation by population groups. This implies how conditions are articulated in the different identity groups in order of subjective, cultural, and other material mediations.

In this direction, there is systematicity in the criterion that the pandemic event produces a variation in all students, at all levels; although such deviations from the norm do not materialize in all schoolchildren in the same way. At the same time, at the beginning of the health emergency, there was uncertainty regarding the total effects that the variation in teaching conditions would cause. In this same sense, the displacement of the role of the school teacher to parents is signified as an important aspect, which presupposes competencies in the latter, which do not exist equivalently among all families, and in contexts such as Cuba, the domestic burden has accentuated female (García-Álvarez et al., 2020).

It is necessary to evaluate to what extent the ideal of social policies has been specified within the different territories. In general terms, the health emergency at the point of departure of COVID-19 represents a challenge for the management of social justice. The economic and social effects in the context of this health problem in Cuba include, among others, contractive effect on employment, reduction in family income, reduction of fiscal space, higher inflationary pressure, and impact differentiated by territories. The latter aspect is influenced by those regions in which an important source of employment is tourism. Socially, the impact supposes reduced availability of food, pressures on the public health and social assistance system, potential gender challenges, impacts on education and specific cultural services, and differentiated impact by population groups (Rodríguez & Odriosola, 2020). The country has defined its government strategy in the National Economic and Social Development Plan until 2030 and the conceptualization of the Cuban economic and social model, which constitutes the vision of the Cuban nation for this period (Díaz-Canel, 2021). At the same time, a strong articulation between scientific advice and political management has been progressively promoted. This science-political interface constitutes the benchmark for action for the country's leadership in updating the Cuban social-economic model. An important part of this process is the monetary order that began in January 2021, which is linked to the pernicious effects of a global crisis that systemically affects all dimensions of human development.

The development scheme that combines scientific activity with that of political decision-makers has led to advances in important areas of human development such as health and education. But in the current scenario of the pandemic, these areas of the greatest progress in the country, along with other areas of human development, face challenges, complexities, and bottlenecks, among which are guarantees for a distributive operation of products that satisfy basic demands of the population to contain and subvert development inequities. Likewise, sustainability in the progress of population segments that, due to generational, gender, local conditions, health problems, and employability, find greater vulnerability to the effects of the pandemic in different areas.

The reversal of these effects means overcoming historical gaps between academic activity and other sources of knowledge and the state management of governments to solve these problems. At the country and regional levels, community projects aimed at positively influencing human development have been carried out, but generally, there is no work to integrate development objectives. Although from the perspective of local development, there has been working aimed at equity, it has not always been deepened in all its dimensions, nor has it been a political objective on this scale (Fundora, 2021).

At present, macro-programs are being projected that should make the National Development Plan viable, such as Human Development, Equity, and Social Justice. From its project perspective, it works on integrated management that includes attention to the different human dimensions, that is, health, education, and resilient development spaces, on the basis of recognition of difference.

For a better understanding of Cuban reality, it is important to contextualize here fundamental aspects of economic activity in the current national scenario, referring to the purchasing power of the population. In this sense, it is important to note that starting in 2010, the non-state sector of the economy developed progressively in Cuba, cooperatives, especially non-agricultural ones (the latter have traditionally existed) and self-employment that stimulated an increase in the labor force within this sector. Records of 2021 report that in the country, there are more than 600,000 people hired in this labor modality, which formally represents 13% of the occupation in the country (Granma, 2021), a figure that does not account for the vast majority of contracts of this kind, a type that operates informally. Sources corresponding to 2020 specify that 36.2% of the population of working age (a greater number of women than men) is doing well in the informal sector, in unpaid care activities, voluntarily unemployed, or residing outside the country, although they maintain their status migratory as a resident in Cuba (Rodríguez & Odriosola, 2020).

The activities in which women are generally inserted are those with the lowest remuneration, tending to reproduce typical female patterns. Among them, domestic work, especially in rental houses for foreign tourism and the sale of imported clothing, activities that are depressed in the current context of the global crisis. All of this was articulated with the monetary system in Cuba as of January of this year, which meant an increase of five times the minimum wage, which mainly favored the labor force assigned to the state sector, although it triggered strong inflationary tensions that have affected the purchasing power of wages.

The significant number of labor force belonging to the non-state and informal economy (in which a young labor force predominates) has been left at the mercy of the multidimensional crisis that accompanies the pandemic context. The situation that, as a mechanism of adaptability of this group to the effects of the crisis, has produced a disproportionate increase in the prices of sales of basic products marketed by this sector. Generalized practice constitutes the expression of the inter-neighborhood economic violence that is at the epicenter of the community social problems of Cuba today. The Cuban scenario in dealing with the pandemic also includes distortions that cause unresolved internal problems, such as shortages, corruption, illegalities, hoarding, diversion of resources, and uncontrolled price volatility. Complexity is faced by the rigorous application of the regulatory framework (Arias, 2020). The behavior described for pandemic peak phases that survive, even with higher levels of negative effects.

In the problems found, conditions of vulnerability, threats, and setbacks in the fulfillment of the Development Goals of the 2030 Agenda are identified, co-implicated with equity both by gender and by other identity determinants such as skin color in areas such as education, employment, family life that presupposes domestic work, among others related to human well-being. Namely:

- Goal 1 is aimed at reducing poverty by gender and age groups, including building resilience to economic and social shocks; finds setbacks, particularly, in groups of the informal economy that have lost, displaced, or varied, due to worse remuneration, the economic activities to which they are dedicated. Case of many women in this group is employed in deactivated work within the framework of the current pandemic and the current Cuban economic and social context. Many of these women are subcontracted, which is why they are not covered by regulatory frameworks that support labor guarantees.
- Objective 2 is dedicated to nutritional guarantees, finds its purposes distorted due to the extreme volatility of food prices in the informal market, which is more supplied than the state market. The commercialization of products, as an economic activity of the informal sector, is superior to the productive activity of food. At the same time lower than the demand of the population, whose ability to pay is insufficient with respect to prices. This production deficit is combined with the existence of underutilized urban and periphery land. Areas with population settlements largely depend economically on informal activity. The implications in terms of meeting this goal are articulated with Goal 8, linked to sustained economic growth and decent work. Similarly, it relates to Goal 11, which is aimed at inclusive human settlements,
- Objective 3 is aimed at the health and well-being of all ages, coupled with Goal 5 and the corresponding Goal 17 with the elimination of all forms of violence against all women and girls in the public and private spheres; as well as the valuation of care and domestic work; plus, shared responsibility at home; finds complications in the context of the health emergency due to more forced coexistence in homes. In this sense, a higher level of conflict and family violence is detected with a greater risk for boys and girls and women who are violated in their relationship with their partners. Similarly, the intensification of domestic work reproduces the traditional sexual division.
- Objective 4 is aimed at inclusive and equitable education, also implies intensifying vulnerabilities with respect to historically disadvantaged groups. Cuban social policy is highly inclusive, however, there is an underrepresentation of the black population in well-paid positions (Fundora, 2021) in correspondence with the underrepresentation of people of black skin in universities. Axis

of inequality of the least addressed in Cuban studies, which is nevertheless included in a program as part of the National Development Plan until 2030. As part of coping with the changes produced by COVID-19 in school education, which implied suspension of school activity for several months, a program of teleclasses was deployed from primary education to upper secondary. In the case of the university, teaching resources were used on free digital platforms. In all the variants, technological means are required; in some cases of a certain level of development, plus preparation of the family. Conditions that do not exist equitably among all schoolchildren in primary, secondary, upper secondary, and university education. A situation that is aggravated by territory, it has been detected that in the municipalities with the largest population of black skin, access to the university decreases high school and college.

The implementation and monitoring of these objectives in the current conditions of existence are also transversal with Objective 16, which expresses facilitating access to justice for all and building effective and inclusive institutions that are accountable at all levels.

Regarding academic development has been mentioned, the evolution of learning was mediated by: technological accessibility and cultural heritage; capital distributed differentially between groups according to different criteria such as family composition, and financial status, among others, in turn, mediated by gender and skin color. As an effect, the behavior of the development has been different according to the conditions referred to above. It must be specified that even in Cuba there are development gaps as the level of education increases. In the order of gender, there are profiles of feminized careers, a delay in women compared to men in obtaining scientific degrees and certain specialties, and consequently, differentiation in job positions and remuneration. The situation increased in the pandemic context, fundamentally for the non-state sector of the economy. In relation to skin color, there are also development gaps to the extent that one advances in educational level and according to the social prestige of the career, whose access continues to be mostly meritocratic (Almeida, 2021).

Although a characteristic of the Cuban context is the female presence at the tertiary level of education, this presence is outlined among certain racial groups. And as the most important data in the direction of this reflection, it should be noted that at the postgraduate level and subsequent professional development, the gender gaps open in favor of the masculine condition (Calcerrada et al., 2022). An articulation between skin color and gender in the Cuban context leads to a lower presence of black women in conditions of professional progress. We do not fail to recognize that, at least in our research in this regard, within the group of tertiary-level students not recognized as white-skinned, we have found more female youth than male youth, especially in the regular daytime course. But, they have been mestizo women and descendants of one or both university-level parents (Calcerrada et al., 2022). The integration of the above results in fewer women and men of black skin in advantageous socio-professional conditions.

Regarding this last reality, the University of Holguín as of September 2021, has contributed to the "Second and Third Campaign to Overcome Racism in

Higher Education" coordinated by the UNESCO Chair for "Indigenous and Afro-descendant Peoples of the National University of Tres of February" from Argentina. The Cuban contribution (coordinated experience for Cuba by the authors of this text) has been aimed at favoring – from the intersectional perspective that gender analysis supposes – the development of sectors of the community racialized in an exclusive way in the collective unconscious. This population does not reach a majority in universities, both as directors and as students and teachers. Equally, The Campaign is aimed at perfecting the preparation of teachers for their formative work with an inclusive character. In this same way, it stimulates the recognition of productions in the field of the academic community, historically neglected, by overcoming nuances of epistemic racism originating in hierarchically established regional conditions, such as those produced outside the capital.

In conjunction with the fundamental guidelines of this text, one of the fundamental actions of the Cuban experience regarding this Latin American campaign has been to start mainstreaming the perspective of racial and gender justice in university curricular training. It is worth saying that in the Cuban academic teaching programs, progress has been made in the inclusion of the gender perspective, incorporated as a transversal in some careers of different universities in the country, however, the racial perspective has not been integrated in the same way. In this regard, we consider the need for an epistemological turn in teaching.

The binary, contrasting, hierarchical character that since antiquity typified thought constitutes an androcentric and racial fate that typified the history of science. The production of knowledge and its legitimacy have been skewed by essentialist systems that ponder certain types of knowledge as more dominant based on their identity matrices, from which conditions such as the feminine, black culture, and the popular have been dismissed, an example of epistemic racism.

The hierarchical and exclusive order between reason and experience (the affective, the body) is also expressed generically and racially. The reason, expresses the intellect, since ancient times connoted as the eternal, was linked to the masculine, not to any kind of masculinity, but to hegemonic masculinity. Meanwhile, the experience, which is particularly, changing, goes through the affective dimension and the body. It was cataloged as an expression of the feminine and the feminine as a symbol of the subordinate in which not only women enter, but also other identities historically inferiorized by mechanisms of domination. There are also men phenotypically different from the referenced Euro model, that is, non-white men.

The black as well as the feminine, the latter with a much longer history of devaluation, is dismissed, along with its intellectual productions. That is to say, in the history of ideas and academic productions, the contribution of non-white men and women has been devalued and omitted, because they are considered inferior by nature for intellectual production. This has represented not only delegitimizing the merit of their knowledge, but the dismissal also includes the issues that affect them (e.g. those of an emotional nature) and the knowledge that emerges from their cultural traditions that imply a source of their own knowledge. But like the experience, what affects, the experience of the bodies, it is particular and belongs to the private, to the level of microhistory, has no social importance. In a world of knowledge that, for our Western culture, it originated in the public realm; what was not included in that debate took place with a secondary importance. Despite the lack of merit that has occurred in academic production, Darwinian social theory contributed to the continuity of the patriarchal and racist tradition from antiquity. Asymmetric logic has occurred in the history of science and its teaching.

Therefore, the paradigmatic purpose toward which we are working includes the subversion of the feminine devaluation and what it represents along with racism in its different versions. Similarly, deconstruct discrimination based on phenotypic traits, the inferiorization of expressions corresponding to black and mestizo cultural memory. Likewise, epistemic racism for demeriting knowledge that comes from sources not scientifically recognized, such as good popular knowledge, or, within the scientific ones, those that are proposed from places and people not recognized for their relationship with the type of knowledge that is legitimated. For this, we incorporate in the teaching of careers such as Psychology and Specialties of the University of the Arts – in the order of Philosophical Thought, Research Methodology, and Social-Community Discipline – historical-theoretical foundations corresponding to feminist thought as a current of modern thought that has contributed in multiple ways to the erosion of different expressions of racism. In this same way, we incorporate decolonial thought as an original Latin American contribution to epistemic development and the subversion of unequal differences determined by excluding essentialist conditions. In parallel, among other actions in compliance with this purpose, since December 2021 we have developed the section Beyond the Skin on the university website on a monthly basis (www.uho.edu.cu). In the improvement of this project, we are expanding the system of actions in teachings that precede the university. The subversion of the development gaps implies a systemic approach in the history of the different processes that are inherent to them.

Peruvian Experience from the NGO the way is Made by Walking in the Inclusive Management for the Equitable Development of Migrants

The inclusion management carried out by the non-profit Peruvian Civil Organization Se hace camino al andar articulated with the UNHCR-Peru has as its objective to advise, integrate, and protect the refugee and migrant population in Peru, fundamentally in the direction of their integration into the national market to become, in the short- and medium-term, the engine of the economy. In the direction of this purpose, it creates helplines through support networks and digital platforms, identifies refugee and migrant populations who need counseling in the migration context.

The mission includes school reinforcement and economic inclusion, directions that have been particularized in the face of the complex effects of the health emergency caused by COVID-19. The pandemic event coincided with a strong migratory wave from Venezuela; hence, the reference chosen for this text is this population group. In the context of COVID-19, the students of this migrant population have experienced a setback in their school courses as a consequence of accentuated limitations in access to technology, a condition of substantive inclusion during the pandemic event. This situation is expressed differentially by gender.

According to the Survey aimed at the Venezuelan population residing in Peru (ENPOVE) carried out by the National Institute of Statistics and Informatics (INEI)– with support from the United Nations Refugee Agency (UNHCR), the United Nations Population Fund (UNFPA), the International Organization for Migration (IOM), the United Nations Children's Fund (UNICEF) and the World Bank (WB) – between November and December 2018, differences were reported since before the health emergency of gender in the economic participation corresponding to this population. The source confirms that according to sex, men achieve greater insertion in the labor market (96.5%) compared to women (89.9%). The unemployment rate for women was 10.1%, being three times more than that of men (3.5%). According to the same survey, one of the main needs expressed by the Venezuelan population is the generation of income/employment (54.4%), followed by education and training (37.7%). We assume that the explanation of these statistics is related to the perceived needs of the population, since contrary to what these figures express, the possibilities of access to successful employment are preceded by training through education and training. As a result of deficits in training for insertion into the labor market from their context of origin, Venezuelan migrant women residing in Peru face greater barriers to access the labor market, followed by education and training (37.7%).

In a recent survey carried out by the GRANMAV organization, the previously described behavior has been identified. In a population of Venezuelan refugee and migrant women, only 27.4% are currently employed. About 12% refer to having a non-formalized venture, while 9.6% had a venture and want to activate it. Likewise, 26.5% express their intention to undertake its development. The most frequently mentioned undertakings are styling and beauty, confectionery, handicrafts, and computing. From the effects of the pandemic, one of the main focuses of work of this NGO has been the inclusion management of this population.

As part of the accompanying strategies for this migrant population, both the direction oriented toward educational development and integration mechanisms that favor their daily subsistence has been articulated. In general terms, migrant populations, as a tendency, in their initial phases of integration into a new territory are characterized by a subsistence economy. This condition is opposed to progress, particularly for migrant women in the Peruvian context. Based on this behavior, the NGO Se hace Camino al Andar makes viable actions such as the following:

- Train adult Venezuelan refugee and migrant women through training courses in different trades, offering them adequate tools for job placement.
- Promote the conditions to access new jobs that allow them to have a dignified life and achieve proper integration with the host community.
- Have a safe space so that, in addition to training and education, they can socialize and share spaces for personal growth.
- Include school accompaniment projects for children and adolescents residing in the country that allow them to level and access the different options offered by education in Peru in order to achieve proper integration in the host community.

- Develop integration strategies with the most vulnerable populations within refugees and migrants, specifically people with disabilities, children and adolescents, and women victims of violence and/or human trafficking, among other historically vulnerable groups.
- Define employability and formalization strategies for the refugee and migrant population in Peru.
- Create massive information campaigns about rights and duties in the host country; as well as access to public services that Peru provides, especially health and education.

That is to say, a system of actions directed to the formation of capacities, among others, cognitive, compatible with employment opportunities that in turn contemplates the different conditions of the feminine and migrant plurality in a general sense.

Experience of the Association of Education for Inclusive Management of the Province of San Luis: A Window into the Educational Field of Argentina in the Pandemic Context

The experience of the Educational Civil Association of Inclusive Management of Argentina (ACEGI) anchored in the province of San Luis, Argentina— co-participating body in the aforementioned Cuban campaign against racism in Higher Education, which has been articulated with overcoming sexism. Its corporate purpose is to carry out educational and advertising projects through actions of social-cultural development of the community, vertebrated by the inclusion and recognition of authentic collective identities from the affirmation of their potentialities. In this direction, ACEGI has carried out projects such as "Training for heterogeneous educational contexts as part of the transition towards inclusive education." Action aimed at training teachers and management personnel regarding, among others, comprehensive sexual education in the classrooms of various educational levels. Likewise, it incorporates in making educational management relations with the Huarpes of San Luis, one of the original population groups.

The policy that supports the work perspective of this association prioritizes inclusive training for different educational contexts. They stimulate the transition from the mixed school corresponding to the twentieth century toward a truly inclusive institution that ponders the recognition of difference and its adequate personalized treatment. In achieving this purpose, from the management carried out by this instance, the methodological training and epistemic conceptions of education agents are affected, mainly in schools.

Among their actions, they propose updating the curricula of the cultural characteristics of the different contexts to favor the authentic assimilation of different training axes. In this direction, they include in the training of educational agents supports sociological, psychological, pedagogical, and cultural, in such a way that the recognition of differences and their integration become viable.

In the work perspective of this association, the explanation of the dynamics of heterogeneous groups and the active involvement of the main socializing agents are incorporated. In this sense, it offers a vision of how to organize the teaching-learning process from the recognition of differences as a genuine form of human respect and the healthy transition toward inclusive educational spaces. Complementarily, it includes the characterization of the methodological procedures that are used regularly as part of the personological and group diagnosis, from a process perspective and not isolated moments that statically label people. Dialectical approach that allows updating didactic and methodological variants in training.

During the first year of the pandemic event, ACEGI's work was carried out fundamentally through virtual platforms, a modality that in itself constituted a bias by requiring technological inputs. In 2020, from the articulation with The Distance Training Institute (IFAD) carried out a set of training actions:

Interviews with teachers aspiring to cover positions in training, postgraduate degrees, and diploma courses offered by IFAD. Creation of the IFAD page – San Luis Designs of informative plates of IFAD training offers attention to the public in the ACEGI office in reference to different topics of interest. Training of IFAD teachers in the different subjects to be taught. Offer, free of charge, of the virtual training, provided through the ACEGI virtual platform, oriented to topics such as learning problems, comprehensive sexual education, conflict resolution, attention to diversity, initial literacy, etc. (acegi.guia-didactica.net). At the same time, counseling was implemented for teachers regarding inclusion situations in the different schools, providing pedagogical and guidance material free of charge.

In 2021, the contract with IFAD (based in Buenos Aires) was terminated due to the instability in its operation from the states of confinement and the uncertainty in all social activities derived from the pandemic produced by COVID-19. However, virtual training continued in the direction of subverting the historical gaps in education, which increased by the health emergency. To the directions of work carried out in 2020, the improvement of the work toward overcoming racism was added in a more conscious way. In the direction of raising the quality of inclusive management in this critical context, the Board of Directors was trained in May 2021 at the Fundación Huésped on the subject of Comprehensive Sexual Education for all educational levels.

ACEGI, in addition, during the aforementioned time, has co-participated in the evaluation of the inclusive educational project that is developed in the Self-managed Public Schools (EPA) No. 15, 16, and 17 (San Luis, capital). Specifically, it has analyzed its weaknesses and strengths, shared results in different academic and scientific fields in Latin America and Europe.

How Has the Development by Study and Employment Been Affected by the Gender Condition in the Pandemic Context of San Luis?

During this period, in the age population corresponding to the first stages of development, childhood, adolescence, and youth, mainly residents in marginalized areas, the evolution of educational processes has been affected due to lack of technology to access classes virtually, illiteracy of the parents in school subjects that prevented them from accompanying their learning, lack of communication between families and teachers in the advisory department, due to economic problems that made it difficult to use the telephones.

In women, more situations of family violence were evidenced and in some cases in boys and girls, abuses were found in their own families. Situation combined with the lack of fiscal control, the judicial services did not work with the usual speed and in some cases were suspended. Similar to the situation described in the Cuban experience, families that depended on self-employment experienced damages by not being able to open these services (stores, restaurants, bookstores, etc.) due to confinement. Those without financial support went bankrupt, in contrast to financially solvent families with state-mandated jobs, which were more resilient.

On the other hand, in the case of the native peoples of San Luis, adaptive mechanisms were appreciated in the face of the critical event. The native peoples have assimilated the facilities of modernity (e.g. preserved food, etc.) appropriation that has contributed to deferring their ancestral customs. However, during the pandemic, there was a recovery of old customs reappropriated in the direction of the development of economic enterprises, for example, carob flour alfajores and among other things. Practice that is not strange to the progress that had begun since 2017 when the first pilot experience was carried out in San Luis in EPAS No. 15, 16, and 17, with the purpose of systematizing the ancestral teachings of these populations with the participation of leaders of these identity groups.

As a result of this experience, in 2018, an agreement was instituted between the University of San Luis and indigenous peoples aimed at "pedagogical" training that integrates non-academic cultural matrices, an expression of overcoming epistemic racism. However, although these actions favored these people, there has not been a "common" school education, the adults of these communities have continued in their homes preparing their offspring for the traditions and care of our Earth. This dissociation, although it is not absolute, from our understanding hinders to a certain extent the progress for authentic occupational and professional integration in contemporary societies, since occupational demands are structured on referential patterns corresponding to modern societies. The regulatory framework, although it alternates with our recognition of differences and the cultural autonomy of minorities without historical power, cannot ignore what modern technologies contribute to development, for which reason their integration must be considered. Despite this critical observation, the progress made by the Huarpes group, the main native population with which ACEGI works, cannot be ignored, as they have managed to insert themselves into a development program, the Indigenous Cultures Program. The system has been involved in the construction of schools, hospitals, livestock programs, and among others. Areas of development that, although they express a level of achievement and cultural autonomy, at the same time, they imply training the original population in the successful performance of the tasks required in these spaces. Which, as noted above, would represent true cultural integration. The challenge to what ACEGI contributes through the exchange with Huarpe schoolchildren and the management of training in decoloniality, racism, and sexism in education contributes to the erosion of vertical hegemonic conceptions, not only with respect to universal identity models but also with respect to patriarchy. Traits present in these communities of ancestral tradition. There is still a sexual gender division in these populations, that is, subjectively internalized as complementarity between women and men, however, it maintains a hierarchical structure that limits the progress of Huarpe women.

Policy Recommendations Aimed at Equitable Education and Employment Opportunities

- Update, in teaching staff and public decision-makers in the educational area, positions in paradigms of socio-critical knowledge, not dominant from canons: philosophical, political, scientific that have turned out to be patriarchal, colonial, and racist. Instead, adopt as a platform the politics of equitable difference conceived from the de-essentialization of identities and cultural integration.
- Promote an alter-globalizing conception in the formative management of educational institutions, surpassing classist, androcentric, and ethnocentric conceptions. Stimulating a sense of distributive justice based on both a policy of recognition of the specific person located and the granting of resources that enhance their development according to their history and integration needs.
- Regarding the didactics of teaching at all levels, we consider it interesting to strengthen, through dialogic participation, the understanding (in teachers and students) of the formative matrices of identities, conceived in their plurality. To do this, incorporate aspects of critical thinking such as decolonial into the curricular updating of teachers. Likewise, from those critical positions that value the place of micro-histories, articulate teaching practice with students' experiential experiences in order to contextualize teaching, not reproduce universal models and subvert rational logic that prefers affectivity as a source of knowledge.
- Explicit in the normative order of educational and labor organizations a sense of equality, an alternative to the exclusive sameness, that as a principle of access to fundamental rights of life supposes the specific situated condition of people, determined plurally by factors such as gender, skin color, geographical, religious origin, and among other conditions of identity determination, which express different needs and potentialities.
- In the field of organizational policies, deconstruct the domination of patriarchal job selection and evaluation parameters that divide reason and affection, public and private space, and they essentialize success from the canon of hegemonic masculinity.
- Strengthen, through regulatory systems, the level of micro-agency development of subjectivities in the different socialization institutions, by promoting the exercise of autonomy from early childhood without gender judgments.
- Defer the categorization of students and work personnel based on fixed, extemporal parameters, instead determine their development needs and potential according to their uniqueness, cultural, and social context.

References

Almeida, Y. (2015). Higher education, race and social policy: A brief reflection from Cuba. In P. Vommaro & V. Labrea (Eds.), *Youth, participation and social development in Latin America and the Caribbean* (pp. 125–137).

Arias, L. M. (2020). Strategic perspective in the management of Covid 19 in Cuba. https://www.clacso.org/perspectiva-estrategica-en-la-gestion-de-la-covid-19-en-cuba

Brunet, R., Ferras, R., & Théry, H. (2005). *Les Mots de la Geographie. Dictionary Critique.* Reclus-La Documentation Française (3rd ed.).

Butler, J. (2002). *Bodies that matter.* Paidós.

Calcerrada, M., García, J. M., & Suárez, N. (2022). Higher education in Cuba: An intersectional analysis from the conditions of gender and skin color. In L. Lafortune, V. Paez, N. Sorin, M. C. Guillot, E. Rose-Nadié, & M. Calcerrada (Eds.), *Femmes en situations professionnelles. Cuban and Québécoise experiences* (pp. 135–152).

Claval, P. (1999). *Geografía cultural.* Barcelona: Paidos.

Collins, P. (1990). *Black feminist thought, knowledge, consciousness, and the politics of empowerment.* Unwin Hyman.

Di Meo, G. (1993). Les Territoires de la Localité, Origine et Actualité Revista L'espace. *Géographique, 22*(4), 306–317.

Díaz-Canel, M. (2021). Why do we need a government management system based on science and innovation? *Annals Magazine of the Cuban Academy of Sciences, 11*(1). http://revistaccuba.sld.cu/index.php/revacc/article/view/

Espada, J. P., Orgilés, M., Piqueras, J. A., & Morales, A. (2020). Good practices in child and adolescent psychological care before COVID-19. *Clinic and Health Advance.* https://doi.org/10.5093/clysa2020a14

Foucault, M. (2005). *Discipline and punish: The birth of the prison.* New York: Vintage Books.

Fundora, G. (2021). Configuration of local equity policies in updating the Cuban development model. *Annals Magazine of the Cuban Academy of Sciences, 11*(1). http://revistaccuba.sld.cu/index.php/revacc/article/view/

García-Álvarez, L. et al. (2020). Will there be changes in alcohol and tobacco consumption during the COVID-19 lockdown? *Adicciones, 32*(2), 85–89.

García, M., Castellanos, R., & Álvarez, J. (2020). *Physical isolation in homes due to Covid 19: Psychological effects on Cuban children and adolescents.* UNICEF.

Grupo Estudios del Trabajo (GrET). (2020). *Report of the observatory of the labor dynamics of the General Pueyrredon Party. The impact of mandatory isolation on work, income and care. No. 2.* National University of Mar del Plata.

Granma. Official Organ of the Central Committee of the Communist Party of Cuba. www.granma.cu/cuba/2021-02-12/cuba-pasa-de-127-a-mas-de-2000-actividades-por-cuenta-propia-gran-salto-en-favor-de-la-economia--yel-empleo-video-12-02-21-13-02-42

International Labor Office. (2012). *Gender equality and decent work: Key ILO conventions and recommendations for gender equality 2012.* International Labor Office, Bureau for Gender Equality, International Labor Standards Department, ILO.

Menéndez, D., & Figares, J. L. (2020). *International Journal of Education for Social Justice, 9*(3e).

Montañez, G., & Delgado, O. (1998). Space, territory and region: Basic concepts for a national project. *Geography Notebooks, 7*(1–2), 121–134.

Montañez, G. (2001). *Reason and passion of space and territory: Spaces and territories: Reason, passion and imaginaries.* National University of Colombia.

Montanchez, M. (2015). Education as a right in international treaties: A reading from inclusive education. *Peace and Conflict Magazine, 8*(2), 243–265.

Mouffe, C. (1999). *The return of the political.* London: Verso.

Rojas, M. (2011). *Cultural identity and integration: From the enlightenment to Latin American romanticism, philosophical.* Series No. 19. University of San Buena Ventura, Editorial Bonaventuriana.

Rodriguez, J. L., & Odriozola, S. (2020). *Economic and social impacts of COVID 19 in Cuba: Policy options.* UNDP.

Rodríguez, D. (2010). Territory and territoriality: New category of analysis and didactic development of Geography. *UniPluriVersidad, 10*(3).

Trepat, C., & Cómes, P. (2000). *Time and space in the didactics of social sciences.* Graó.

Chapter 4

A Spectre Haunting Academia: Management and Masculinities Among Chilean Universities

Marcela Mandiola Cotroneo, Nicola Ríos González and Aleosha Eridani

Abstract

In this chapter, the authors analyze the relationship between academia, organization, and gender in Chile. In particular, the connection between academic practices, management, and hegemonic masculinity throughout the history of Chilean universities. The authors took a critical approach from the field of gender and organizational studies, shedding new light on a longstanding problem: gender-based violence in universities. The authors will discuss how the centrality of management in Chilean universities makes sense in a late and globally connected capitalist scenario, characterized by the introduction of managerialism and business logic in higher education. Consequently, the practice of management acquired a central and hegemonic status that articulates the rest of the academic practices, organizing them not only in terms of the hegemony of management but also in terms of male hegemony.

Keywords: Gender; higher education; organization; management; masculinity; hegemony

Introduction

In this chapter, we analyze the relationship between academia, organization, and gender in Chile. In particular, the connection between academic practices, management, and hegemonic masculinity throughout the history of Chilean universities.

Economy, Gender and Academy: A Pending Conversation, 61–76
Copyright © 2023 by Marcela Mandiola Cotroneo, Nicola Ríos González and Aleosha Eridani
Published under exclusive licence by Emerald Publishing Limited
doi:10.1108/978-1-80455-998-720231010

We take a critical approach from the field of gender and organizational studies, shedding new light on a longstanding problem: gender-based violence in universities. The issue in question has gained relevance as it reflects political demands that have reshaped the agendas of higher education institutions. Yet within this transformative process –which has resulted in significant content-based and institutional measures– the academic practices and rationales governing them have remained all but untouched. This chapter addresses the need to develop a critical understanding of this issue, unveiling what remains persistently out of sight in the field of feminist political demands at universities. We therefore aim to expose a "spectre" of sorts haunting academia.

From an organizational perspective, universities may be understood as fields of practice organized around a variety of purposes, from the training of professionals to the production of scientific knowledge. The definition of these purposes has consequences on the bodies and relations brought about by each routine and organized practice, with special emphasis on those that affect and refer to academics as university workers. Therefore, by focusing on universities from an organizational perspective, we will refer to the specific set-up of the academic practices carried out by those who work in them.

In view of the above, we may distinguish two unavoidable academic practices in universities: teaching and research. A third practice trails after them: extension, which is typically subservient to the first two. The above shows how the practices carried out by academics in Chile articulate through the metaphor of the "cassata."[1] Even though there is a simultaneous demand for these three practices, they are not weighted equally: while research is linked to privileged positions within the hierarchy, teaching bestows a kind of recognition that is secondary and undervalued, all the while extension remains at the periphery due to its ambiguity and lack of form (Mandiola, Ríos & Varas, 2019).

Nevertheless, we should also refer to a fourth practice that, despite its increasing presence in Chilean academia, does not get to be acknowledged as a practice in its own right; it is not even made visible by universities on an official level and is often taken for granted by academics themselves. A fourth practice that is permanent, one might even say, persistent; a task that struggles to be considered as formal and yet is easily recognizable by all academics. It is there, it operates, but it does not constitute a defined, recognized, or even remunerated duty. It is uncomfortable because it is time-consuming. It is a practice that conditions work to the point of becoming essential, yet remains difficult to identify; a practice that seems inevitable and lacking in alternative forms of articulation. We are talking about management, an imperative way of conducting academic work.

By management, we mean a practice that encompasses the tasks, procedures, rituals, demands, stages, formalities, requirements, etc., that give substance to the three aforementioned academic practices. Yet, at the same time, by management, we also mean a style, a "way of doing" that shapes other practices and subjugates

---

[1] The name for a popular three-layered ice-cream dessert, mixing chocolate, vanilla, and strawberry. Also known as Napolitan Ice-cream.

them. A practice and at the same time a crucial style that drives university organization and monopolizes the process of organizing the entire range of academic practices. In short, an "hegemonic academic practice," insofar as it obscures the contextual origins of its power and hides away the precarious foundations of its articulation to sustain its centrality (Meriläinen et al., 2008).

We will discuss how the centrality of management in Chilean universities makes sense in a late and globally connected capitalist scenario, characterized by the introduction of managerialism and business logic in higher education. This is understood in light of the historical transformations resulting from the free market reforms under the Chilean dictatorship and the dominant position they achieved in its wake, intertwined with a hierarchical and conservative university tradition. Consequently, the practice of management acquired a central and hegemonic status that articulates and subjects the rest of the academic practices, organizing them not only in terms of the hegemony of management, but also in terms of masculine hegemony.

This organizational pact between management and masculinity has become so entrenched in higher education that it has been kept out of the reach of feminist advocacy in universities, rendering the gendered nature of management invisible and uncontroversial (Acker, 1990). It is in this relationship forged between feminisms and the university that we must adopt a critical organizational approach, which will allow us to trace how academic practices are organized and the resulting political implications that this entails –in our case, gender-based ones (Mandiola et al., 2022; Ríos, Mandiola y Varas, 2017).

Management, Gender, and Academia: A Conceptual and Political Entwining

Drawing from critical organizational studies, management refers not only to a practice that bureaucratizes work but also to one that manifests a managerial ideology; that is, one that is exclusively oriented toward optimizing resources governed by the principles of efficiency and effectiveness in pursuit of productivity (Alvesson & Willmott, 2003; Gonzales-Miranda & Martinez, 2019; Parker, 2002). Therefore, we claim that the emergence and expansion of management at universities points to the introduction of business and neoliberal rationales that permeate and affect the whole of academia and the way it is organized, disrupting the educational and the economic, reflective and profitable, the right to education and the educational market (Alves Sousa & Hendriks, 2008; Anderson, 2008).

In this line of organizational critique, the expansion and preponderance of management in universities may be viewed as an ideological practice that supposes a managerial way of organizing and "subjecting" the whole of academic practices, eclipsing other forms of organization. It is an ideological practice, as it normalizes the social and political process that put it at the very center, together with its ability to hegemonize research, teaching, and extension (Mandiola et al., 2019). It is through this normalization that managerial ideology has managed to take a foothold at universities, challenging academics to transform themselves into entrepreneurial ventures, seeking economic incentives and public recognition, to become more desirable and better suited to these new corporate universities (Fardella et al., 2016).

One of the processes that nurtures and reinforces managerialism and managerial ideology in universities has been called "academic capitalism," a concept that illustrates how knowledge has become a saleable, hoardable product that generates surplus value. In the context of academic capitalism, labor is organized not only as a form of exploitation of academics according to the economic interests of the educational market but also as a system that directs academic practices according to the standards of competition, profitability, and attractiveness of the knowledge market (Slaughter & Leslie, 1997; Slaughter & Rhoades, 2004).

Still, the organizational critique denouncing the managerial transformation of the university, in which management becomes a hegemonic practice, has also been nourished by other perspectives that provide new complexities to explore. In the case of Chile, we would like to point out the contributions of the gender lens, since universities have been a focal source of neoliberal critique. They have also been at the center of various criticisms raised by feminist struggles, in line with the demands for transformation by social movements, against market logic, sexism, and gender violence in education (Zerán, 2018).

Since the early 2000s, feminist and gender studies in Chile have started to make relevant contributions by targeting universities and academia as fields of research. They have analyzed issues such as academic careers and the performance of women in managerial positions, university prestige systems, or scientific production statistics classified by gender (Berrios, 2007; Krauskopf, 2008; Saracostti, 2006). However, from an organizational and labor perspective, something in common to the aforementioned studies and most of those that followed is their understanding of gender as a category akin to women's studies or one that refers to the feminine and the masculine as a reified dichotomy (Mandiola et al., 2019). These insights are best reflected in studies on the specific difficulties and gaps experienced by women in academia, or alternatively on issues such as the glass ceiling and the sexual division of labor, including the horizontal or vertical distribution of men and women in academia and the emphasis on equity (Bustos et al., 2018; Gaete, 2015; Pino et al., 2018).

Without detracting from the importance and contributions of the aforementioned gender perspectives and approaches, our proposal adheres to a critical understanding in the field of gender and organization studies, in which gender is understood as a social practice that is relational and contextual, rather than a category that allows for the delimitation of discrete and quantifiable identities (Butler, 2006). By understanding gender as a social practice, this perspective emphasizes its contextual nature, without overlooking its binary norm. The distinctive feature of this perspective, therefore, is that it challenges the binary gender norm, turning our attention to how notions of the feminine and the masculine are produced, stabilized, and "naturalized."

Following this critical perspective, and starting from periods similar to those of the aforementioned research, we may find organizational studies concerned with going beyond the male–female or masculine–feminine duality, exploring the fluidity of gender from a non-essentialist position that focuses more on "undoing" than "reifying" it (Alvesson & Due Billing, 2009; Knights & Kerfoot, 2004; Linstead & Brewis, 2004). By focusing on the question of how gender is produced in everyday organizational life, this perspective discusses gender as something that exists insofar as it is acted upon in relation to its normative context (Butler, 2006; Kelan, 2009). In other words, gender is understood as a social practice that is "organized" with regard to the practices and routines that define a given organizational regime. Following Connell (1995), we can state that

> there is a gendered configuration of recruitment and promotion, a gendered configuration of the internal division of labour and monitoring systems, a gendered configuration of policy formulation and practical routines. (p. 73)

From this perspective and in previous works, we have analyzed how academic trajectories within the gendered organization of academia produce and reproduce the binary, distributing positions of power and recognition in what we have metaphorically dubbed the *cassata*: a concept that speaks not only of practices that carry different weights, but which are gendered in specific ways: masculinization of research, feminization of teaching, and ambiguity of extension (Mandiola et al., 2019; Ríos, Mandiola & Varas, 2018). Given this *cassata* and the invisibility of management among the "three flavors" that comprise it, it is relevant to further analyze how this fourth practice and its hegemony brings with it a hegemonic organization and production of gender.

Theoretical cues are useful for this purpose, as they help to explore the relationship between gender and the managerial organization of universities in greater depth. We specifically focus on the literature that has addressed management at universities from a gender perspective, drawing on the field of masculinities studies (Kimmel et al., 2005). It is from here that the organizational practices of academia may be understood as mechanisms to produce and reproduce gender relations that underpin both male domination and managerial hegemony (Whitehead & Moodley, 1999).

In masculinities studies, the category of masculinity is understood as a process that shapes practices structured by inherently historical gender relations, and whose process of formation and reformation is political in nature. In other words, it is a definition that helps to understand masculinity as a set of practices embedded in academic organizations, organizational history, and their "gender politics" (Connell, 1995). This refers not only to the university as a domain that, from its very inception, has been conceived as male-dominated but also to how it continues to organize practices that facilitate the reproduction of male privilege and the patriarchal dividend (Syrett, 2007).

A critical gender analysis of the masculinity category does not imply focusing on the positions held by men and women in academia, but rather on the organizational rules that place them in these positions and how the consolidation of these rules contributes to the production and reproduction of the binary that consolidates male privilege. These rules simultaneously eclipse, subordinate, and marginalize other forms of organizing gendered life, affecting not only women but also men and other bodies and practices that go beyond the binary.

In this respect, the organizational rules that managerial hegemony brings about deserve to be discussed on their own. Several authors have pointed out that managerial ideology is structured in a masculine key, closely linked to the rationales of management and business schools (Fotaki, 2013). This suggests that the gendered masculine character of managerialism shows up whenever universities articulate the interests of capitalism, focusing their attention on the rationale of "business" or "productivity" (Carvalho & Machado, 2010; Martínez Alemán, 2014). Similarly, the male symbolic order emerges when management practices are combined with neoliberal values or discourses such as "competition" or "individualism," as well as liberal discourses that emphasizes "autonomy" or "independence" (Connell, 2010; Connell & Messerschmidt, 2005; Morley, 1999; Prichard, 1996; Thomas & Davies, 2002).

In addition to the neoliberal capitalist side of masculinity in academic management, we may add other traits linked to the scientific method, such as "objectivity," "rationality," and "instrumentality" (Barry et al., 2006; Ross-Smith & Kornberger, 2004). By promoting these rules in the production of knowledge and the organization of academic work, the ideal worker emerges as someone detached and disengaged from responsibilities other than a strict dedication to academic production (Martínez Alemán, 2014). As feminist literature from critical organizational theory has warned, this ideal worker obscures his (male) gender marker, appearing incorporeal, abstract, and immaterial, a process by which he ensures his centrality and hegemony.

Another characteristic aspect of hegemonic masculinity is expressed in practices of "homosociality," which have also been identified and analyzed in university management (Martínez Alemán, 2014; Prichard, 1996). Such homo-sociality can be observed in what Cress and Hart (2009) have called "sport metaphors" linked to athletic competition. This implies characterizing academic practices in sports codes where categories such as "team," "strategy," "scoring," "competition," "ranking," among others, blur management's economic origin, making it a practice more akin to a gentlemen's club of sorts (Thomas & Davies, 2002).

Finally, masculine hegemony in university management has also revealed how the quest for "positional power" and "high-ranking positions" is synonymous with a discursive centrality that constitutes hegemonic masculinity (Acker & Webber, 2006; Connell & Messerschmidt, 2005; Martínez, 2014). All of the above shows us how the dominant managerial and masculine organization has marginalized and excluded other practices and forms of organization in academia, even if there are experiences of organization and resistance to such domination (Sliwa & Johansson, 2014; Taylor & Lahad, 2018).

In short, as we have seen thus far, the managerial organization of academic practices, which has become extremely normalized, can be read in terms of gender: insofar as these practices are organized from the centrality and hegemony of the fourth management practice, the root of the managerial rationale underlying this organization –including competitiveness, individualism, and elitism– is how the university as a domain has been historically and continually masculine. What is left, then, is to give an account of this history for a specific and distinct territory, such as Chile.

Cassocks and Briefcases: Tracing the History of an Invisible Endeavor

Asking ourselves about the articulations between managerialism and masculinity in Chilean academic organizations requires us to briefly put the history of its universities into context. An overview of how these institutions came into being and developed further reveals how managerial and masculine discourses shaped the entirety of academic practice. This historical overview shows two main discursive fields giving shape to academic work, notwithstanding other modes of construction that have remained on the sidelines throughout Chilean history. We refer to the Catholic and business discourse, which have strongly influenced the consolidation of masculine managerialism up to the present day.

The influence of the Catholic Church in universities has been present since their inception, and remains to this day a hegemonic field of articulation, providing not only worldviews and values but also ways of structuring power and academic work through hierarchies and concrete regulations. The early days of higher education in Chile were part of a period that Bravo (1992) calls the Pontifical University (1622–1747), marked by the control of the Catholic Church, its evangelizing character, and from there the importance of the teaching of theology and a hierarchical structure built around ecclesiastical criteria.

This was followed by the establishment of a Royal University in Chile (1747–1843), under the command of the Spanish Empire, which remained glued to a Catholic worldview. This second stage introduced the possibility of studying secular subjects, including Law, and the collegiate nature of leadership, supervised by a cloister made up of corporations or guilds participating in the university, with a rotating position of the rector (Bravo, 1992). Upon the country's independence and the beginning of the Republic, colonial tutelage was replaced in 1843 by the Chilean state. This change did not initially entail democratization processes; on the contrary, "all university employees were removable at the will of the President" (p. 93), and it was he who chose the rector.

Nevertheless, it was around this time that the Amunátegui decree was enacted (1877), making Chile the first Latin American country allowing women to obtain university degrees. Thanks to this decree, women's secondary education was recognized, allowing them to take entrance exams for higher education. This achievement, however, granted access only to a limited group of women from certain

68 Marcela Mandiola Cotroneo et al.

educational establishments and on grounds related to the deep-rooted belief that women possessed a "natural advantage" for certain trades related to caregiving. This precedent is, perhaps, the first milestone marking the insistent gendering of fields and professions, which still pervades the trajectories of university students and scholars to this day.

It was not until 1927 that the state relinquished its power, granting economic and administrative independence to the institutions. The rector became the leading figure in each of the universities, and the academic practices that characterize them to this day began to take shape: research and extension began to develop in parallel to teaching, which had until then monopolized unversity endeavors in Chile. Paradoxically, this independence from the State triggered bureaucratization processes designed to manage economic resources and decision-making. Professor Juan de Dios Vial Correa stated in this regard that "the spiritual demise of the university has been felt for a long time, as it has gradually developed into an office-university, conceived as a gigantic higher education service" (Vial Correa in Bravo, 1992, pp. 216, 218).

Nevertheless, from the 1960s until 1973, the university in Chile began to commit themselves strongly to the transformation of the structures of political and economic domination, both within academia and society at large. In this brief period, both students and workers denounced the elitist character of the student body and the oligarchic nature of university governance (Garretón & Martínez, 1985), which gave way to the University Reform (*Reforma Universitaria*) process from 1967 onward, seeking to democratize the organization and curricula of universities and connect them to the major social and political problems of the time. This process was abruptly interrupted by the 1973 coup d'état and the civil-military dictatorship under General Pinochet for 17 years.

Just three weeks after the coup, the eight existing universities were intervened through the appointment of military personnel to the rector's offices, who took over the management of these institutions. Entire academic departments, particularly in the social sciences, were dismantled; fields such as sociology, political science, anthropology, and political economics were completely wiped out. Institutional independence, freedom of expression, and pluralism vanished (Santos, 2005). According to the dictatorship, Chilean higher education was a virtually monopolistic state system, which escaped any form of economic efficiency checks. Thus, in 1981, a broad, predominantly market-oriented education reform was imposed under the premises of neoliberal ideology (Bellei & Orellana, 2014; Brunner, 1997). This led to the creation of new private universities, whose funding and administration were completely disconnected from the State. State funding was slashed, and competition was introduced as a leading economic principle in all universities. Institutions were encouraged to meet their financial needs by charging tuition fees, while a public loan scheme was set up to facilitate access for low-income students. The change in funding mechanisms also changed how universities organized themselves internally. This not only refers to the creation of private universities emerging as companies within the context of market-based education, but also to the incorporation of business rationales into pre-existing universities (Santos, 2006).

The governments following the dictatorship did not dismantle the business orientation of higher education. This resulted in social movements between 2006 and 2011 demanding public, free, non-profit, democratic, and secular education (CONFECH, 2011). To date, however, these demands have not clearly translated into structural changes to the way universities have been organized since the dictatorship (Salazar & Leihy, 2017). The reforms implemented are only just underway and have not necessarily altered university organization, as they have overlooked the democratizing nature of the university (Da Corte, 2015). This is in line with the silence, invisibilization, or inability of those working at universities to challenge the organizational transformations of academic practices in the neoliberal university (Mandiola, Varas, Ríos y Salinas, 2014). Furthermore, post-dictatorship governments have until very recently continued to push for reforms to consolidate neoliberalism, thus reinforcing the penetration of managerialism in universities (Fardella-Cisternas et al., 2017).

As Berrios (2007) pointed out early on, the "age of access" –a description used to refer to the process whereby university enrollment massified and increased female numbers– brought with it greater demands for equity and the incorporation of marginalized sectors from a class lens; yet, this has not substantially transformed the gender regime at universities. According to the author, despite the increased participation of women academics in higher education, gender inequality "is expressed in the constant distinction process that establishes hierarchies in academic work" (Berrios, 2007, p. 40).

In the same vein, the student demonstrations of the so-called Feminist May 2018 in Chile (Zerán, 2018) questioned university organization through a new lens, emphasizing the gender-based violence that takes place in academic contexts. They denounced how such aggressions relate to the masculine governance underlying these organizations. The mass protests, the occupation of physical spaces, and the various *"funas"* or *"escraches"* (call outs) against male students and academics over the last few years, forced universities to respond by managing the conflict through new institutional procedures aimed at creating gender policies. These policies sought, above all, to generate response protocols for dealing with violence. In some cases, they also sought to develop action plans aimed at promoting gender equality at an organizational level. Nevertheless, these policies are still under development and their implications have not been evaluated (Gaba, 2020; Mandiola et al., 2022).

In this brief overview, we may observe how Catholic and business discourses have permeated the history of universities in Chile. Currently, there are 58 universities in Chile (SIES, 2020). More than 68% of them are private and 24% are Catholic. These discourses can be found in aspects such as the owners, the subjects taught, the authorities who preside over them, and the hierarchical system that governs them, among others. However, management has emerged within this narrative as a way of organizing universities in collusion with those discourses. It is an organizational management commanded to a large extent by cassocks and briefcases, permeating all academic practices and affecting academic staff, the student body, and their families. Colonial sovereignty and Catholic evangelization were inextricably linked to the bureaucratization of various academic strata, which served as the foundation for establishing economic rationales based on economics and, above all, on the competition and productivity of each university. The governance of these organizations never ceased to be male-dominated; on the contrary, this history managed to blend religious conservatism with market individualism. The milestones of protest and the forces of change have been interrupted, neutralized or suppressed, yet they remain latent to this day in the wake of an unfinished uprising (Mandiola et al., 2014).

The Articulations and Challenges of a Spectral Haunting

As mentioned in the Introduction, the analysis of academic organizations in Chile cannot be separated from the context of transformations that have led to both market dominance and the perpetuation of conservative rationales in higher education. It is against this background that we can witness a special type of management take shape, in this case, managerial and masculine, which has been consolidating in academic organizations. Following this historical overview, we may notice the prominent role that the Catholic Church and business groups have played in the direction and shaping of Chilean universities. Although the role of the State has historically strained these two hegemonic blocs, even in the 1960s when they seriously challenged this order, after the dictatorship and the reforms carried out back then, the organizational structures of universities in Chile have not shifted away from the interests of these groups. Evangelization, conservatism, and the pursuit of surplus value unfettered by the State combined with an authoritarian, hierarchical, elitist organization that demands not only obedience from its workers and students, but also competitiveness, individual success, and entrepreneurship.

Our contribution to the organizational study of academia from a gender lens goes beyond a gendered understanding of identity to its intricate articulation in academic practices. The image of the cassata (Mandiola et al., 2019) as evidence of the gendered hierarchization of academic practices failed to analyze in detail the factors birthing the contingency of this articulation, and whether it is an ideology that binds them together. The approach to university management –that broad and pervasive administrative practice, omnipresent, inescapable, and normalized– allows us to continue our general analysis of academic practices.

From this perspective, we argue that academic work is sustained through its articulation with a masculine and managerial discourse. We have highlighted the presence and insistence of a fourth academic practice that cuts across and conditions the traditional university trilogy. This practice is readily acknowledged by Chilean scholars, it is spontaneously criticized, yet not seen as a problem (Mandiola et al., 2019). Its depoliticized normalization raises the question of how it has come about through history (Mandiola & Varas, 2018) and provides an opportunity for a contextualized discussion of how masculine managerial logic has developed within Chilean academia, as well as the material evidence of its implications.

Management specialization refers to a context that puts managerial and entrepreneurial models in universities at the center (Brunner & Uribe, 2007).

It requires embracing the principles of business management to increase organizational efficiency and reinforce managerial tasks (Mandiola & Varas, 2018). It is precisely this specialization that responds to the establishment of a dominant university management model, reshaping the way in which academic practices are understood and organized (Mandiola et al., 2019). Thus, management has gained a foothold among scholarly duties, emerging ambiguously as an interference to academic work and as a formal power within organizational dynamics at universities. The emergence of this practice as a representation of the managerial transformation of Chilean academia may be interpreted and analyzed from a gender lens. The way in which this ambiguity is resolved and the role played by management in academic career paths is nuanced, thus leading to a patriarchal dividend that perpetuates a gendered system for opportunity allocation (Ríos et al., 2018).

However, we must also ask ourselves how it is possible that this particular form of organization within Chilean universities can be perpetuated in a context that would seem to force it into constant transformation, considering the influence of discourses such as innovation, the backdrop of educational reforms, or the feminist critical debate launched since May 2018. There have certainly been changes in recent years, but the relationships between management, managerialism, and masculinity remain at a structural level that is not even visible.

The invisibility of management as a proper academic practice undoubtedly serves the reproduction of a conservative and neoliberal way of organizing universities. This invisibility has indeed been fostered by those who govern universities, most of them are men, to retain their positions of dominance and privilege. However, the reproduction of such a mode of organization is only possible to the extent that the invisibility of management also extends to the whole of academic practices and to those who make up the different strata of the university. It is not only about hiding those who govern but, above all, about normalizing the mode of governance imposed on faculty, staff, and students. Therefore, university organization in Chile should be understood less as the mere sovereign will of a group of men, and more as an intertwined process that reproduces managerial practices embedded in the day-to-day activities of most of those who make these organizations come to life. Drawing from the category of hegemonic masculinity and how it manifests within academic management is useful, as it reveals how this mode of organization is upheld in day-to-day academic work, notwithstanding the actors of formal governance.

In research, teaching, and extension, we may catch management red-handed in its attempt to merge and blend in with other practices. In research, we perceive it in the copious amount of paperwork required to apply for research funds, in the collection of quantitative evidence, in the monitoring of a project's financial deployment, and in the generation of products that can be accumulated and ranked. In teaching, we see it in the preparation of classes, in the design of the syllabus and module evaluations, in how grades are recorded, and in teaching performance evaluations, among others. In extension, we often sense it in the production of academic events, which take the form of business ventures aimed at selling an academic product and marketing a syllabus. In each of these arenas, management is performed in a "parallel" time period, not one defined by a "workload," but rather a fuzzy interval that blurs the separation of work from the personal, the public from the intimate, and the utilitarian from leisure. It is the hegemonic masculine nature of managerialism –articulated through these different academic practices– that underlies its natural and invisible presence. The desire to be published in the best journals or to climb the academic ladder speaks of the quest for positions of power typical of hegemonic masculinity. Moreover, the emphasis on financial control, the self-management of resources, and the demand for profitable productivity are indicative of the individualistic, corporate, and competitive nature of the masculine within the context of neoliberal capitalism. The quantitative and measurable logic of evaluations and audits –which try to account for a publication's impact or the effective use of resources– confronts us with positivist objectivity and the prevalence of instrumental rationality so typical of scientist masculinity, and which also happens to coincide with the hegemonic masculine. Finally, the constant individual competition that governs university accreditation, academic promotion, and student approval is consistent with the kind of athletic or sporting masculinity that is also found in these organizations. It is not only a question of masculine governance, but also, more importantly, a hegemonic masculine management that permeates practices and commands them.

However, various authors have reported on the relationship between masculinity and invisibility (Anahita & Mix, 2009; Badinter, 1993; Butler, 2017; Kimmel, 2010). In this case, it is not about invisibilization excluding, marginalizing, or eradicating the presence of women or other subjectivities or populations, but rather the invisibility of women in science, or the invisibility of glass ceilings. This is another type of invisibility that acts in favor of sustaining the practices that keep men in their hegemonic positions. Elisabeth Badinter points out that this is "the traditional 'invisibility' of the male gender that has done so much to equate it with what is considered human" (1993, p. 24). Judith Butler (2017) argues that this universality of hegemonic masculinity is produced through the disregard and denial of its body, thus, "the masculine is presented as a disembodied universality" (p. 63). It is this invisibilization of the male body, as an inescapable aspect of gender that causes us to treat "men as if they had no gender" (Kimmel & Messner in Badinter, p. 24). As Sine Anahita and Tamara Mix point out: "the gendered aspects of men's activities [are] invisible to casual observers, (...) this underlines how masculinity is generally not seen at all, it remains invisible" (2009, p. 511).

The invisibility of management works in a similar fashion. It insists on its universality as a managerial model running through, governing, and overseeing all academic endeavors. Yet it is an abstract universality that does not manifest itself as an academic practice per se; it is not recognized as a separate field to be acknowledged concretely as a workload beyond those of research, teaching, and extension. It simultaneously dominates and organizes the university while at the same time remaining incorporeal when trying to tackle it as a specific practice, given that it is acted out of complicity with a hegemonic masculine order. It is a disembodied, incorporeal management that seems not to exist, yet never ceases to insist. This is why we argue that it is a spectre haunting academia. A spectre that we fear and loathe, yet whose existence we cannot prove.

Through the ideas discussed thus far, we wish to emphasize the unnoticed, imperceptible, and normalized aspects left untouched by the promise of the transformation of Chilean universities. This is especially the case as the promise is a response to the student movements and feminist struggles that have been a hallmark of the last decade. The commodification of education and the profit motive, together with the various expressions of sexual and gender-based violence that drove the student movements from the early 2000s until the so-called Feminist May of 2018, were translated into political demands that aimed, among other things, at reforms, laws, and institutional measures such as the creation of bodies, commissions, protocols, and new university programs and policies.

However, this raises a few caveats when donning a critical gender and organizational lens, specifically with regard to the processes of gender institutionalization. Indeed, by attempting to define, institutionalize, and educate with respect to gender, there have also been insistences, elisions, omissions, and implementations of forms of organizational violence that denude a clear necessity for critical assessment through the gender lens (Ríos et al., 2018). The buzz around student and feminist demands, as well as the "culture of compliance" (Marine & Nicolazzo, 2017) that shapes university responses, have overshadowed the experiences of academic and administrative bodies with respect to the managerial and masculine organizational pact that runs through academic life as a whole, facilitating the continuity of forms of violence embedded in management as an ideological practice. By not focusing on the promise of university transformation, management becomes a practice that guarantees the university's complicity with the patriarchy and neoliberal ideology corroding academic practices. In conclusion, and drawing from the contributions outlined throughout this chapter, we believe that there is an urgent need to critically expand the concept of gender beyond its conservative, binary, identitarian, and quantitative interpretations. We must reclaim its political capacity and ability to question modes of organization, in this case, of academic practices and the gendered, ideological and "spectral" articulation haunting the neoliberal university.

References

Acker, J. (1990). Hierarchies, jobs, bodies: A theory of gendered organizations. *Gender and Society, 4*, 139–158.

Acker, A., & Webber, M. (2006). Women working in academe: Approach with care. In C. Skelton, B. Francis, & L. Smulyan (Eds.), *The Sage handbook of gender and education* (pp. 483–496). Sage.

Alves Sousa, C., & Hendriks, P. (2008). Connecting knowledge to management: The case of academic research. *Organization, 15*(6), 811–830.

Alvesson, M., & Hugh, W. (2003). *Studying management critically*. Sage.

Alvesson, M., & Due Billing, Y. (2009). *Understanding gender and organizations*. Sage.

Anahita, S., & Mix, T. L. (2009). Retrofitting frontier masculinity for Alaska's war against wolves. In M. En Kimmel & M. A. Messner (Eds.). *Men's lives* (pp. 504–520). Allyn & Bacon.

Anderson, G. (2008). Mapping academic resistance in the managerial university. *Organization*, *15*(2), 251–270.

Badinter, E. (1993). *XY: La Identidad Masculina*, Alianza Editorial.

Barry, J., Berg, E., & Chandler, J. (2006). Academic shape shifting: Gender, management, and identities in Sweden and England. *Organization*, *13*(2), 275–298.

Bellei, C., &Orellana, V. (2014). What *does "education privatisation" mean?* Conceptual discussion and *empirical review of Latin* American *cases*. Centro de Investigación Avanzada en Educación, CIAE.

Berríos, P. (2005). El sistema de prestigio en las universidades y el rol que ocupan las mujeres en el mundo académico *Calidad en la Educación*, (23), 349–361.

Berríos, P. (2007). Análisis sobre las profesoras universitarias y desafíos para la profesión académica en Chile. *Calidad de la Educación*, (26), 39–53.

Bravo, B. (1992). *La Universidad En La Historia De Chile, 1622–1992*. Pehuén Editores.

Bustos, J., Hernández, F., Orihuela, P., & Cárdenas, H. (2018). La desigualdad de género en el cuerpo académico de las universidades chilenas. *Contribuciones Científicas y Tecnológicas*, *43*(1), 29–34.

Butler, J. (2006). *Deshacer el género*. Paidós.

Butler, J. (2017). *El género en disputa: el feminismo y la subversión de la identidad*. Paidós.

Brunner, J. J. (1997). La educación superior chilena como objeto de análisis y de políticas. *Estudios Sociales CPU*, *91*.

Brunner, J. J., & Uribe, D. (2007). *Mercados universitarios: Los nuevos escenarios de la educación superior*. Editorial Universidad Diego Portales.

Carvalho, T., & Machado, M. d. L. (2010). Gender and shifts in higher education managerial regimes. *Australian Universities' Review*, *52*(2), 33–42.

CONFECH. (2011). *Demandas de los estudiantes agrupados en la CONFECH, 30 de abril de 2011*. Centro de Estudios Miguel Enríquez.

Connell, R. (1995). *Masculinities*. University of California Press.

Connell, R. (2010). Building the neoliberal world: Managers as intellectuals in a peripheral economy. *Critical Sociology*, *36*(6), 777–792.

Connell, R., & Messerschmidt, J. (2005). Hegemonic masculinity. Rethinking the concept. *Gender & Society*, *19*(6), 829–859.

Cress, Ch., & Hart, J. (2009). Playing soccer on the football field: The persistence of gender inequities for women faculty. *Equity & Excellence in Education*, *42*(4), 473–488.

Da Corte, M. (2015). 2016: El año decisivo para la reforma y el movimiento estudiantil. *El Dínamo*, 27 de octubre.

Fardella, C., Sisto, V., & Jiménez, F. (2016). Nosotros los académicos. Narrativas identitarias y autodefinición en la universidad actual. *Universitas Psychologica*, *14*(5), 1625–1636.

Fardella, C., Sisto, V., & Jimenez, F. (2017). La transformación de la universidad y los dispositivos de cuantificación. *Estudos de Psicologia (Campinas)*, *34*(3), 435–448.

Fotaki, M. (2013). No woman is like a man (in Academia): The masculine symbolic order and the unwanted female body, *Organization Studies*, *34*(9), 1251–1275.

Gaba, M. (2020). Nuevas arquitecturas de género(s) en las universidades chilenas como respuesta a las movilizaciones feministas estudiantiles del 2018. *Symploké*, *1*, 22–30.

Gaete, R. (2015). El techo de cristal en las universidades estatales chilenas. Un análisis exploratorio. *Revista Iberoamericana de Educación Superior*, *17*(6), 3–20.

Garretón, M., & Martínez, J. (1985). *Universidades chilenas: Historia, reforma e intervención; Biblioteca del movimiento estudiantil, t. 1*, ed. Sur, *Santiago* Chile.

Gonzales-Miranda, D., & Martínez, G. (2019). *Tratado de estudios organizacionales* Volumen 2. *Exploración de las temáticas* – Edición de la versión en español. Editorial EAFIT, Universidad Autónoma Metropolitana, Red Mexicana de Investigadores en Estudios Organizacionales, Sage.

Kelan, E. (2009). *Performing gender at work*. Palgrave Macmillan

Kimmel, M., Hearn, J., & Connell, R. (2005). *Handbook of studies on men & masculinities.* Sage.

Kimmel, M., & Messner, M. A. (2010). *Men's lives.* Allyn & Bacon.

Kiss, D., Barrios, O., & Álvarez, J. (2007). Inequidad y diferencia. Mujeres y desarrollo académico. *Estudos Feministas, 15*(1), 85–105.

Knights, D., & Kerfoot, D. (2004). Between representations and subjectivity: Gender binaries and the politics of organizational transformation. *Gender, Work and Organization, 11*(4), 430– 454.

Krauskopf, E. (2008). Indicadores de productividad por sexo generados en Chile, en algunas disciplinas del área científica y tecnológica. Conicyt.

Linstead, A., & Brewis, J. (2004). Editorial: Beyond boundaries: Towards fluidity in theorizing and practice. *Gender, Work and Organization, 11*(4), 355–362.

Mandiola, M., Ríos, N., & Eridani, A. (2022). El Género Administrado: lecturas feministas y críticas a la reorganización de la academia y las universidades en Chile. En Varios Autores *Mucho género que cortar: Estudios para contribuir al debate sobre género y diversidad en Chile.* Programa de Investigación de Género y Diversidad Sexual GEDIS Universidad Alberto Hurtado.

Mandiola, M., Ríos, N., & Varas, A. (2019). "Hay un tema que no hemos conversado". La cassata como organización académica generizada en las universidades chilenas. *Pensamiento Educativo, 56*(1), 1–16.

Mandiola, M., & Varas, A. (2018). Educar es gobernar: Explorando los inicios del managerialismo masculino en la academia chilena. *Revista de Ciencias Sociales, 31*(43), 57–78.

Mandiola, M., Varas, A., Rios, N., & Salinas, P. (2014). (Im)possible identities in the movement for Chilean Education: Positions and antagonism in academia. *Journal of Workplace Rights, 17,* 411–425.

Marine, S. B., & Nicolazzo, Z. (2017). The rise of compliance culture: A dead end for addressing sexual violence. *Praxis: The Blog of the Journal of Critical Scholarship on Higher Education and Student Affairs.* https://jcshesa.wordpress.com/2017/06/27/the-rise-of-compliance-culture-a-dead-end-for-ending-campus-sexual-violence/

Martínez Alemán, A. (2014). Managerialism as the 'new' discursive masculinity in the university. *Feminist formations, 26*(2), 107–134.

Meriläinen, S., Tienari, J., Thomas, R., & Davies, A. (2008). Hegemonic academic practices: Experiences of publishing from the periphery. *Organization, 15*(4), 584–597.

Morley, L. (1999). *Organising feminisms: The micropolitics of the academy.* Palgrave McMillan.

Parker, M. (2002). *Against management.* Polity Press.

Pino, S., Vallejos, R., Améstica, L., & Cornejo, E. (2018). Presencia de las mujeres en la alta gestión universitaria. Las universidades públicas en Chile. *Páginas de Educación, 11*(2) 176–198.

Prichard, C. (1996) Managing universities: Is it men's work?. In C. En David & H. Jeff (Eds), *Men as managers, managers as men: Critical perspectives on men, masculinities, and managements* (pp. 227–238). Sage.

Ríos, N., Mandiola, M., & Varas, A. (2017). Haciendo género, haciendo academia: Un análisis feminista de la organización del trabajo académico en Chile. *Psicoperspectivas, 16*(2), 114–124.

Ríos, N., Mandiola, M., & Varas, A. (2018). Regímenes sexuales, regímenes organizacionales: De la denuncia del acoso sexual a la denuncia de la organización de la sexualidad en la universidad. In G. Perez-Arrau, P. Isla, M. Mandiola, R. Muñoz, & N. Ríos (Eds.), *Nuevas formas de organización y trabajo: Latinoamérica frente a los actuales desafíos económicos, sociales y medioambientales* (pp. 81–88). Red de Posgrados de Investigación Latinos en Administración y Estudios Organizacionales, 82–88.

Ross-Smith, A., & Kornberger, M. (2004). Gender rationality? A genealogical exploration of the philosophical and sociological conceptions of rationality, masculinity and organization. *Gender, Work and Organization, 11*(3), 280–305.

Salazar, J. M., & Leihy, P. S. (2017). El largo viaje: los esquemas de coordinación de la educación superior chilena en perspectiva. *Education Policy Analysis Archives/Archivos Analíticos de Políticas Educativas,* (25), 1–29.

Santos, J. (2005). *La universidad chilena desde los extramuros: Luis Scherz García.* Universidad Alberto Hurtado.

Santos, J. (2006). Anomalías del modelo neoliberal en Chile. La universidad chilena hoy: El espejismo de su progreso. *Estudios Avanzados Interactivos, 5*(7), 1–12.

Saracostti, M. (2006) Mujeres en la alta dirección de educación superior: Posibilidades, tensiones y nuevas interrogantes. *Calidad en la Educación,* (25), 243–259.

SIES (2020). Instituciones de educación superior en Chile vigentes – 31 de diciembre de 2020. www.mifuturo.cl/instituciones-de-educacion-superior-en-chile/

Slaughter, Sh., & Leslie, E. (1997). *Academic capitalism: Politics, policies & the entrepreneurial university.* The John Hopkins University Press.

Slaughter, Sh., & Rhoades, G. (2004). *Academic capitalism and the new economy: Markets, state, and higher education.* John Hopkins University Press.

Sliwa, M., & Johansson, M. (2014). The discourse of meritocracy contested/reproduced: Foreign women academics in UK business schools. *Organization, 21*(6), 821–843.

Syrett, N. (2007). Academia. In M. En Flood, J. Kegan, B. Pease & K. Pringle (Eds.) *International encyclopedia of men and masculinity* (p. 1). Routledge.

Taylor, Y. & Lahad, K. (2018). *Feeling academic in the neoliberal university.* Springer.

Thomas, R., & Davies, A. (2002). Gender and new public management: Reconstituting academic subjectivities.*Gender, Work & Organization, 9,* 372–397.

Whitehead, S., & Moodley, R. (1999). *Transforming managers: Gendering change in the public sector.* Routledge.

Zerán, F. (2018). *Mayo feminista. La rebelión contra el patriarcado.* Lom.

Chapter 5

Case of Policies for Gender Equality in Latin America Andean Community of Nations – CAN (Colombia, Bolivia, Peru, Ecuador)

Diana Mercedes Valdés Mosquera and
July Alexandra Villalba Rodríguez

Abstract

The theoretical context is necessary to understand the process that frames the gender perspective. It must be studied from the pillars of human rights, those that are inherent to the human being and that do not discriminate against age, sex, social status, etc. Being considered Universal, human rights do not contemplate political ideologies, economic systems, or cultural differences; furthermore, as it is irrevocable, it is not possible to delegate or renounce them; human rights are indivisible, that is, they are related and interconnected with each other, but they are formed as a whole. In addition, due to their nature, they are legally enforceable and recognized by the states, therefore, they require respect and compliance.

Keywords: Gender equity; Andean Community of Nations; equality; human rights; womens rights; social roles; gender inequality; gender discrimination

Introduction

To talk about gender requires an understanding of the biological context because when the contributions of biology are taken into consideration, awareness of the complexity of the distinction between sex/gender increases.

Economy, Gender and Academy: A Pending Conversation, 77–92
Copyright © 2023 by Diana Mercedes Valdés Mosquera and July Alexandra Villalba Rodríguez
Published under exclusive licence by Emerald Publishing Limited
doi:10.1108/978-1-80455-998-720231011

From the concept of gender, theories are built to create the principles of what is called "gender," this same promotes the gender perspective and defines it as

> the approach or conceptual content that we give to gender to analyze reality; there are diverse phenomena, evaluate policies, legislation and the exercise of rights, design strategies and evaluate actions, among others. (Guzmán & Campillo, 2004)

In addition, it is important to recognize the historical process involved in the debate on the institutionalization of gender in the context of development practice and the international agenda. Its beginnings date back to what was called "Women in Development", within the framework of the Women's Decade declared by the United Nations Organization in 1975, to determine the "Gender in Development" approach, at the end of the 1980s and beginning of the 1990s.

At the same time, in the Latin American context, the Mexico Declaration on Equality of Action for Women and the World Plan of Action (1975) and the approval of the Convention on the Elimination of All Forms of Discrimination Against Women (UN, 1979), discussions began on the need to establish

> an interdisciplinary and multisectoral machinery within government, such as national commissions, women's bureaus, and other bodies, with adequate staff and resources, which can be an effective transitional measure for accelerating the achievement of equal opportunities for women and their full integration into national life.

This historical framework in turn reveals the creation of the first "women's offices" in some Latin American countries, influenced by the "Women in Development" (WID) approach and by the characteristics of the States where they were created. The objective was to promote the integration of women into development processes and the activists of the time spoke of "integrating women into development".

But it was not until the 1990s that the "institutionalization of gender aspects" or "gender mainstreaming" in development planning and policies was formalized. This shift in emphasis stems from the recognition that institutions are not gender-neutral so they reproduce and produce inequalities and hierarchical structures of male privilege. Thus, it is recognized that without institutional change that reflects and represents the interests of women, it will not be possible to achieve the goal of gender equity and equality.

Establishing a comprehensive view of the gender equity issue in Latin America and the entire world is the call and the struggle that has been developed by women's movements and organizations worldwide, which has allowed the prioritization of the issue in government agendas; support that is enshrined in the constitutional precepts of the different countries from where determining laws are mentioned that have made it possible to advance in generating awareness and to achieve spaces for greater social inclusion in the gender issue. (Red Nacional de Información, 2022).

In this sense, there are many laws and public policies from the basis of constitutional precepts in these Latin American countries, which enact gender equity as a way of rectifying and generating vindicatory advances on this issue, as is the case of the laws of quota and gender parity among others, where inequality is recognized. Thus, in Peru through the law 28869/2006, Ecuador in the Political Constitution 2008 article 116, Bolivia in the Law of the electoral regime 26/2010 and Colombia law 1475/2011; but that still reflects myopia in its projections as the case of the policy of abortion interruption in Colombia, which affects the reproductive autonomy of women fall short in recognition of health rights and deepen situations of violence and discrimination against women (CEPAL, 2014).

This chapter aims to analyze the conditions of public policies present in the Andean Community – CAN, aimed at promoting gender equity between 2018 and 2022. to achieve this end, the following structure is contemplated for the chapter:

1. Contextualization of the CAN and its relevance in Latin American trade.
2. Gender equity in the CAN.
3. Gender equity in the case of member countries.
4. Strategies for strengthening gender equity in the Andean Community.

The research methodology of this project is qualitative-descriptive, making use of a documentary analysis technique, the purpose of which will focus on gathering, selecting, and analyzing the required information on the current policies of gender equity in the countries belonging to the Andean Community – CAN; on the other hand, the interview technique will also be applied with the objective of analyzing the institutional perspective within one of the oldest economic blocs in Latin America.

Contextualization of the CAN and its Relevance in Latin American Trade

The Andean Community – CAN is the Regional Integration Agreement that emerged in 1969 through the signing of the Cartagena Agreement, the constituent treaty, by Bolivia, Colombia, Ecuador, and Peru; today, the CAN is a large free trade zone, 100% of the originating products can circulate through the Andean countries without the payment of tariffs and constitutes one of the most advanced forms of political, economic, commercial, legal, technological, and environmental cooperation in Latin America.

As an economic bloc, the CAN's objectives are focused on promoting development and improving the quality of life of the citizens of the Andean countries, boosting growth and the generation of quality jobs, improving the bloc's position in the international environment and facilitating the participation of member countries in regional integration processes that will allow them to move toward more advanced degrees of economic integration, such as a common market.

The Andean Integration System (SAI) is a mechanism that promotes the integral, autonomous, and balanced development of the countries that make up the Andean Community, whose adoption was necessary to guarantee the effective coordination of the bodies and institutions that make up the Andean Community, such as the management and control organizations, the community bodies and institutions, and the participation and consultative bodies of civil society; focusing the work agenda on key factors for the Andean countries such as trade, services, investments, transport, electrical interconnection, mobility of people, and Andean identity.

In terms of regulations, the establishment of an Andean legal order with rules that must be adopted by the member countries has been achieved; in terms of mobility of persons, Andean citizens can move throughout the community only with their identity document, without the need for a passport or visa; in terms of international cooperation, resources have been channeled to projects of regional scope, among other achievements in telecommunications, dispute settlement, and support for Pymes, which in each of the Andean countries generate around 60% of jobs (Cancilleria, 2022).

From the trade point of view, the importance of CAN is reflected in the numbers that support it; in 2021, CAN exports to the world increased by 42.1% compared to 2020 (136,448 million USD), intra-community exports increased by 32.2% compared to 2020 and extra-community exports increased by 42.9%; Colombia was the country with the second largest share of exports to the world (30.3%), behind Peru (42.3%). In terms of intra-community exports, Colombia is the leading country with 34.2%, followed by Peru with 29%, Bolivia with 19%, and Ecuador with 17%. Among the most exported intra-community products are soybean oil, copper, animal feed, wood planks, medicines packaged for retail sale, and iron. (Comunidad Andina, 2022).

The similar productive characteristics of the Andean countries lead us to think that their integration through the CAN increases their capacity to compete in world trade, making possible through their actions greater participation in the volume of commercial exchanges and a better position compared to the other regional blocks; in addition, the characteristics of the economies that confirm it make it an attractive market for foreign investment and the emergence of new industries, the CAN is a market of about 114.12 million inhabitants, with an annual GDP of approximately 608,858.1 million US dollars (Mincomercio, 2021).

Given the dynamics of the world, regional integration is seen as a clear strategy to face global challenges, including those related to gender equity, because supra-national organizations are required to dictate the guidelines to be followed in terms of gender equality, and these guidelines must then be adopted and implemented by the countries in the national, regional, and local context of their territories.

Gender Equity in the Andean Community – CAN

The pillars that have been forged over time in the CAN trade bloc have been guided by the reports of the World Health Organization (WHO), whose statistics show that in the world one-third of women have suffered violence, mostly physical and sexual; such statistics are even more crude when stating that 40.63% of women in Latin America are the most representative victims of this type of violence.

Taking into account the above, the Andean Community of Nations CAN through the Andean Council of High Authorities on Women and Equal

Opportunities – CAAAMI, have devoted their efforts to carry out social actions in member countries and have also created strategies to quantify through the Andean Indicators on Gender Violence, these initiatives allow to guide the generation of public policies that focus on monitoring and evaluation of actions and programs in benefit of Andean women.

The economic block has also proposed movements to monitor and follow-up on acts of violence against women, most of which are perpetrated by someone other than the partner or ex-partner, and to identify, by age group, the type, and methodology of violence inflicted throughout life.

All these activities have resulted in a percentage of women who have begun to require some type of help due to violence by their husband/partner. The numbers indicate that women between 15 and 49 years of age who have been married or who live with their aggressor confirm that they have suffered physical and/or sexual violence in the last 12 months.

On the other hand, the representatives of the Andean Community will start working together to promote gender equity policies in the member nations, to guarantee and allow equal access to educational and employment opportunities for women and men, focusing on the denominated economic and digital inclusion.

From this perspective, CAN countries consider that the focuses of attention to contribute to the gender equity gap are:

- Guarantee access to equal opportunities for women and men.
- Economic and digital inclusion.
- Eliminate gender barriers.
- Promote a greater female presence in the labor force and in foreign trade.
- Support small businesswomen and promote economic autonomy in the region.

In addition, the post-pandemic situation requires the economic bloc to involve women in economic reactivation and development; in fact, it has been pointed out that, although the member countries continue to generate and assume more and more actions and policies aimed at strengthening gender equality, the challenges that were identified thanks to COVID-19 show the inequality gaps that must be minimized, since out of the 111 million Andean citizens, 56 million are women.

Gender Equity in the CAN, A Close Look at the Realities of the Member Countries

Colombia

To contextualize the Colombian regulations on gender equity public policies, it is inherent to take a look at the 1991 Political Constitution as a legal framework support: thus, article 13 of the Constitution states:

> All persons are born free and equal before the law, shall receive equal protection and treatment from the authorities and shall enjoy the same rights, freedoms and opportunities without any

discrimination on grounds of sex, race, origin, nationality or family, language, region, political or philosophical opinion. (Constitución Política de Colombia [Const]. Art. 13, 1991)

In the same way, Article 43 refers to the equality of rights and opportunities between men and women, and the impossibility of women being subjected to any kind of discrimination.

This has allowed the country to contextualize and support the progress of the legal framework as well as the formulation of public policies to provide guarantees in terms of gender equity and to socially equalize the rights of women, girls, and people with diverse identities.

In this sense, public policies have been oriented to emphasize gender aspects, involving in state institutions the management of indicators discriminated by age groups (girls, elderly women), gender, race (Afro and indigenous women), and geographic location; evidencing progress in relevant aspects such as the orientation of specific programs, as in the case of Law 731/2002 for the empowerment of rural women, among others.

Similarly, the depth of violence against women in the social life of the country, where the gender aspect has been used as a weapon of power in the context of the conflict and the internal war experienced during the last six (6) decades in Colombia, allowed to include in the framework of the peace agreement signed in 2016 between the government and the former FARC – EP, the gender approach as a cross-cutting element to prioritize the recognition as subjects of rights, especially of women victims of the conflict and the differentiated impact of the conflict in the country, for the promotion of equality, and guarantee the special protection of women and men, the participation of women and their organizations in the construction of peace (Procuraduría General de la Nación & Defensoría del Pueblo, 2021).

State institutional guidelines have materialized agreements and implemented specific actions through the CONPES documents, which make it possible to coordinate and coordinate actions to make possible and implement public policies, which propose strategies for sectoral and multisectoral institutional strengthening, for cultural transformation and social imaginaries that allow overcoming gender gaps.

Major topics of incidence have been worked on in the country such as economic autonomy (Conpes 4080/2022), sexual and reproductive health and prevention of teenage pregnancy (Conpes 147/2012), life free of violence (Conpes 161/2013), rights of women victims of the armed conflict (Conpes 3784/2013), salary equality between men and women (Law 1496/2011), participation of women in the decision-making levels of the different branches and organs of public power (Law 581/2000), among others. Colombia has adopted international regulations as a sign of its commitment to advance the generation of gender equity; however, there is a lack of greater appropriation, sensitivity, awareness, effectiveness, and efficiency of the State institutions to appropriate and implement pedagogy and affirmative actions, the existing regulations in the country and make them more effective, generating greater justice and social equity.

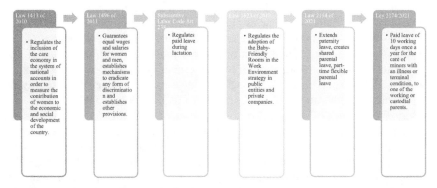

Fig. 5.1   Labor Policies Impacting Gender Equity in Colombia. *Source*: Own elaboration, 2022.

The Global Gender Gap Index analyzes the division of resources and opportunities between men and women in 155 countries. It measures the size of the gender inequality gap in participation in the economy and skilled labor, in politics, access to education, and life expectancy; in the latest measurement, Colombia ranked 75th with a gender gap index of 72.50% (Datosmacro, 2022a), evidencing the urgent need to reduce the differences between men and women, going beyond policies, to actions.

Gender equity is measured in the labor context; Colombia's legal framework is broad and establishes laws for the protection of women, most of which are shown below (Fig. 5.1).

While the policies described above should be sufficient to guarantee an equitable working environment for women and men, the numbers reveal that actions are needed to ensure that these policies have a real impact.

In Colombia:

- The unemployment rate in women is higher than in men (22.9% vs. 13.8%), especially among young people between the ages of 18 and 24 years.
- The labor market insertion gap between men and women is 20.8% points. Half of the women of working age are outside the labor force.
- Women have a higher level of education, but they also have the highest representation in the percentage of informal labor.
- Women in Colombia receive at least 12.1% less in salaries compared to men.
- In Colombia, the value of Unpaid Domestic and Care Work - DCNR amounts to 186 billion COP, 77% of which is carried by women's work.

Other policies in the country are aimed to protect women and their physical autonomy, such as:

- C-055-22: Decriminalization of Abortion.
- Law 2172/2021: Measures to guarantee women victims of extreme gender violence priority access to housing subsidies.

- Law 1761 of 2015: Criminalizes femicide as an autonomous crime.
- Law 1257 of 2008: This law establishes rules for awareness, prevention, and punishment of forms of violence and discrimination against women.
- Law 1542 of July 5, 2012: Guarantees the protection and assistance of the authorities in the investigation of alleged crimes of violence against women.
- Law 1639 of July 2, 2013: Strengthens measures to protect the integrity of victims of acid crimes and adds Article 113 of Law 599 of 2000.

The issue of discrimination and labor and social inequality of gender in Colombia also transcends to educational and higher education spaces such as the academy, where it also strongly marks the entrenched "sexism" with its irregular stereotypes in gender equity and social justice; a situation that is contradictory from the dynamics and social and educational role that the academy should play to promote changes in mentalities and construction of better citizenship and country.

In this sense, statistical data from the country's National System of Higher Education indicate that the private sector attracts and employs more women in higher education (39%) than the public sector (37%). This indicates that the higher education sector has a percentage of less than 40% of women in its educational institutions, and this representation varies according to the disciplines and educational institutions.

The same scenario is presented in the field of access to management positions and positioning in the area of research, where the percentage of women involved in the scientific process in universities does not exceed 40%.

It is mentioned in this regard that Colombia, with a percentage of 46%, is at the lower end of the scale of women's participation in academia in Latin America and the Caribbean (Guarín, 2020).

The review of the numbers in the access of women to higher education graduated in undergraduate and postgraduate courses shows that the percentage has been increasing considerably over the years; from 2013 to 2019, the percentage of female participation grew by 48%, going from 24,900 to 37,048 undergraduate university graduates; in postgraduates, from 3,125 magisters they went to 7,825 with a growth of 150%; Similarly, for participation in doctorates, the number of women graduates went from 73 to 244, with a growth of 230% (Laboratorio de Economía de la Educación, 2021).

Along the same lines, according to the Ibero-American Observatory of Science, Technology and Society (OCTS, 2018), Colombia ranks 14th with 38% female participation in research processes, above other Latin countries, such as Peru, Chile, and Mexico.

Finally, a review of the Colombian legal framework in terms of gender equity reveals that it is the country in the Andean Community of Nations (CAN) with the highest number of laws to guarantee gender equity from a constitutional basis, taking into account factors such as economic autonomy, protection of women and physical autonomy. However, a review of the numbers regarding crimes against women, the wage gap, the participation of women in decision-making positions and the percentage of women participating in the labor market, highlight the urgency of generating strategies that become actions to achieve a more equitable country in practice.

Ecuador

Considering that Article 70 of the Constitution of the Republic of Ecuador, which promulgates "the formal and material development towards the effective enjoyment of rights to achieve equality between women and men" (Asamblea Nacional Constituyente, 2008).

According to the National Survey of Family Relations and Gender Violence against Women, conducted by the Ecuadorian Institute of Statistics and Census (INEC) in 2011, six out of 10 women have experienced some type of gender violence by any person, nationwide. This survey of women and adolescents over 15 years of age, in the 24 provinces of the country, found that one in four women has experienced sexual violence. However, it should be noted that psychological violence is the most recurrent form of gender violence, reaching 53.9% (Ministerio de Relaciones Exteriores y Movilidad Humana, 2008).

Based on the above, the Ecuadorian State has progressively and systematically implemented in its legal system and public policies, the commitments on human rights to promote the eradication of all forms of discrimination against women, the Government has committed to implement in the 2030 Agenda and the Sustainable Development Goals, gender equality is a pillar within the State plans, the main objective is specifically gender equality and the empowerment of women, girls, and adolescents.

Although in recent years, the government has carried out awareness-raising actions and created national institutions to work on the prevention and eradication of gender violence against women, the country is beginning to evaluate the progress made and thus generate initiatives to improve the living conditions of women in Ecuadorian territory, since statistics show a stark reality despite the efforts made (Fig. 5.2).

This being so, the National Assembly approved on January 27, 2018, the "Comprehensive Organic Law to Prevent and Eradicate Violence against Women," which creates the "Comprehensive National System to Prevent and Eradicate Violence against Women" (Asamblea Nacional Constituyente, 2008). This policy is based on four pillars: prevention, attention, protection, and reparation.

In addition, the last Foreign Policy Agenda 2017–2021, in accordance with the gender approach outlined in the National Development Plan 2017–2021 - Toda un Vida, contemplates gender equality as a transversal axis, defending and

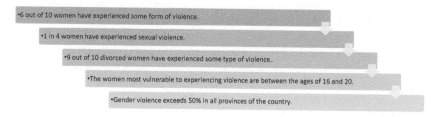

Fig. 5.2 Statistics of the Female Context in Ecuador. *Source*: Own elaboration based on the United Nations Gender Equity Report 2019.

promoting women's rights in all areas, services and work environment; since the studies carried out by (Ministerio de Relaciones Exteriores y Movilidad Humana, 2008) determines that as of January 2018, the total number of ambassadors in active service (68), only 11 are women, representing 16%; a similar situation occurs in the ranks of Ministers and Counselors, where women represent on average 34% of the total in each case. This pattern of inequality is replicated in diplomatic systems at the international level. As an example, of the 44 Embassies accredited in Ecuador, only 12 are headed by female Ambassadors (27%), while of the 26 International Organizations with offices in Ecuador, 12 are represented by women (46%). (Ministerio de Relaciones Exteriores y Movilidad Humana, 2008).

For these reasons, it is important to promote the institutionalization of crosscutting gender equality policies, which will make it possible to meet this objective internally and in all areas of employability management. Other bodies or policies to promote gender equality in Ecuador are:

- The 2008 Political Constitution. Article 116 determines that for multiperson elections, the electoral system indicates the principles of proportionality, equality of the vote, equity, parity, and alternation between women and men (Asamblea Nacional Constituyente, 2008). The Political Constitution also recognizes women's participation of 20% in the lists of multiperson elections.
- The Women's Labor Protection Law establishes the obligation to appoint a minimum of 20% of women to the Superior Courts of Justice, Courts, Notaries, and Registries.
- Gender equality policy promotes non-sexist language, awareness for the elimination of patriarchal cultural patterns, and strengthening training in human rights, especially women's rights, as well as strengthening human talent units to eradicate discrimination and harassment.

Peru

Peru has made some progress in terms of gender, based on Article 2 of the National Political Constitution of 1993, as the guiding letter of the legal basis, which states that:

Every person has the right: To equality before the law. No one shall be discriminated against for reasons of origin, race, sex, language, religion, opinion, economic condition or any other reason. (Congreso Constituyente Democrático, 1993)

Regarding this legal framework, Peru has Law No. 28983 on equal opportunities between women and men, which establishes "that the Executive Branch, regional governments and local governments, in all sectors, adopt policies, plans, and programs, integrating the principles of the aforementioned Law in a cross-cutting manner", this in its 6th article.

Similarly, there is the National System of Gender Indicators (SNIG) implemented through Supreme Decree No. 005-2015, which aims to perform at the national level the follow-up, monitoring, and evaluation of policies on gender equality.

Along these lines, for the definition and implementation of public policies and laws, the Peruvian State has also relied on international treaties, such as the Inter-American Convention on the Prevention, Punishment, and Eradication of Violence against Women (Belém do Pará), the Declaration, the Platform for Action of the Fourth World Conference on Women (UN WOMEN, 1995) and the Convention on the Elimination of All Forms of Discrimination against Women – CEDAW, among others.

The national legislation on gender equity in this country is not nourished, just as there is little notable progress in the application of existing national regulations.

The concept of Sustainable Development Goals (SDGs) introduced by the United Nations has dimensioned environmental sustainability and equality as structural axes that should make inroads in the global economic dynamics, to generate real development with sustainability in Latin America.

From this vision and from the United Nations agenda for post-2015 development and Rio+20 (2013), the development of countries is closely related to social and gender balance and equity, with the predominance of the inclusion and real incursion of women in public and private institutional life, as well as in the political, labor, economic, cultural, and social dynamics of the people, and in all spaces of relevance and guarantees of existing rights, where from their visible empowerment and spaces of power, they are protected, valued, and respected.

Regarding the country's position in the Global Gender Gap Index, in the last measurement, Peru ranked 37th in the gender gap ranking with an index of 74.9% (Datosmacro, 2022b); this means that there is still an opportunity to work to reduce the differences between men and women to improve the country's position compared to the global average.

From the point of view of labor policies that impact gender equity, the lack of women's autonomy and empowerment in the different spheres and especially in the economic sphere, which responds to the inequalities and social injustice previously mentioned in this document, slows down and hinders the real participation of women in all decision-making links, affecting in particular, the quality of life of women and their families and in general the development of their community environment and the country.

Article 26 of the Political Constitution of Peru, in relation to labor equity, indicates that the country respects the principles of equal opportunity without discrimination, the inalienable nature of the rights recognized by the Constitution and the law, and the interpretation in favor of the worker in case of insurmountable doubt about the meaning of a norm (Congreso Constituyente Democrático, 1993).

Similarly, State Policy No. 11 of the National Agreement reveals the commitment of the Peruvian state to combat all forms of discrimination, strengthen the participation of women as social and political actors, and give them equal access to productive resources and employment.

On the other hand, through the Supreme Decree No.068-2017. PCM called Diagnosis of Wage Inequality in Peru, provisions were decreed for state bodies, including ministries, autonomous constitutional bodies, regional, and local governments, to carry out a diagnosis of the wage gap between women and men and the causes in each of the entities, which allow formulating actions to close the gap for wage reasons; along the same lines, Law 30709 of December 28, 2017, prohibits discrimination between men and Women in terms of remuneration, a policy also aimed at reducing the gender pay gap.

In addition, the sectoral plan for equality and non-discrimination in employment and occupation of Peru 2018–2021, constituted a key tool to generate and promote opportunities for women and other vulnerable groups in the framework of equality in access and stability in the labor dynamics for the effective enjoyment of rights, strengthening capacities of the people who are objects and of the institutionality, to energize and facilitate the inclusion of these vulnerable groups (Quiñones, 2019).

The adoption of international provisions ruled by the International Labor Organization- ILO, such as Convention No.100 of 1951 on equal remuneration; Convention No. 111 of 1958 on discrimination (employment and occupation); Convention No. 156 of 1981 on workers with family responsibilities; and Convention No. 183 of 2000 on maternity protection., show the legislative work that has been done from the State in this country, to equalize the inequitable differential issue between men and women in the field of participation in the labor market and economic income. In 2020, the gender gap between men and women in terms of income for work performed, taking into account equal factors such as education, working hours, and occupation, was set at 15% difference; in management positions, it was 56% and in participation in the labor dynamics it reached 21% (Beltrán, 2021).

Finally, it is worth highlighting the role of academia in research on gender equity, because such studies are decisive for the formulation of public policy regarding this gap.

According to the Research Center of the Universidad del Pacífico in Peru, inequity in job opportunities in different fields of academia, such as research, access to management positions, salary equity, opportunities for recognition and career advancement for women, is also limited; the study revealed that in the academic world in Peru, women have difficulties to stand out and achieve academic prestige, as well as to access positions of responsibility, due to the male bias in the discipline and the few possibilities of access to research groups, the lack of experience and, in general, the few opportunities; The gaps are also notable in salaries, in the recognition of the scientific work they produce, the domestic burdens socially indicated more to women, the dynamics of the fertility of couples, or the time dedicated to procreate and form a family, which falls on women in greater proportion and hinder their labor development (Centro de Investigación Universidad del Pacífico, 2022) (Fig. 5.3).

Bolivia

Bolivia has proposed the National Plan for Equal Opportunities "Women Building the New Bolivia, To Live Well" which is the product of a process of reflection

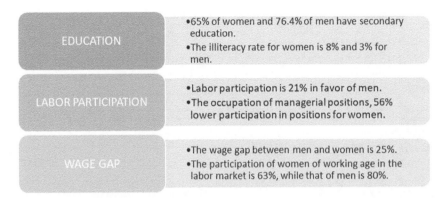

EDUCATION
- •65% of women and 76.4% of men have secondary education.
- •The illiteracy rate for women is 8% and 3% for men.

LABOR PARTICIPATION
- •Labor participation is 21% in favor of men.
- •The occupation of managerial positions, 56% lower participation in positions for women.

WAGE GAP
- •The wage gap between men and women is 25%.
- •The participation of women of working age in the labor market is 63%, while that of men is 80%.

Own elaboration based on figures from the National Institute of Statistics and Informatics- INEI, 2021.

Fig. 5.3   Gender Equity in Figures in Peru, 2020. Own elaboration based on figures from the National Institute of Statistics and Informatics – INEI, 2021.

and joint work between the National Government and women's social organizations throughout the country, in this process the problems faced by women were identified, to design a long-term strategy aimed at mitigating or eradicating these problems.

This country is characterized by a wide cultural diversity, but also has a gender gap of 73.4%, in fact, in 2015 there were 30,176 cases of violence against women, only 0.7% came to have a formal indictment, statistics show that the year with more femicides was 2017 with 111 cases.

In 2017, nine out of 10 women suffered psychological violence throughout their lives, so much so that in rural areas 82.5% of women have suffered some type of violence; according to the UN Women report for 2018, 7 out of 10 economically active women in the country work in informality or without all labor guarantees and rights being respected.

According to the World Bank, in 2015, 84% of the companies led by women were microenterprises with less than five employees and according to the National Institute of Statistics (INE), women in the private sector have an average remuneration 30% lower than that of men in 2017 (Comisión Especial de la Mujer, 2018).

Based on the above, the government has decided to create a plan that strengthens development strategies with a common vision: Bolivia fully recognizes the contribution of women to the development of the country. This recognition should be expressed in equal opportunities for access to services, full participation in decision-making spaces, the equitable distribution of economic, technological, and patrimonial resources, creating the conditions for a life free of violence due to gender (Viceministerio de Género y Asuntos Generacionales, 2018).

To achieve this vision, the Bolivian government is committed to developing six pillars in its policy (Fig. 5.4):

This strategy has been built, step by step, with the broad participation of various sectors of women, and has placed special emphasis on the need to build a society where cultural diversity is its main wealth.

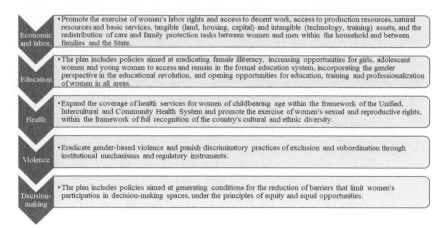

Fig. 5.4   Vision of Gender Equity Policy in Bolivia. *Source*: Own elaboration based on figures from the National Institute of Statistics and Informatics – INEI, 2021.

In addition, it joins the other laws that ratify the commitment of the State, such as:

- Law 26, Law of the Electoral Regime determines the Principle of Equivalence, which sustains gender equity and equal opportunities between women and men, applying parity in the lists of candidates for all government positions.
- Law 25, Law of the Judicial Branch, establishes that nominations to the Plurinational Legislative Assembly, the Supreme Court of Justice and the Agro-environmental Tribunal must have 50% women.
- The new Political Constitution of the Plurinational State of Bolivia determines that participation shall be equitable and under equal conditions for men and women.
- Law 2.771 of Citizen Groups and Indigenous Peoples, which establishes that the Citizen Groups and Indigenous Peoples shall establish a quota of no less than 50% for women.

Strategies for Strengthening Gender Equity in CAN

To give some recommendations to promote gender equity in the Andean Community of Nations (CAN) is a challenge of an institutional and academic nature, since for the effective incorporation of the gender perspective in projects, programs, and agreements, the gap between theory and practice must be closed; it is necessary to agree on guidelines for the effective integration of the gender perspective in the economic bloc; it is necessary to incorporate the mandates, plans and national policies of the member countries, to promote the use of non-sexist language in all academic, social, and labor activities.

It is necessary to carry out a massive awareness-raising process on the relevance of the gender approach to avoid the reproduction of patriarchal cultural patterns and thus gradually include equality and reduce the levels of gender violence. This certainly helps to strengthen the exercise of women's rights in general, and especially those related to equality and non-discrimination, through training that promotes knowledge on the subject, as well as specific training related to the approach and gender equality in management and public policy.

It is necessary to work through training to raise awareness in the Human Talent Management units, to attend and assist employees in cases of discrimination and harassment, as well as, if necessary, to correctly refer cases to the appropriate institutions and take the corresponding disciplinary measures.

References

Asamblea Nacional Constituyente. (2008). *Constitución 2008.* Asamblea Nacional Constituyente. https://www.asambleanacional.gob.ec/sites/default/files/documents/old/constitucion_de_bolsillo.pdf

Beltrán, A. (2021). *Brecha de género: Balance 2021 y proyecciones al 2022.* Centro de Investigación Universidad del Pacífico. https://ciup.up.edu.pe/analisis/balance-2021-y-proyecciones-al-2022-brecha-de-genero/

Cancilleria. (2022). *Ministerio de Relaciones Exteriores.* https://www.cancilleria.gov.co/international/regional/can

Centro de Investigación Universidad del Pacífico. (2022). *8M: ¿Qué inequidades persisten en la academia?* Centro de Investigación Universidad del Pacífico. https://ciup.up.edu.pe/analisis/8m-que-inequidades-persisten-en-la-academia/

CEPAL. (2014). *Políticas públicas para la igualdad de género: Un aporte a la autonomía de las mujeres.* https://www.cepal.org/es/publicaciones/37226-politicas-publicas-la-igualdad-genero-un-aporte-la-autonomia-mujeres

Comisión Especial de la Mujer. (2018). *Información estadística.* ONU Mujeres.

Comunidad Andina. (2022). *Estadísticas de Exportaciones Intra y Extra Comunitarias 2021.* Secretaria General Comunidad Andina. https://www.comunidadandina.org/DocOficialesFiles/DEstadisticos/SGDE941.pdf

Congreso Constituyente Democrático. (1993). *Constitución Política del Perú.* https://cdn.www.gob.pe/uploads/document/file/198518/Constitucion_Politica_del_Peru_1993.pdf

Congreso de la República. (1991). *Constitución Política 1 de 1991 Asamblea Nacional Constituyente.* https://www.funcionpublica.gov.co/eva/gestornormativo/norma.php?i=4125

Datosmacro. (2022a). *Índice global de brecha de Genero Colombia.* https://datosmacro.expansion.com/demografia/indice-brecha-genero-global/colombia

Datosmacro. (2022b). *Índice Global de Brecha de Género Perú.* https://datosmacro.expansion.com/demografia/indice-brecha-genero-global/peru

Guarín, A. (06 de Marzo de 2020). *Universidad de los Andés.* Obtenido de ¿Para cuándo el cierre de la brecha de género en la academia?: https://uniandes.edu.co/es/noticias/brecha-de-genero-una-deuda-pendiente-de-la-academia

Ibero-American Observatory on Science, Technology and Society (OCTS). (2018). *Overview of gender equality in Colombia.* OECD. https://www.oecd-ilibrary.org/sites/99444453-en/index.html?itemId=/content/component/99444453-en

Laboratorio de Economía de la Educación. (2021). *La brecha de género en investigación en Colombia. Informe Análisis Estadístico LEE No. 30.* Pontificia Universidad Javeriana. https://economiadelaeducacion.org/informe030/

Mincomercio. (2021). *COMUNIDAD ANDINA (CAN)*. Mincomerio. https://www.mincit. gov.co/getattachment/8d2d6dc4-f268-4f1b-b790-fcf6e8f73058/CAN.aspx

Ministerio de Relaciones Exteriores y Movilidad Humana. (2008). *Política para la igualdad de genero*. ONU Mujeres.

Pacheco, G., Torres, I., & Tojo, L. (2004). Los derechos humanos de las mujeres: Fortaleciendo su promoción y protección internacional De la formación a la acción. *San José C.R: Instituto Interamericano de Derechos Humanos*. chrome-extension: //efaidnbmnnnibpcajpcglclefindmkaj/https://www.iidh.ed.cr/iidh/media/1831/los-derechos-humanos-de-las-mujeres-2004.pdf.

Procuraduría General de la Nación & Defensoría del Pueblo. (2021). *Informe sobre la incorporación del enfoque de género en la implementación del Acuerdo de Paz*. PuntoAparte Editores. https://www.procuraduria.gov.co/portal/media/file/Informe%20 de%20g%C3%A9nero_2021_completo_abr26.pdf

Quiñones, S. (2019). *El marco institucional y normativo de la igualdad de oportunidades por razón de género*. https://cdn.www.gob.pe/uploads/document/file/413497/boletin_ informativo_laboral_N_94.pdf

Red Nacional de Información. (30 de Junio de 2022). https://cifras.unidadvictimas.gov.co/ Cifras/#!/hechos

UN WOMEN. (1995). *Beijing and its Follow-up. UN WOMEN*, Beijing. https://www. un.org/womenwatch/daw/beijing/

Viceministerio de Género y Asuntos Generacionales. (2018). *Plan Nacional para la igualdad de oportunidades*. UNESCO.

PART III

Gender Equity Within Latin American Organizations in the Context of the SDGs (Internship – Productivity)

Chapter 6

Alternatives for Organization Change with A Gender Perspective

Alejandra Elizabeth Urbiola Solis

Abstract

This chapter starts with two initial questions: Why, despite the fact that most large companies and organizations have protocols and instances for handling complaints to address gender violence, on many occasions, asymmetric relationships persist and no structural changes are observed in most of them? Can the culture of the environment determine resistance to change within organizations, or are the new processes part of an isomorphic organizational response to environmental pressures? To answer these questions, macroeconomic indicators of development and the gender gap are shown, to later explore the relationship between the construction of gender as a product where multiple variables converge and the gap that exists between women and men in organizations. Regardless of the economic wealth of a country, the incorporation of gender protocols does not always yield positive results. From a neo-institutional theoretical perspective and gender studies, the existence of a structural pressure to align subjects in dichotomous categories is proposed. Added to the visible asymmetries are the invisible costs for women and men: violence, invisibility, and underrepresentation. It is proposed to recognize the cultural conditions and the different degrees of organizational porosity to promote an intervention on three levels: from the subject in the organization; in the organizational field, structure, positions, processes, and products, and through a political praxis.

Keywords: Gender gap; organizations; violence; invisible costs; cultural conditions; organizational intervention

Economy, Gender and Academy: A Pending Conversation, 95–110
Copyright © 2023 by Alejandra Elizabeth Urbiola Solis
Published under exclusive licence by Emerald Publishing Limited
doi:10.1108/978-1-80455-998-720231012

Introduction

The objective of this chapter is to explore the relationship between gender construction and the gap between women and men in organizations. Based on a review of macroeconomic indicators of development and the gender gap, it identifies the groups of countries where gender asymmetry is most acute, as well as the challenges of development. This chapter begins by recognizing that, within organizational fields, as a result of environmental pressure, the conditions for women in the public sphere have changed. The changes have been gradual and are not necessarily related to a country's economic wealth indicators, that is, there may be countries with macroeconomic indicators of economic growth, but with a large gender gap. The chapter explores how the incorporation of gender protocols does not always have optimal results; from a neo-institutional and gender studies theoretical perspective, it is argued that there are mechanisms that reproduce structural inequality, even if measures are taken to legitimize organizations in terms of gender equity. The immediate consequence of this condition is the development costs of not favoring equity and the hidden costs for women and men in organizations with heteropatriarchal dynamics.

According to the World Bank (2022a), the asymmetries and roles played by women and men in the private sphere contribute to persistent gender violence in organizations: violence and exclusion are replicated in the public sphere. Social relations reproduce personal relations (Izquierdo, 2010), and subject remain anchored to structures that impose an exclusionary dichotomous binary system (Maffia, 2016), unless within organizations there are mechanisms that ensure equity. Data from the World Bank (2022b) in relation to income and participation indicate that women obtain only two-thirds of the income of men throughout their lives (p. 3), which impoverishes women heads of household and reduces the possibility of breaking poverty; the institution adds that a more egalitarian legal environment is associated with greater economic participation in entrepreneurship and a reduction in domestic violence and femicides.

Why is it that despite the fact that most large companies and organizations have protocols and complaint instances to address gender violence, asymmetrical relationships persist on many occasions and structural changes are not observed in most of them? Can the culture of the environment determine resistance to change within organizations, or are the new processes part of an isomorphic organizational response to environmental pressures?

The possible answers to these questions lead us, on the one hand, to the analysis of the gender gap between women and men within organizations and in the workplace, a gap that has been denounced worldwide and which public policies are trying to modify; on the other hand, we must reflect on the transversal effect of environmental conditions that modify the gender relationship: the cultural assignment of sexual difference, legal changes, and other variables such as religion or ethnic identity. Organizations are inserted in fields of socio-economic and legal interrelationships and legislation on working conditions for women and men, but also in cultural fields of gender mandate and processes of cultural globalization. There are economic and non-economic mechanisms of globalization and resistance (universalism vs. cultural relativism) which, when speaking of gender, establish jus cogens norms that imply adopting gender equity norms and practices to facilitate economic integration and world institutional organization.

Gender Gap

It can be said that the gender gap is an indicator that shows inequity, asymmetries, and the areas where it is possible to work on public policy to improve the living conditions of women and men. It would be expected that a country with a high development indicator would also have a good indicator of gender equality and low-income concentration. However, we can find countries where cultural elements influence the gender gap more than economic elements: countries with good HDI indicators, but with a large gender gap: Iran (HDI of 0.783 and 143rd place in gender gap) and Algeria (HDI of 0.748 and 140th place in gender gap, UN data, 2022) are examples.

Considering the possible relationship between economic development conditions and the gender gap, four categories can be identified:

(a) Rich countries with low gender gap – Iceland and other Nordic countries.
(b) Rich countries with a large gender gap – Iran and other Muslim countries.
(c) Poor countries with a small gender ga– – Rwanda and Burundi.
(d) Poor countries with a large gender gap – Niger, Chad, Mali, and other African countries.

Among the main macroeconomic indicators showing the living conditions of women and men that can guide public policies in addition to the overall gender gap index and the human development index is the Gini coefficient. The HDI includes the variables of life expectancy, education, and gross domestic product. It classifies countries according to three categories according to the highest rating or level of development (equal to one): countries with high human development (HDI greater than 0.80); countries with medium human development (HDI between 0.50 and 0.80) and countries with low human development (HDI below 0.50). In this chapter, rich countries were considered to be those with HDI above 0.70 and poor countries with HDI below 0.56, respectively.

The gender gap involves a quotient that measures the distance between women and men in relation to variables related to education, work, health, and political participation; it involves respect for rights gained and lost or the search for them, the use of resources, and access to opportunities. Finally, the Gini coefficient is an indicator that measures inequality in income or income per percentile of the population; with a result of 0, the index indicates maximum equality, and with a result of 1, maximum inequality, is when all income is concentrated in a single citizen.

According to data from the United Nations (UN), by 2022, the five countries with the best indicators in the global gender gap index out of a total of 146 countries were, in order of importance, Iceland, Finland, Norway, New Zealand, and Sweden. These countries also had high indicators in the HDI and low indicators in the Gini coefficient, indicating that in their territory there are public policies that generate low-income concentration and gender equity.

In relation to Latin America, the countries with the best indicators in the global gender gap index were Nicaragua (7), Costa Rica (12), Mexico (31), Argentina (33), Guyana (35), and Chile (47) out of a total of 146 countries. Other geopolitically important countries in the region, but with low gender equity were Colombia (75) and Brazil (94). All the countries mentioned above had high HDI indicators, with Chile, Argentina, and Costa Rica standing out in the group with development levels of 0.851, 0.845, and 0.810 in that order. Costa Rica was the only country in the Latin American group that can be compared with the Nordic countries in terms of reducing the gender gap and development conditions, as well as New Zealand. On the other hand, Nicaragua, with a short gender gap, did not reach optimal levels of development.

If we look at income concentration, the difference between the Nordic countries and New Zealand with low gender gap and high levels of development, compared to the Latin American countries, Nicaragua and Costa Rica with the low gender gap, have high-income concentration. In other words, there is high-income inequality. All the other countries in the group, Colombia, Brazil, Mexico, Chile, and Argentina, register Gini coefficients above 42.0 being the most unequal countries Colombia (54.2) and Brazil (48.9), close to the most unequal country in America, Suriname (57.9) and higher than Haiti (41.1), UN data for 2012, 2014, and 2020, respectively.

In relation to the gender condition, based on the above indicators, we can infer that those countries with low Gini coefficients and high HDI indicators and with a low gender gap have optimal resource distribution conditions. Here would be Iceland, Finland, Norway, New Zealand, and Sweden, with Gini coefficients ranging from 23.2 (2018 data for Iceland) to 26.8 (2021 data for Sweden). Indicating the global gender gap index good conditions for women in the public and private spheres.

The second group of countries are those with wealth, but with a significant gender gap, Saudi Arabia (127th place), Iran (143rd), Algeria (140th), Tunisia (120th), and Egypt (129th). Iran is the country with the highest Gini coefficient, 40.9 (2017 data), indicating a great inequality in income concentration, while the other countries remain in a range below 32.8 in the indicator (UN data for 2011, 2015, and 2017). Saudi Arabia with an HDI of 0.854 has a significant gender gap, although there is no data for the Gini coefficient.

The explanation for the status of women in Iran and Saudi Arabia is related to religious norms and their secular application in constitutions, in the first case, as a theocracy and in the second, with an absolute monarchy. The countries that apply the Sharia (Iran, Afghanistan, Saudi Arabia, and Yemen) in secular legislation, reproduce asymmetric dichotomous categories between women and men (see Table 1 Annex); with an androcentric orientation, they translate into sexist and heteropatriarchal regulations (Martel, 2021).

Afghanistan is a country with an HDI of 0.511 in HDI by 2022 (UN) and a gender gap that places it at the bottom of the UN list. No data on the Gini coefficient is found, but it is inferred that after the armed conflict and religious reorganization, there are no available or reliable statistics. In the case of Japan, cultural elements have an impact on the gender gap. With an HDI of 0.919, it ranks 116th in the gender gap, with an income concentration of 32.9 (data for 2013). Data that corroborate the importance of religious and/or cultural variables.

The UN reports for 2022, poor countries with a small gender gap: Rwanda (6), Namibia (8) and South Africa (20), African countries that, however, have very high Gini coefficients: 43.7 (2016 data) for Rwanda; 59.1 (2015 data) for Namibia, and 63.0 (2014 data) for South Africa. How can we explain the existence of a small gap but a high-income concentration? Perhaps, the gap indicator includes women who are in the public sphere, highly educated, and occupy high positions with good incomes, while the Gini coefficient indicates that there is a large part of the population of women and men in precarious and poor living conditions.

Finally, countries with large gaps and low development indicators such as Niger, do not necessarily have a high Gini coefficient (37.3 in 2018); other countries in this group would be Chad (37.5 in 2018); Mali (36.1 in 2018); and Pakistan (29.6 in 2018). This clearly tells us that these are excluded countries and economic regions and that their population in general faces challenges in achieving adequate development indicators. The HDI of the above countries was for Niger at 0.394; Chad at 0.398; Mali at 0.434; and Pakistan at 0.557, as shown in Table 6.1.

Based on the above, it is necessary to explore the conditions in which public policies affect the gender gap, specifically in those countries that have good HDI indicators with a wide gender gap, which for Latin America is the case of Brazil and Colombia. If we add the distribution of wealth, we would have countries in the region that in addition to a wide gender gap have a high concentration of income, this would be the case of Colombia.

According to data from UN Women (2022), in Colombia, unpaid work per week for women is 33 hours, while men report 11.5 hours per week. 39.3% of the female population over 15 years of age has no income of its own, while only 17.4% of men have no income of their own. The unemployment rate for women is 14.5% and 9% for men. The salary gap in Colombia ranges from 4% to 35% for women in equal conditions (academic qualification or preparation). The double workday is also present, since women reported in 2021, 18.2% of their time was dedicated to housework while men only 5.3% to this activity.

With the pandemic, the double and triple workday revealed violence in the private sphere and unemployment in the public sphere, which in both cases harmed women more than men. A direct relationship between violence and confinement is reported. A study conducted in 2021 reported that 63% of Colombian women experienced some type of violence. These gaps in organizational spaces also occur in the other countries of the region and are exacerbated by the pandemic, the economic crisis derived from it, and the market mechanisms of the income distribution. UNICEF data for Colombia indicate that one out of every four women has a partner or marries before the age of 18, and that for every 10 unemployed men, only one woman has been able to do so.

Table 6.1.   Main Economic Indicators: HDI, Global Gender Gap Index and
Gini Coefficient.

Country	Human Development Index	Place in the Global Gender Gap Index (Total 146)	Gini Coefficient[a]	Sahara Desert	Islamic Countries With Sharia[b] in Constitutions
Iceland	0.949	1	23.2 (2018)		
Finland	0.938	2	25.7 (2021)		
Norway	0.957	3	25.3 (2020)		
New Zealand	0.931	4	No data		
Sweden	0.945	5	26.8 (2021)		
Nicaragua	0.660	7	46.2 (2014)		
Costa Rica	0.810	12	49.3 (2014)		
Mexico	0.779	31	45.4 (2014)		
Argentina	0.845	33	42.3 (2020)		
Guyana	0.682	35	45.1 (1998)		
Chile	0.851	47	44.9 (2020)		
Colombia	0.767	75	54.2 (2020)		
Brasil	0.765	94	48.9 (2020)		
Rwanda	0.543	6	43.7 (2016)		
Namibia	0.646	8	59.1 (2015)		
South Africa	0.709	20	63.0 (2014)		
Burundi	0.433	24	38.6 (2013)		war
Mozambique	0.456	34	54.0 (2014)		
Tunisia	0.740	120	32.8 (2015)	Tunisia	
Níger	0.394	128	37.3 (2018)	Niger	
Egypt	0.707	129	31.5 (2017)	Egypt	
Morocco	0.686	136	39.5 (2013)	Mororcco	
Benin	0.545	138	37.8 (2018)		
Oman	0.813	139	No data		
Algeria	0.748	140	27.6 (2011)	Algeria	
Mali	0.434	141	36.1 (2018)	Mali	
Chad	0.398	142	37.5 (2018)	Chad	
Iran	0.783	143	40.9 (2012)		Iran
Republic of Congo	0.574	144	48.9 (2011)		
Pakistan	0.557	145	29.6 (2018)		Pakistan
Afghanistan	0.511	146	No data		Afghanistan

Table 6.1. (Continued)

Country	Human Development Index	Place in the Global Gender Gap Index (Total 146)	Gini Coefficient[a]	Sahara Desert	Islamic Countries With Sharia[b] in Constitutions
Libya	0.724	No data	No data	Libya	Libya
Mauritania	0.546	No data	32.6 (2014)	Mauritania	Mauritania
Sudan	0.510	No data	34.2 (2014)	Sudan	
Irak	0.674	No data	29.5 (2012)		
Saudi Arabia	0.854	127	No data		Saudi Arabia
Yemen	0.470	No data	36.7 (2014)		Yemen
South Sudan	0.433	No data	44.1 (2016)		War
Central African Republic	0.397	No data	56.2 (1999)		War
Democratic Republic of Congo	0.480	144	42.1 (2012)		War
Japan	0.919	116	32.9		
Kuwait	0.806	130	No data		

Source: Own elaboration with data from the UN, HDI, Global Gender Gap Index. Expansión Datosmacro.com. Guini Index. https://datosmacro.expansion.com/demografia/indice-gini; https://datosmacro.expansion.com/idh; https://datosmacro.expansion.com/demografia/indice-brecha-genero-global

[a] The current statistical information and those available on the Internet were reviewed. When data were not available, a statistical trend comparison between countries was sought. It is considered that due to the COVID-19 pandemic, statistical information is not available for all the countries compared. Also for issues of internal conflicts. The analysis of transmigrant groups to countries of destination is left out.

[b] Azerbaijan, Bangladesh, Algeria, Chad, Libia, Malasia, Senegal, Sudan and Tunisia do not have Sharia (Islamic religious law for public and private aspects by gender) as the source of legislation, that is, they do not declare themselves as Islamic republics, although they do include it in the application of the law.

Gender, The Cultural Construction of Sexual Difference

Gender as a cultural assignment to sexual difference (Lamas, 1994, 2000), has had different expressions according to the historical context and, in most of them, women have been excluded and discriminated against socially and legally (Maffia, 2007). We speak of a patriarchal order when there is male domination for activities that are necessary for the reproduction of the domestic nucleus, as well as in relation to the rules on the use of the body (Rubin, 1986). Since the end of prehistoric times with the Sumerians and in ancient times with the great empires of Mesopotamia (Sumerians, Akkadians, Babylonians, Assyrians, Persians) and the Nile Delta (Egyptians), productive surpluses allowed for a division of labor and assignment of tasks by sex. This situation was also present in the other great cultural areas of the world (Mesoamerica, Andean Region, India, and China).

Subsequently, the rules of behavior by sex, the assignment of tasks to each sex, and the regulation of the female body, as well as the control of group reproduction, were institutionalized through religion and theocratic governments. In the first monotheistic Abrahamic religions, women were excluded from those activities that were already considered male activities. The reading of the Torah and the discussion of Jewish mysticism or kabbalah were forbidden even for unmarried men under the age of 40 (Iriarte, 1992). Sumerian law and the code of Hammurabi regulated the status of women in various aspects such as space, body conditions, purity and impurity, the (patriarchal) family, prostitution, and economic activities. It is recognized that the legislation was not always favorable to women, but it allowed them to have some independence; depending on their social status, they could own property, marry and have rights over assets, as well as engage in trade and public administration activities (Lereth de Matheus, 2011).

Among the cultures of the Mesoamerican region, the sex–gender relationship began shortly after birth, the midwife presented in a ritual to the newborn those elements that would accompany him throughout his life according to his place in the world. Thus, women were destined to preserve the warriors through activities such as food preparation and their relationship with the earth was closer. The characteristics of a woman made her similar to the earth, cold, dark, and humid like caves; while, for men, war, and the search for spaces of conquest identified them with the forces of nature that break and penetrate. Women and men were assigned activities and use of the body in relation to the deities and the environment; their bodies wore skirts reminiscent of the earth or paint to represent male deities. Roles and activities could not be easily broken and were historically imposed in the pre-classic, classic, or theocratic, and post-classic periods or military states (Arroyo, 2004; Ruz, 2004).

Some authors affirm (García, 2008) that the private spheres of affection and motherhood, and the public sphere of war, commerce, and public administration activities did not function rigidly between women and men, nor did they have the connotation that both spheres have today. There were cosmogonic, religious, and prestige elements to be considered. On the other hand, Pool Cab and Hernández (cited in García, 2008), refer that, among the Mayas, the public – private dichotomy was not rigid, it was adjusted to the circumstances, the same case for the Zapotec zone (González, 2007, cited in García), where prestige, abundance, and growth are related to the subordination of women (González, 2007, cited in García).

The cultural assignment of gender finds in economic conditions and cosmogonic-religious explanations the origin of the differences between women and men. The sex–gender division of labor was an alternative to accumulate production surpluses that allowed economic development. It is not directly associated with a specific mode of production, but it begins to show more asymmetries and resorts to structural violence with the advent of market economies. Before imposing itself as the dominant mode of production, the mechanisms of gender perpetuation were legal and religious structures.

With the conversion of Flavius Valerius Constantine to Christianity, the Roman Empire gradually adopted the Christian religion as well as its gender norms. Women became a bargaining chip and the use of their bodies was regulated to reproduce patriarchal structures of domination. The Renaissance and modernity implied a rethinking about the role of women, the church, and the form of cultural assignment by gender; John Stuart Mill pointed out the condition of inferiority in which women lived (Lereth de Matheus, 2011) and with it, the need to rethink whether the culturally assigned dichotomous categories could change (Table 6.2 and Fig. 6.1); Little by little, women's non-conformity and the struggle to improve living conditions, political participation, recognition of citizenship and the right to vote, as well as respect for fundamental rights, became more visible. The worldwide domination of the capitalist mode of production implied changes in the public and private spheres that have not been homogeneous in all countries and that are transversally crossed by the type of government and the dominant religion.

The incorporation of women into production and the modifications in the private sphere, as well as the multiple configurations in power relations, are expressed in everyday asymmetries: sticky floor, glass ceiling, glass walls, glass borders (Burin & Meler, 2010; Burin, 2004, 2015). What has been called the "Wollstonecraf dilemma" entails arguing in relation to property: first of all, over one's own person, one's own body, and one's own sexuality.

Equal economic participation between women and men would increase world GDP by 26% and 2.4 billion women could have greater economic opportunities,

Table 6.2. Exclusive Dichotomous Categories.

Dependent	Independent
Emotional	Unemotional
Passive	Aggressive
Sensitive	Insensitive
Calm	Competitive
Graceful	Uncoordinated
Innocent	Experienced
Weak	Strong
Insinuating	Active
Educated	Self confident
Self-critical	Hard
Soft	Sexual aggressive
Sexually submissive	Rebel
Accommodating	Independent

Source: Own elaboration with Gender and Identity data: https://www.plannedparenthood.org/esp/temas-de-salud/orientacion-sexual-y-genero/genero-e-identidad-de-genero#sthash.jMpXjbcv.dpuf.

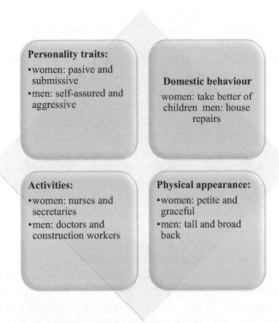

Fig. 6.1.   Gender Stereotype. *Source*: Own elaboration based on Maffia (2016).

empowerment, autonomy, and well-being (UN, WB, 2022). Women's participation in the public sphere in conditions of asymmetry implies a lag in HDI
indicators and a reduction in the potential multiplier effects derived from their
participation in the economy. Exclusion has a woman's face: management positions are preferentially reserved for men; women's salaries show gaps compared to
men's salaries; reported cases of sexual harassment are higher among women and
minorities. In the private sphere, there are unwritten codes and rules of behavior
for women that include body changes even against their health. It is common to
hear sexist, misogynistic statements, while homophobia, transphobia, and lesbo-
phobia emerge with greater force.

If we have a stereotype of what a man is and a stereotype of what a woman is
and we also hierarchize these categories, we are reinforcing the hierarchy of women
with respect to men in inferiority. It is said, for example, "she is extremely emotional to assume a public position", "she is too emotional to occupy a function of
such responsibility" (Maffia, 2016, p. 3). Table 6.2 for the dichotomous categories.

The Organization: Visible Asymmetries and Invisible Costs

An organization refers to a group of people with common objectives: the family,
the school, the church, the army, and the company are some examples. Within it,
there is a structure, a division of labor, and power relations. In their day-to-day
work, leaders in organizations face situations of uncertainty and make decisions;
they establish policies and programs to preserve the organization and the changes

that are generated as a consequence have an external origin, they seek to reduce uncertainty within. In organizations, there are power relations, violence, and sexism is present. For its analysis, we have analytical categories: gender, the sex-gender system, and patriarchy. Of the three categories, we suggest using the gender category. According to Burin (2015), the category is relational, that is, it involves subjects in interaction and intersubjectivity; it is not an ahistorical category, it acquires particular connotation depending on the historical-cultural context and serves us as a tool to analyze the bases of asymmetries and stereotypes for women and men, which reproduce women and men crossed by class condition, ethnicity, religion, geographic space, and economic context (Burin, 2015; Izquierdo, 2010).

Violence is institutionalized by reproducing the surrounding culture through perpetrator mechanisms of gender asymmetries: structures such as the family, the church, the army, the school, or the company; cognitive structures in bodies and minds and the cultural assignment of gender. A patriarchal, homophobic, and misogynistic sociocultural structure reproduces gender mandates on women and men in specific activities in the organization. The public sphere reproduces the exclusion and dichotomous categories assigned to women. The prevalence of gender asymmetries and violence suggests that protocols, policies, and instances of attention reflect the myths rationalized in the organizational field or institutional environment rather than the demands of violence and/or gender gaps in work activities. Thus, processes, programs, and offices, among others, are incorporated into the formal structure, ceremonially adopted, and become routines that are carried out considering the type and the actor.

In the workplace, protocols for intervention in gender-based violence tend to be part of the organizational routine and become the rules of the game for the actors. In gender relations, power, and personal and institutional violence are exercised not only physically and emotionally, but also in terms of sexual and financial harassment, deprivation or neglect, patrimony, intimidation, or discrimination, among the most frequent.

Gender intervention protocols constitute the rules of the game that facilitate interaction inside and outside the organization, in that sense, they fulfill a function of denunciation or demand for equity. However, if we analyze in more detail the number of complaints that are successful and achieve a sanction on the violator, it seems that the protocols and departments are isomorphic and seek to legitimize the organization in a field, but do not necessarily reduce gender asymmetries.

Table 6.3 shows two extremes of the organizational model and dynamics, on the one hand, an organization where efficiency is the most important, achieving the established goals with the least possible expenditure of resources, linked to bureaucracy, the administration in this type of organization is vertical, scientifically oriented in the administration of work, with coercive decisions and a pyramidal chain of command. Violence is part of the organizational work and cases of adhocracy are rare. The vision linked to efficiency in relation to gender is androcentric, blinded to any other alternative "not recognized" in the dominant structure. There is greater gender vigilance, on the should be for women and men, invisibilization or underrepresentation of those subjects that do not fit into the dichotomous should be, and, therefore, there is greater symbolic violence.

Table 6.3.   Organizational Model and Organizational Dynamics.

EJES	Efficiency		Effectiveness
Gender	Androcentric, blind		Diverse
Structure	Bureaucratic, rigid		Flexible
Decision-making	Coercive power	Organizational model	Collegiate
Chain of command	Pyramidal		Adhocratic
Proxemia	Distant		Close
Normativity	Imposed		Consensual
	Masculinization		Feminization

Source: Urbiola, Cázares y Vázquez (2022).

On the other hand, effectiveness, or the pursuit of goals through paths that can be flexible, allows for a porous and diverse organization that can include non-binary genders. Being more flexible allows for the resolution of micro-aggressions, is more proactive, involves the actors within the organization more, allows them to express performative alternatives to gender stereotypes, and therefore tends to be adhocratic and of a matrix nature. These organizations tend to have communication departments and open and novel forms of communication so that information flows in all directions. The configurations of masculinity are usually not only the hegemonic ones, as there is room for other non-heteropatriarchal expressions.

Organizational duty linked to efficiency relates to an essentially masculine occupational culture, which revolves around categories related to being a man: strength, virility, sharpness, intelligence, fortitude, decisiveness, fortitude in the face of adversity, among others. Occupations linked to efficiency are surveillance operator, police officer, caretaker, and custodian. On the other hand, effective organizational dynamics, more tolerant, with less emphasis on force than on persuasion, with multiple channels of communication are portrayed in occupations such as nurse, educator, secretary, and assistant.

The existence of these organizational dynamics and models does not mean that all organizations must present all characteristics as a unit, since some departments in large corporations may have more aggressive characteristics than other departments. Likewise, we can affirm that as a model of structure and dynamics, it is subject to changes in the organizational field, hence the importance of carrying out a detailed study on the functioning of gender equity departments and gender intervention protocols. The dynamics reflect the structural organization where women and men are confronted with organizational models that do not favor them. Organizational suffering comes from the different types of violence that are exercised on subjects who do not adapt to the dominant schemes and from the symptoms of suffering that can be experienced: gastritis, headache, tachycardia, shortness of breath, weight loss or gain, insomnia, alopecia, and psoriasis, among others.

The challenges of the incorporation of women into the labor market and the organizational changes that occur due to the demands of gender violence force us to rethink the way in which power relations and gender asymmetries or gaps are reproduced and institutionalized within organizations, such as companies, public organizations, and universities. According to Meyer and Rowan (2001), "institutionalized products, services, techniques, policies, and programs function as powerful myths and many organizations adopt them ceremonially" (p. 79). This means that within organizations there are cultural mechanisms that reproduce the gender gap, beyond technology or the production process. Most organizations have moved from a scientific, pragmatist, and positivist organization of work to organizations with multiple rationalities in ambiguous and uncertain contexts. Powell and DiMaggio (2001) claim that strategies for organizational change involve, in the first place, public policies focused on reducing the gender gap and approving and/or promoting legislation that seeks equity. In the organizational fields, transparency mechanisms and audits to analyze the condition of education, prevention, and possible sanction programs and protocols. In the educational aspects, routines and ritual language stand out, as well as the practices that become the rules of the game within organizations. Secondly, work within the organizations, with inter-subjective models that allow individuals to identify with the values of the organization.

The rejection of rational actor models and the recognition of limited rationality, as well as the contexts of uncertainty and ambiguity, underline the importance of exogenous aspects, of context in the organizational field. Among them, culture is a central element in shaping organizational reality. Culture, understood as a "system of cognitive maps" (Romero, 2001, p. 17), is above the organization, and in relation to the gender gap, it forces to rethink the forms of leadership, the organizational structure, the job descriptions and the activities performed by women and men.

Organizational Options

Organizations as systems with interdependent activities cannot override the cultural structures that are the basis of the society that contains them, that is, the level of autonomy of organizations may vary in relation to their capacity for adaptation and/or modification. Some maintain diverse identities within them, while others seek to reproduce an ideal type through corporate organizational culture.

There are different levels of organizational exclusion and, on the other hand, of organizational porosity. These extremes imply the coexistence of diverse identities with systemic institutional logics. Intervention can be promoted at three levels: the first is related to the subject, involving aspects of the psychic, subjective, libidinal, or desire structure. The second is in the organizational field, in the structure, positions, processes, and products. Finally, the third is that of an economic-cultural field or structure that contains the organization. Each of these three levels means interaction of the organization's members and different possibilities for permanent change as suggested in Fig. 6.2.

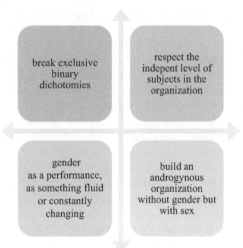

Fig. 6.2.   Suggestions in Organizational. *Source*: Own elaboration.

In order to increase the possibilities of greater gender equity, intervention is required at all three levels: the first one related to the subject is psychological support and recognition of the challenges posed by the post-pandemic and the new normality. It also implies a non-discriminatory policy for alternative gender expressions. Likewise, in the case of service organizations such as schools and universities of programs and departments of gender education and openness to heteropatriarchal dissidence. This involves modifying curricula and syllabi, launching gender refresher programs for staff members, and providing psychological support in specialized departments.

The second is related to what has been explained in this chapter about the need for external organizations to certify progress in reducing the gender gap since the members of organizations with already institutionalized tasks tend to routinely repeat behaviors that may be considered exclusionary. It is possible to work based on gender intervention protocols and internal complaints departments, as well as human rights and psychological assistance, but beyond that, it is necessary to unlink gender assignment with positions and activities, that is, to change the traditional gender assignment associated with the sex of the organization's members.

Finally, the third will be the result of political praxis involving gender, sustainability, and post-pandemic issues in relation to aspects of economic growth (investment, employment, wages, purchasing power, among others). Thus, fiscal and monetary public policy impacts the labor and legal status of women and men through political work. In the face of public pressure or denunciation, they can change processes and products.

When women enter the labor market or become heads of households or self-employed entrepreneurs, they face a gender gap that reaffirms inequality in the family nucleus.

Final Reflections

Gender-based violence is a daily constant for millions of women around the world. Although their economic participation has increased, the lack of gender equity causes economic losses and backwardness in welfare levels around the world. Closing the gender gap requires not only economic growth, that is also, having optimal macroeconomic indicators: gross domestic product growth, inflation below double digits, and low unemployment rate, among others; in addition to economic indicators, it is necessary to work on those that seek the equal incorporation of women and minority groups that do not assume a binary gender identity and remain excluded. Thus, in addition to the Gini coefficient or income concentration indicators, there are changes in human development and global gender gap indexes. These changes at the macroeconomic level are related to the development plans and public policies of each government. At the mesolevel, in organizational fields, there are two levels where it is possible to contribute to change. On the one hand, with respect to the use of exclusionary dichotomous categories that minimize the contribution of women and non-binary groups to the economy: making the categories visible and providing elements to expose the working conditions of women and members of groups excluded because of their gender and sexual orientation. Through exposure as a starting point, to have elements that can modify the working conditions of the subjects in the organization, to incorporate new non-binary, non-exclusionary gender visions that recover the value of labor activity without relating it to sex or gender.

At the level of the subjects, re-considering the changes in the environment and the personal aspects of each subject; reviewing the departments and protocols of attention to gender violence is an essential activity to ensure equitable working conditions.

References

Arroyo, G., S. (2004). Retrato de lo humano en el arte mesoamericano. *Arquelogía, XI*(65).
Burin, M. (2004). Género femenino, familia y carrera laboral: Conflictos vigentes. *En Subjetividad y Procesos Cognitivos, 5*, 48–75. http://dspace.uces.edu.ar:8180/xmlui/handle/123456789/263
Burin, M. (2015). Prólogo. Actualización en Estudios de Género: El programa Post-doctoral en Estudios de Género en UCES. *En Revista Científica de UCES, XIX*(1), primavera 2015. https://dspace.uces.edu.ar:8180/dspace/bitstream/handle/123456789/3313/prologo_burin.pdf?sequence=1
Burin, M., & Meler, I. (2010). *Género y familia. Poder, amor y sexualidad en la construcción de la subjetividad.* Paidós.
Expansión Datosmacro.com. (2022a). *Índice de Gini.* https://datosmacro.expansion.com/demografia/indice-gini.
Expansión Datosmacro.com. (2022b). *Índice de Desarrollo Humano.* Retrieved, August 29, 2022, from https://datosmacro.expansion.com/idh

Expansión Datosmacro.com (2022c). *Índice Global de la Brecha de Género.* Retrieved, August 29, 2022, from https://datosmacro.expansion.com/demografia/indice-brecha-genero-global

Hechos y cifras: Empoderamiento económico. *ONU-MUJERES.* Retrieved, July 27, 2022, from https://www.unwomen.org/es/what-we-do/economic-empowerment/facts-and-figures

García, R. (2008). Las mujeres en Mesoamérica prehispánica. *Cuicuilco, 15*(43), 223–229. Retrieved, September 2, 2022, from http://www.scielo.org.mx/scielo.php?script=sci_arttext&pid=S0185-16592008000200010&lng=es&tlng=es

Iriarte, M. (1992). Mujer y Ministerio: Antiguo Testamento. *Diakonia* (63), 43–58. http://repositorio.uca.edu.ni/id/eprint/3874

Izquierdo, M. (2010). Las dos caras de la desigualdad entre mujeres y hombres: Explotación económica y libidinal. *Quaderns de Psicologia, 12*(2), 117–129. http://www.quaderns-depsicologia.cat/article/view/759.

Lamas, M. (1994). Cuerpo: diferencia sexual y género. *Debate Feminista, 10.* https://doi.org/10.22201/cieg.2594066xe.1994.10.1792

Lamas, M. (2000). Diferencias de sexo, género y diferencia sexual. *Cuicuilco Nueva Época, 7*(18), 1–24. http://www.redalyc.org/pdf/351/35101807

Leret de Matheus, M. (2011). *La discriminación social y legal de la mujer.* Editorial Leret de Matheus María Gabriela.

Maffía, D. (2007, February). Género y ciudadanía. En: *Encrucijadas,* no. 40. Universidad de Buenos Aires. Disponible en el Repositorio Digital Institucional de la Universidad de Buenos Aires. http://repositoriouba.sisbi.uba.ar

Maffía, D. (2016) *Contra las dicotomías: Feminismo y Epistemología crítica.* In C. Korol (Ed.), *Feminismos populares, pedagogías y políticas.* Editorial Chirimbote, Ciudad Autónoma de Buenos Aires: América Libre.

Martel, I. (2021, August 19). *En qué países del mundo se aplica la ley islámica.* https://www.abc.es/internacional/abci-en-que-paises-aplica-ley-islamica-nsv-202108191209_noticia.html?ref=https%3A%2F%2Fwww.abc.es%2Finternacional%2Fabci-en-que-paises-aplica-ley-islamica-nsv-202108191209_noticia.html

Meyer, W. J., & Rowan, B. (2001). Organizaciones institucionalizadas: La estructura formal como mito y ceremonia. InP. W. y Dimaggio, P., *El nuevo institucionalismo en el análisis organizacional.* México. Fondo de Cultura Económica.

Powell, W., & Dimaggio, P. (2001). *El nuevo institucionalismo en el análisis organizacional.* Estudio introductorio de Jorge Javier Romero. Fondo de Cultura Económica.

Romero. (2001). Estudio Introductorio: los nuevos institucionalismos, sus diferencias, sus cercanías. In *El nuevo institucionalismo en el análisis organizacional.* FCE.

Rubin, G. (1986). El tráfico de mujeres: Notas sobre la "economía política" del sexo. *Nueva Antropología, 8*(30), 95–145.

Ruz, M. (2004). De cuerpos floridos y envolturas de pecado. *Arqueología Mexicana, XI*(65), 22–27.

Urbiola, A., Cázarez, I. y, & Vázquez, A. (2022, 4 de agosto). *Estructuras Socioculturales en las Organizaciones desde las Masculinidades. Conferencia en el Seminario de Estudios Críticos Organizacionales.* UAM Iztapalapa México.

World Bank (2022a). *Aproximadamente 2400 millones de mujeres en el mundo no tienen los mismos derechos económicos que los hombres.* Retrieved, August 2, 2022, from https://www.bancomundial.org/es/news/press-release/2022/03/01/nearly-2-4-billion-women-globally-don-t-have-same-economic-rights-as-men

World Bank (2022b). *La mujer, la empresa y el derecho.* Retrieved, August 2, 2022, from https://wbl.worldbank.org/es/wbl

Chapter 7

Toward an Essential Museum: The Fight of Two Women for Holocaust Education

Laura Velez

Abstract

This chapter reports on the difficulties and challenges faced by a woman in Mexico to generate an enterprise whose objective is education. This is achieved by taking up the story of Sharon Zaga and Mili Cohen, two Jewish women who set themselves the goal of founding a museum that would speak of the relevance of historical memory, but also of the importance of tolerance. The emergence of COVID-19 presented them with a new challenge: the museum had to remain closed for more than a year. We will explore the strategies that allowed them to keep their organization afloat, a circumstance that can be taken up by more Latin American women who intend to undertake also on their own.

Keywords: Female entrepreneurship; Latin American women leaders; women in organizations post-COVID-19; Holocaust education; discrimination on the basis of gender bias; anti-Semitism

> Our responsibility as a minority for having a millenary history of persecution, is to fight to be defenders of Human Rights, to prevent discrimination.

The Museum of Memory and Tolerance, in Mexico City, has hosted essential meetings to guarantee the democracy of the Mexican nation, as well as the real exercise of Human Rights, such as the Forum The Americas at the Crossroads: more security, less rights? by Amnesty International, the Forum Challenges for the Reconstruction in Mexico: Transparency and Accountability (2017), by the Government of the CDMX, and the Forum Journalism and Challenges for Freedom of Expression in Mexico (2019), by various civil associations.

Economy, Gender and Academy: A Pending Conversation, 111–122
Copyright © 2023 by Laura Velez
Published under exclusive licence by Emerald Publishing Limited
doi:10.1108/978-1-80455-998-720231013

The instance, which stands peacefully on Juarez Avenue, in front of the Alameda Central, in the historic center of the city, has managed to position itself as an emblematic site, aimed at promoting peace, diplomacy, and tolerance toward diversity. It is the only place in Mexico, created by private initiative that has these characteristics. In June 2022, for example, after the terrible news broke that a large group of immigrants had been abandoned to their fate inside a trailer on a rural road near San Antonio, Texas, resulting in the death of at least 53 of them (Weber, Lozano, & Spagat, 2022), it was in the museum's plaza where relatives of the victims gathered to demand justice.

This chapter, through documentary compilation and interviews, gives an account of the process of founding a museum that, emerging in a country bathed in blood by daily violence, took on the mission of spreading a message of tolerance, respect, and inclusion. Mexico is also a profound misogynist nation not only an academic education but also undertaking a project of one's own as a woman is extremely complex.

Through a qualitative approach, and taking as a frame of reference the story of Sharon Zaga and Mili Cohen to found an educational institution, we will observe the complexities that a woman must face to generate entrepreneurship. We will discover the discriminatory elements that intertwine to shape these complexities and what circumstances, in particular, allowed them to overcome the exclusion they were subjected to to achieve their goal.

Therefore, the objectives of the study are:

• Determine the aspects of gender inequity that combine to hinder women's entrepreneurship in Mexico, in the educational field.
• To discover if, in the light of the post-COVID-19 pandemic scenario, these same difficulties are repeated when trying to start up an educational institution founded by women.
• To provide elements that can be used by women in the process of entrepreneurship, using the case of Sharon Zaga and Mili Cohen.
• To put dots on the map about the situation of women in the field of organizations after the organizations in the aftermath of the COVID-19 pandemic.

In the following lines, we will describe the trajectory that led to the foundation of MYT, the numerous obstacles that had to be overcome, and how the COVID-19 pandemic affected the organization and we will contribute elements that can be taken up by other women who, like Sharon Zaga and Mily Cohen, have the objective of influencing the field of organizations in this country and in Latin America.

A Grandmother's Confidence

Sharon was just a child when one day while talking to one of her great aunts, she told her about the difficult time she experienced when she was taken to the Auschwitz concentration camp and was one of the human beings with whom the infamous "Angel of Death," the doctor Josef Mengele, carried out experiments

(Sadurní, 2022). This talk deeply marked Sharon, who finds in the event the seed that would germinate years later in the Museum of Memory and Tolerance:

> The museum was born out of my great-aunt's openness to tell me about her experience when I was 12 years old, even though she didn't tell anyone. She didn't tell anyone about it; she was open with me. And from that was born a very overwhelming interest in me in the subject of the Holocaust. Once I started studying the Holocaust, I realized that it is something that has happened in history, that it repeats itself, that it has never been avoided, and hence my commitment to create a space for tolerance, for diversity, for inclusion, for promoting awareness. (Sharon Zaga, Interviewed by the MYT Academic Direction, 08/15/22)

A second event added to the talk she had with her great-aunt: at the age of 16 years, Sharon headed to Poland to be part of the contingent that would walk the "March of Life" that year. The event commemorates the victims of the Holocaust who perished under the strategy known as "the Final Solution": derived from the Germans' infatuation with annihilating the Jews, the strategy implied that they were taken en masse to the gas chambers, mainly those built at Auschwitz. They were transported by train from the place where they were deported: they were informed that they could take their belongings with them in no more than one suitcase and, upon arrival, they were separated into two main categories: those who were forced to perform forced labor, and those who were destined directly for death. From the train station, the latter walked about three kilometers, in a real "Death March"; they were informed that they would receive a shower, for which they were asked to undress and, upon entering the chambers, they were exterminated in minutes.

The March of Life, therefore, commemorates the existence of these people through their surviving descendants, redefining the terrible actions of the Nazi army with a lively walk of young people on their way to a more promising destiny.

Sharon recalls the occasion when she first attended:

> I was proud to be able to do it. It was hard to get there, we were in the middle of a war, the Gulf War, and there was a lot of hesitation from all the parents to let us go, but I really lived it to the depths of my being. Everybody said 'she transformed here'. It's not that I couldn't smile, but I was completely in a state of reflection. It hit my soul to be there. Before I left, I was already thinking that I wanted to learn more and teach about this, and when I came back, there I said (right at the school, at a ceremony), 'I'm going to make a museum. (Sharon Zaga, Interview with Oso Trava, 03/02/22)

A Mother's Consciousness

Mily Cohen is Sharon's partner in the adventure that has been the museum. Even though the Jewish community in Mexico is not excessively large (the 2020 Census counted 58,876 Jewish people in this country), Mily and Sharon did not know each other during the first years of their lives.

If Sharon's point of no return was the trip to Poland, Mily's happened on national territory but, not for that reason, it was of lesser importance:

> My son, the first one I had, was born exactly around the time of the genocide in Rwanda. And it was a driving force for me to decide to do something. When I saw the pictures on the news, he was a newborn baby; I held him in my arms and thought: well, what kind of world did I bring him into? I promised that baby that I was going to do something. That was my trigger.(Mily Cohen, Interview for DW, 10/15/2018)

Mily consulted with the Jewish Community Central Committee regarding what she could do to channel that impetus. There, she was informed that there was another girl with a similar interest. Mily decided to seek her out and talk to her; it took her about three months to find her.

They met at Sharon's house, where she had set up a small museum and was giving talks to students.

Mily and Sharon hit it off immediately. For Mily, the main thing was finding someone who supported her initiative from the beginning:

> It was the first time I found someone equally or more willing than me to get things done. I was impressed by the confidence I saw in her. Because everyone, before I met Sharon, was telling me, "Oh, Mily, you and your crazy ideas! You're not going to make it." I lacked that drive. (Mily Cohen, Interview for Diario Judío, 2014)

> Another aspect that played in her favor was the understanding that Mily found in Sharon regarding the concept of the museum, as they were able to agree on it without problems. Both agreed that their organization would be different from the others, from the beginning: "It is not going to be a museum of dates and characters. We want to ask: at what point does a doctor, who has taken an oath to heal, decide to experiment on children? What makes a peasant who has lived well all his life with those next door, suddenly decide to kill his neighbors? What makes the hero or the monster come out in some?" (Mily Cohen, Diario Judío, 2014)

Fighting Prejudice

The race to the top had just begun ... and it wouldnt be easy. The first challenge the two women encountered was their age: it was complicated to make themselves heard or to be taken seriously because they were not yet 30 years old (Sharon was 21 years old when they joined forces and Mily, 26). However, that didnt stop them. Sharon shares:

The more people we went to see who said 'look, why don't you come back in a year' (they saw us young), they said "if you continue with the same idea I support you," the stronger we became. We did not have that feeling of hopelessness, that we would not be able to do it. We were more eager to say: next time, let's say we are older, let's dress more formally. We are going to look older, to see if they believe us. But we weren't coming out hopeless, we were coming out very confident. (Sharon Zaga, interview for DW, 10/15/2018)

Curiously, e-mail became one of their best weapons: through it, the people they contacted did not realize how old they were. This helped them to tackle the second obstacle: raising the income that would allow the museum to materialize.

Both Mily and Sharon used their own resources to visit museums around the world on the theme of memory and tolerance, and were inspired to form their own. They discovered that no organization as such combined the two concepts: either there was a museum of memory in one country, or there was a museum of tolerance in another. The girls decided that their museum would distinguish itself from the rest by focusing on both at the same time.

With that conceptualization under their belts, Sharon and Mily gathered volunteers, worked first from their homes, and then were able to set up a small office in Santa Fe. This was the most difficult period, as they sought to approach people directly, doing so as best they could. After two years of unsuccessful attempts, Sharon had the courage to follow a Holocaust survivor (and Mexico-based businessman) to his cardiologist's appointment. The risky gamble paid off: the businessman donated $1 million, which became his first donation and served as the basis for other donors to get involved.

A Museum in The Air?

The initial donation, as if it had fallen from the sky, was useful to acquire a property in the Condesa neighborhood, one of the oldest in Mexico City. In it, they had the capacity to attend to up to 100 students at the same time, dedicating themselves fully to disseminating their two main axes:

- Historical memory: about the Holocaust and other genocides, to encourage young people to reflect on the unnecessary nature of wars, so that a seed would be sown in them and they would do their part to never allow them to be repeated.
- Tolerance: the harmonious coexistence of differences, guarantor of diversity.

The museum thus began to take shape and to fulfill its educational mission on human rights issues. However, in a meeting with the then Secretary of Public Education, Reyes Tamez (in office between 2000 and 2006), he pointed out the imperative need to accommodate at least 1,000 students at a time. In this way, they would have the opportunity for the museum's contents to be incorporated into the nation's official curricula, a task that was undoubtedly necessary.

Zaga and Cohen decided, therefore, to put the house in Condesa up for sale and bet on the construction of a larger place. For this purpose, using the resources derived from the sale of the property plus some donations, they acquired a plot of land in the center of the city. The challenge, now, was to raise the funds to build, the architectural design of the museum and the hiring of the professionals who would be in charge of making it a reality.

After two years, and has already laid the first stone, the head of government of the CDMX at the time, Andrés Manuel López Obrador, suggested that the Plaza Juárez, located in front of the Alameda Central, would be a better location for the museum. The available space cost twice as much, but its 7,000 square meters made it the perfect place for the museum.

The costs, however, skyrocketed exponentially. Even though the Arditti studio worked pro bono to realize the architectural design, the economic crisis drove up the price of steel to the extent that the initial construction budget increased by 30%: "we barely achieved a funding goal, when we were already short," says Mily (Mily Cohen, Diario Judío, 2014). The summit seemed unattainable.

Pulling Strength from Nothing

The entrepreneurs did not stand idly by since 1999 they had already legally formalized the constitution of the museum as a civil association. With this background, and while the construction was going back and forth, they realized that requesting funds without acting on their mission would not lead them to anything. So they formed a network to help Holocaust survivors in Mexico. Through it, they dedicated themselves to providing a monthly stipend as well as food to each of them. They also saw to it that their basic needs were taken care of. At the end of each year, they held a special dinner with their beneficiaries to celebrate their lives.

In 2002, after compiling the testimony of 86 survivors of the Nazi terror, they published the book: El Rostro de la verdad.

Testimonies of Holocaust Survivors in Mexico. With this inertia, and after insisting by all means with the Polish government, they managed to bring to the country a wagon used by the German forces to transfer Jews to the concentration camps: a mute testimony of the atrocities committed in the Second World War.

These actions became known in Mexican society, and both Sharon and Mily began to receive calls for help from people eager to cooperate.

The Museum of Memory and Tolerance opened its doors on October 11, 2010, with the President of the Republic, Felipe Calderón, as a guest of honor.

The work of reaching as many people as possible in multiple ways with a message of inclusion was finally a reality. Sharon saw the commitment her people had as a minority, "because minorities tend to be exclusionary as a method of protection and that in turn generates more exclusion." The antidote was to provide them with tools that would show them the diversity of the world and give them resources to create inclusive environments, avoiding at all costs falling into the same morass of prejudice that had caused the Germans to wage a campaign of annihilation against them:

> The Jewish community has benefited, as people understand instead of continuing to hate difference or create barriers: bridges are created, openness is created.

> The museum's position of talking about other genocides, at the same time, combats this prejudice that the Holocaust only happened to Jews or that it's the only genocide and shows that, basically, fear of what's different is what causes the destructive capacity of the human being, in a specific circumstance. (Sharon Zaga, Interview for DW, 10/15/2018)

Currently, Memory and Tolerance has 52 permanent exhibition rooms, divided into Memory (the Holocaust and other genocides) and Tolerance (Human Rights, Inclusion, Our Mexico, among others), MYT Island, created to spread values of harmony and respect among the little ones, an Educational Center where more than 100 free activities are offered every month, as well as a temporary exhibition hall where relevant topics such as arms trafficking, the refugee crisis, sexual diversity, people with disabilities, femicides, and others have been addressed. These characteristics have positioned it as an unparalleled space in the capital. Mily explains:

> The museum is already a reference in the CDMX. It is an incredible surprise. We never thought it would be a reference in Human Rights so quickly, it is an educational reference. The museum has had so much credibility that politicians have also approached it for debates, and it makes me very proud to know that activists like Javier Sicilia, like Father Solalinde, have their headquarters in the Museum of Memory and Tolerance. (Mily Cohen, Interview for DW, 10/15/2018)

An Unexpected Halt

The MYT was days away from opening its most recent temporary exhibition (TicTac: Climate Change is Now) when, on March 20, 2020, non-essential activities in the country had to be put on hold.

The reason? The alarming speed with which the COVID-19 virus was spreading around the world.

The museum management had already foreseen this situation, so much so that they decided to close the museum even a couple of days before the official notification was given. What definitely no one envisioned was that the contingency period would be so extended.

"The museum had an emergency fund for cases like that," says Alex Barky, executive director of the MYT, "however, it proved insufficient when two, three months went by and we saw that the pandemic was still spreading." It was then that they began to do without personnel as a strategy to reduce expenses. "This process was painful because we consider the museum staff to be one big family," says Sharon.

So, what we did was let them go with the promise that we would do what we needed to do to see them come back. But, more importantly, we kept in touch with these people, and if they were having a hard time getting another job, we put together food and basic aid to get it to them. (Alex Barky and Sharon Zaga, New Year's Message, MYT, 2022)

Today, the museum has resumed offering its services to the public. Since the Easter vacations of 2022, it had the opportunity to make a gradual opening: first, with reduced hours and capacity. As the circumstances in relation to the pandemic improved and more of the population was covered by the vaccination program, the panorama became more and more favorable for it. In fact, collaborators who were unfortunately dismissed have been rehired. Such is the case of Karen Alvarez, an accounting assistant, who had been out of the museum for almost two years. Since mid-September, she has been able to return to her job.

The museum had to do without up to 70% of its staff. Gradually, the different areas of the organization are beginning to see the return of their former employees, and it is expected that between 2023 and 2024, the staff will return to its original size.

The road, however, is not an easy one. The obstacles to this recovery are varied and are described below.

A Perfect Storm

The world economy has not faced such an adverse outlook in recent years as the one that began in 2020. Starting in China, then spreading across Europe, COVID-19 forced people of all ages and socioeconomic backgrounds into confinement.

The level of women's employment worldwide plummeted. Of the 12 million jobs lost in April 2020, 42% of them belonged to women (IMCO, 2022). Women, as is often the case in times of crisis, must have borne the brunt: as the primary caregivers, they redoubled these activities, taking care of those who fell ill at home. More than 30% of poor women stopped participating in the labor market due to the overload of care work (ECLAC, 2021).

A difficult condition in itself, being a woman became an endurance race. This had implications even for women in relevant positions within organizations: according to Forbes Women (2021), 54% of women in leadership positions reported feeling exhausted. The reason, in general, they are the only ones in their companies in those positions, so staying present is perceived by them as an obligation. A feeling that, by the way, is never perceived by men.

The situation has become so complex that the number of women engaged in sex work has skyrocketed. In Mexico City alone, from 7,500 workers registered before the pandemic, the figure increased to 15,200 after the spread of the virus and forced confinement (León, 2021).

At the museum, in particular, doing without staff during the pandemic was not enough to keep the organization alive.

Sharon and Mily's leadership was again put to the test. They had to find a way to offer the public a safe, high-quality, and far-reaching experience in order to generate revenue, even during the period of confinement. So they opted for an ambitious, high-cost, high-risk project: creating a virtual museum.

Once again, it required the mobilization of resources, allies, and the search for professionals who could carry out such a large-scale project. The idea was to offer, in addition to the possibility of visiting the museum, the presence of a guide, even if he or she was asynchronously present. Conquering (once again) a new challenge, Sharon and Mily obtained, as a result, the MYT Virtual Tour, an immersive experience in the permanent sections of the museum, which can be visited room by room, according to the visitor's taste. Those who purchase a ticket for this digital option can enter and exit the virtual space of the MYT as many times as they wish during a period of 24 hours (the time in which the access code is valid). A virtual guide accompanies the visitor in each room, explaining (with voice-over) what is found in them.

Where Do We Stand Today?

There is an important lag in the presence of women in the labor market that has been added to the one already existing before the pandemic: the occupation ratio:

> Male jobs lost in the second half of 2020 (about 26 million) are recovered by the third quarter of 2021, but of the 23.6 million female jobs lost only 19.3 million were recovered. This means that just over 4 million female jobs have yet to be recovered. (International Labor Organization, 2021)

If inequality in the labor area is worrisome, the education sector is even more so. In general, access to formal education is considered as a strategy to overcome poverty, also obtaining a more satisfactory standard of living in all areas. The enormous problem we face today is that even this aspiration is seen as excessively complicated. Even before the pandemic, the educational sphere did not look promising: around 50% of 15-year-old students in 10 countries in the region did not reach basic levels of reading proficiency in 2018 (ECLAC, 2022). This implies that, in the wake of the pandemic, we have thousands and thousands of young people thrown into poverty who are not sufficiently prepared even to continue educating themselves. Worse still, data indicate that 3.1 million children in Latin America and the Caribbean are at risk of dropping out of school for good (ECLAC, 2022). In a few years, these children will join the labor market, probably without the ability to perform basic tasks such as adding, subtracting, dividing, and reading.

This will create such a gap that the World Bank has already calculated the income losses that this generation will experience during the rest of their lives: the figure amounts to 17 trillion dollars (World Bank, 2021).

To complicate matters further, on a large-scale, social assistance to the poor and extremely poor sectors requires greater investment than in past years, without this meaning in real terms that the State will actually have an impact in this regard:

> A relevant challenge for 2022 is that the region faces a complex macroeconomic situation with reduced fiscal space, increased debt, and inflationary acceleration, which would lead to lower policy interventions in a context where the population requiring assistance remains high due to the increase in poverty and indigence with respect to 2019. (International Labor Organization, 2021)

Conclusions

As we had occasions to witness throughout these pages, the trajectory of Sharon Zaga and Mily Cohen has been replete with adversity and hardship. However, contrary to the hypothesis behind this work, neither of them showed any signs of having felt discriminated against for being women while they were setting up the foundation of their educational organization.

In the interview conducted on August 15, Sharon was even explicitly asked if she perceived a hint of gender discrimination on the part of the people she was contacting for support. Her answer was a resounding no.

However, we do not have the means to establish whether this was the case or, even if they did not perceive it, whether it is at all certain that at some point both Zaga and Cohen were not discriminated against because of their gender.

The main discriminatory element that these entrepreneurs encountered was their age: both were rejected on numerous occasions for "being young." On the other hand, their accounts did not reveal any circumstance in which they perceived anti-Semitism toward them, that is, discrimination because they were Jewish.

At the level of praxis, what is the main lesson in Sharon and Mily's story? Never give up.

Even from the moment MYT was just an idea, both were aware that the work was not easy: neither because of the environment nor because of their personal circumstances. However, giving up was never an option for them. Sharon puts it this way:

> Without a doubt, it was to say: we are two young women, with small children and we are going to have to dedicate a large part of our lives and we are going to sacrifice many, many things, but this is going to come out. (Sharon Zaga, DW Interview, 10/15/2018)

COVID-19's emergence added one more mark to its record of difficulties ... but also triumphs. Among the strategies that can be delineated from their case, we can highlight:

• *Legally conforming their organization*: in Mexico, registering a civil society organization with the government is the first step for it to subsequently issue tax-deductible receipts. Sharon and Mily made sure that this was one of their first moves, allowing them to implement effective fundraising in the future, established within the parameters of the law.

- *Renewing themselves*: receiving physical visits to the museum was impossible; therefore, the strategy of entering the virtual realm became the only way to offer a new experience to the public and guarantee ticket revenues.
- *Seeing employees as human beings, not just payroll numbers*: cutting staff is always an unpleasant experience when it is the result of financial difficulties. Zaga and Cohen, however, looked beyond the fact that it would lighten the financial burden on the payroll to the person. They did not leave any worker to his or her fate; rather, they kept in close contact with them, to help their circumstances as much as possible.
- *Taking risks*: the investment for the virtual version of the museum was high (although we do not have the credentials to reveal the figure, we can indicate that it exceeds 1 million Mexican pesos). In that sense, if the strategy failed, it would default with the sponsors. Despite this, Sharon and Mily took a step forward, betting on a strategy that managed to work.
- *Patience*: both in the process of building the museum and during the COVID-19 pandemic, both women kept their nerve and composure. Neither process was swift nor quick, and many people would have given up trying. By their example, Sharon and Mily demonstrate that it pays not to despair: the best attitude is to stand tall with confidence about the future.

The main strategy implemented by Sharon and Mily because of the pressures imposed by the pandemic, the MYT Virtual Tour, has paid off, as more than 12,000 people have attended this experience. This, together with the tenacity of its founders (who continue to seek support and sponsors for their project, even though at this point they have been able to open the doors of the museum again), has allowed the Museum of Memory and Tolerance not only to survive but also to begin to recover its staff and to remain as one of the most important emblematic sites in Human Rights in Mexico.

Economists' estimates indicate that it will be until 2024 when signs of recovery will begin to be seen (and that, considering that the Russian–Ukrainian conflict will be solved in the medium or short term). Any organization led by women, therefore, can look in the mirror of Sharon Zaga and Mily Cohen, to see how much can be achieved, even when playing against the odds.

References

CEPAL y OIT llaman a medidas urgentes para apoyar la reinserción laboral de mujeres y jóvenes | Comisión Económica para América Latina y el Caribe. (n.d.). https://www.cepal.org/es/comunicados/cepal-oit-llaman-medidas-urgentes-apoyar-la-reinsercion-laboral-mujeres-jovenes

DW Historias Latinas. (2021, January 29). *Museo Memoria y Tolerancia*. YouTube. https://www.youtube.com/watch?v=aOOHZlDFo_4

Economic Commission for Latin America and the Caribbean (ECLAC)/International Labour Organization (ILO). (2021). CEPAL y OIT llaman a medidas urgentes para apoyar la reinserción laboral de mujeres y jóvenes | Comisión Económica para América Latina y el Caribe. (s. f.). https://www.cepal.org/es/comunicados/cepal-oit-llaman-medidas-urgentes-apoyar-la-reinsercion-laboral-mujeres-jovenes

Forbes Women. (2021). La brecha de género se amplía: 54% de las mujeres líderes se sienten exhaustas https://www.forbes.com.mx/forbes-women-brecha-genero-covid-19-puestos-liderazgo/

International Labour Organization. (2021). América Latina y Caribe: Políticas de Igualdad de Género y Mercado de Trabajo durante la Pandemia. https://www.ilo.org/wcmsp5/groups/public/---americas/---ro-lima/documents/publication/wcms_838520.pdf

IMCO-Instituto Mexicano para la Competitividad. (2022). El empleo femenino a dos años de la pandemia. https://imco.org.mx/el-empleo-femenino-a-dos-anos-de-la-pandemia/

León A. (2021). *Se duplica trabajo sexual durante la pandemia* Reforma. Disponible en: https://www.reforma.com/aplicacioneslibre/preacceso/articulo/default.aspx?__rval=1&urlredirect=https://www.reforma.com/se-duplica-trabajo-sexual-durante-la-pandemia/ar2240585?referer=--7d616165662f3a3a6262623b727a7a7279703b767a783a--.

Oso Trava. (2022, February 7). *Sharon Zaga | Fundadora del Museo Memoria y Tolerancia #160* YouTube. https://www.youtube.com/watch?v=oIkGKZX8bTc.

Sadurní, J. M. (2022, August 25). *Josef Mengele, el cruel médico nazi de Auschwitz.* https://historia.nationalgeographic.com.es/a/josef-mengele-cruel-medico-nazi-auschwitz_17153

Weber, P. J., Lozano, J., & Spagat, E. (2022, June 29). *Mueren 2 migrantes más por la tragedia del tráiler en San Antonio; se eleva el recuento a 53.* San Diego Union-Tribune en Español. https://www.sandiegouniontribune.com/en-espanol/noticias/story/2022-06-28/texas-encuentran-46-personas-muertas-en-un-camion-de-carga

World Bank. (2021, March 9). *La participación laboral de la mujer en México.* World Bank. https://www.bancomundial.org/es/region/lac/publication/la-participacion-de-la-mujer-en-el-mercado-laboral-en-mexico

INTERVIEWS

DW Historias Latinas. (2021, Jan 29). *Museo Memoria y Tolerancia.* YouTube. https://www.youtube.com/watch?v=aOOHZlDFo_4.

Oso Trava. (2022, Feb 07). *Sharon Zaga | Fundadora del Museo Memoria y Tolerancia #160.* YouTube. https://www.youtube.com/watch?v=oIkGKZX8bTc.

MYT Academic Direction. (2022). Entrevista a Sharon Zaga (colección particular, COPYRIGHT).

Part IV

Final Chapter: Challenges, Opportunities for Academia, Gender, SDG Equity, and Organizations

Chapter 8

Asynchronous Dialogues Between Academy, Gender and Economy

Mario Enrique Vargas Sáenz and Marisol Salamanca Olmos

Abstract

This chapter aims to advance the dialogues between academia and economics on gender gaps in organizations, identifying the progress that has been made in this area in Latin America and the challenges that remain, in accordance with the provisions of the Sustainable Development Agenda. The importance of the academy and its role as facilitator is recognized, so that it is there where policies aimed at reducing gender gaps in organizations can be promoted and advanced, and the opportunity that exists in the academy to contribute to gender equity. Emphasis is made on the contributions made by different Colombian universities, which have included gender equity and the linkage of the UNESCO Chair in favor of equal rights, duties, responsibilities, and opportunities. Finally, the challenges that still exist are recognized and must become a commitment on the part of the organizations, if gender equity in the organizations is really to be achieved.

Keywords: Gender equity; gender gap reduction; economy; higher education institutions; organizations; leadership

Introduction

The disarticulation between the academy, gender, and economy, is born from the intention to continue a dialogue, which allows the identification and promotion of spaces regarding the advances that the organizations are moving toward with respect to closing gender gaps. It is in this scenario, that the academy is required to be an ally to assume the role of facilitator so that these good practices can continue to be recognized and contribute from training to recognize the different initiatives of empowerment, participation, and leadership. A view

Economy, Gender and Academy: A Pending Conversation, 125–134

Copyright © 2023 by Mario Enrique Vargas Sáenz and Marisol Salamanca Olmos

Published under exclusive licence by Emerald Publishing Limited

doi:10.1108/978-1-80455-998-720231014

that is intended to be addressed by the advances experienced in Latin American universities. Subsequently, the practices that are being carried out by different universities in Colombia are recognized, and finally, we invite a reflection on this black-and-white gender setting and on the challenges and opportunities that need to be worked on.

Background of Gender and Economy at the Latin American University

The Sustainable Development Agenda (United Nations, 2015), establishes in its objectives number 4 and 5, respectively, quality education and gender equality. In this way, it becomes relevant for the present analysis, from an equity perspective, to understand that if Equality in access to education is not guaranteed, it will be an even broader barrier if the objective to be achieved is to reduce gender gaps.

Therefore, it is important to make visible the advances that have been achieved in terms of women's access to education and the different positions that they can hold in higher education institutions (HEI), regarding the challenges that institutions should begin to consider contributing to the fulfillment of the afore-mentioned objectives. Being able to identify the elements that are causing these barriers becomes a fundamental factor in terms of reducing gaps that can lead to achieving better indicators in terms of growth and development for the econo-mies, which would be pertinent to analyze.

The report "Women in Higher Education: Has the Female Advantage Ended Gender Inequalities?" (UNESCO, 2021), draws some important conclusions that are worth mentioning and analyzing as a point of reference to understand how gender issues are seen from an economic standpoint, take a prominent place and how the exercise should be promoted at both a personal and institutional level. One of the first element is the "glass ceilings" that women continue to face, barriers that persist when holding "key" academic positions in universities, participating in research, and assuming leadership positions, in this regard, it is important to understand that yes, there are policies that promote parity and access, and in this regard, it is worth asking what the barriers are that are preventing women's access in these scenarios.

Looking at the research, it has been found that men publish more articles on average compared to the number of publications made by women, and even more when these correspond to more renowned journals. No less alarming is the per-centage that corresponds to the number of women who study careers related to engineering, industry, construction, information and communication technolo-gies (ICT) – there is an underrepresentation, the percentage is below 25% in more than two-thirds of countries (UNESCO, 2021). Under this view, the promotion of a debate on the role played by HEIs is welcome, within the framework of their social and civil responsibility as a University, regarding whether they really promote the implementation of policies to break these glass ceilings. This, in rela-tion to the points that have been brought up for discussion, or on the contrary, the analysis is more of a personal nature, from the role that women acquire when deciding on one career or another, the real possibility of access to a high-level position or if other factors limit these decisions.

Given the question of why this situation demands a specific agenda for HEIs in a precise, pertinent, and urgent manner, it is enough to review consolidated data before the pandemic – which somehow delayed the statistical updating of some sectors and the public—it is observed that between 2000 and 2018, the gross enrollment rate of women in higher education teaching in the world increased, from 19% to 38%, with greater progress in East and Southeast Asia, as well as Latin America and the Caribbean. If the data are reviewed by gender, the gross enrollment rate for women increased from 19% to 41%, compared to men for which the enrollment rate increased from 19% to 36%. The report highlights that despite the progress made in terms of access to higher education, gaps remain in terms of financial, geographical, and social factors, with the lowest-income groups facing the greatest barriers (UNESCO, 2020).

Curiously, in the statistics presented by the World Economic Forum of 2022 (WEF, 2022) it has been found that Latin America and the Caribbean rank third of all regions, after North America and Europe. The region has closed 72.6% of its gender gap. Based on the current rate of progress, Latin America and the Caribbean will close the gap in 67 years. Within the region, however, only six out of the 22 countries indexed in this edition improved their gender gap score by at least 1 percentage point from last year.

In the same report, it is noted that the educational achievement subindex shows most scores close to parity, but with a growing dispersion between countries toward the bottom of the range. In this dimension, the performance of the countries varied between rates ranging from 48% to 100%. Gender parity in primary education is more frequent in all countries. In tertiary education, 29 countries have closed less than 90% of the gender gap in enrollment, and these countries are concentrated in Sub-Saharan Africa, South Asia, East Asia, and the Pacific. From this year's sample, the only region where performances have moved more toward parity is Latin America and the Caribbean according to the same source (WEF, 2022).

The World Economic Forum (WEF, 2022) additionally points out what is highlighted in the name of the article as an asynchronous dialogue by evidencing that Latin America and the Caribbean on Economic Participation and Opportunity, that gender parity in this sub-index has only reached 64.5% in this region, largely unchanged from the previous edition, even as 13 out of the 22 countries have improved their sub-index scores by at least 1 percentage point. Concerning regional terms rankings in this dimension, Barbados, Jamaica, and Panama occupy the first three places, while Chile, Mexico, and Guatemala occupy the lowest places. At the level indicator, 16 countries report an improvement in gender parity scores in estimated earned income by at least 1 percentage point, yet this measure masks a loss in estimated earned income for women in 13 countries, and for men in 19 countries. In Barbados, Belize, Chile, and Honduras, the drop in estimated earned income levels for men and women is further exacerbated by a decline in gender parity in this indicator, which means that women's estimated earnings fell at a higher rate than those of men. Even so, positive variation is observed in other indicators. For example, there is a general improvement in the perception of equal pay for similar work in 15 countries. Generally speaking, there have been gains in the share of women in senior positions and the proportion of women in technical roles in most countries. In Guyana, Guatemala, and Uruguay, parity among workers in senior positions has increased by at least 10 percentage points. Further, the gender gap between workers in technical roles is narrow in most countries in this region, with 13 countries already reporting parity, and countries like Bolivia and Chile advancing more than 10% pointing toward parity or close to parity on this indicator. The countries of Latin America and the Caribbean showed high levels of gender parity in the Education Achievement Subindex, where, as of 2022, there is less than 0.5% of the gender education gap to be closed. The gender parity scores of each country are also high, with 19 out of the 22 countries in this region have closed at least 99% of their gaps. According to educational level, we see that nine countries have closed their gender gap in primary education, 17 countries in secondary education, and 18 countries in tertiary education. However, the absolute levels of enrollment in the three levels of education in countries such as El Salvador, Honduras, and Guatemala for both genders remain relatively lower than their neighboring countries.

Explanation and opportunity from the Academy in the commitment to close educational gaps also entail a gender perspective in the framework of public policies for digital inclusion, as recorded in the Information System on Educational Trends in Latin America (SITEAL) (Pavez, 2015), the gender gap in the development of STEM disciplines begins with the lack of inclusion that girls have when using and managing information technologies; this is a clear gap with respect to children. In computer literacy, the situation is not so different, since, although new technologies can mean a competitive advantage for people, this is not necessarily respected in education between girls and boys. Women in many Latin American countries still have fewer opportunities to access and use technologies, which largely responds, as has been studied in similar economies, to factors such as educational level, socioeconomic status, cultural aspects, lack of command of English, household responsibilities and child care (Choudhury, 2009). Studies of gender gaps and STEM affirm that women in Latin America continue to be influenced by structural variables that determine culture and institutions, which affect their development possibilities and the role they play in society. Variables linked to the family structure, as well as issues such as school or the world of work, have an inevitable relationship with the gender gap. Women need to make use of new technologies to integrate socially and empower themselves. In fact, if Latin America intends to reduce the gender gap, it needs to focus on enhancing the variable of knowledge in STEM disciplines in the educational and university system and involve the incorporation of women in workspaces related to these areas of knowledge. Once they have completed their studies, it is important to support them so that they overcome the barriers that limit their incorporation into economic life (Arredondo, 2019).

In Latin America, the proportion of women researchers in relation to men has reached 44%. In other words, out of every 100 researchers, 44 are women. Although this figure is not actually low, it is alarming when analyzing the inequality that this percentage implies in the Latin American region. Regarding the gender gap in research, there are countries that stand out more than others; for example, Paraguay (55%), Argentina (53%), and Venezuela (56%) lead in gender parity in research in the region, compared to other countries in the same region, such as Chile (32%), Mexico (32%), Colombia (38%), and Honduras (38%).

Efforts from Latin American universities in recent years include the University of Chile, which created in 2012 the Equality Commission, a three-tier university administrative body that provides support and advice to the proposal and implementation of policies, plans, regulations, and measures aimed at achieving equality of gender. Then, in 2013, the Office for Equal Gender Opportunities was created, under the Office of the Vice-Rector for Extension and Communications, marking a milestone in the University in terms of gender institutionality. The Office, in coordination with various three-tier university administrative instances, prepared studies and promoted policies and measures that place the University of Chile as a pioneer in these matters in the context of HEIs in the country. Said Commission was formalized in 2020 (Universidad de Chile, 2020), its last milestone being the presentation and approval of the Gender Equality Policy by the University Senate in its Plenary Session No. 662, of March 3, 2022, having as principles of gender equality, promotion, respect and recognition of diverse identities, participation, the public role of the University and intersectionality. Likewise, as an objective of said policy, the commitment to overcome the inequalities, discriminations, and gender gaps that exist in all areas of the work of the University of Chile – considering its teaching, research, creation, and extension functions – in order to build a public University that recognizes and promotes substantive gender equality, ensuring the exercise of rights and equitable access to political, economic and symbolic resources for all those who make up the University of Chile, achievable through mainstreaming of the gender perspective with a rights-based approach in institutional work, the promotion of internal and external alliances, effective communication and visibility of women and sexual dissidence, the participation of the university community, intersectionality as an articulating axis and permanent learning that generates knowledge.

A qualitative systematic review of gender policies in higher education in Latin America led by Gina Álvarez and other researchers from the Catholic University of Pereira (Arias, 2021) shows not only the achievements of inclusion fought for by women but also the scarce results of the academic production on these issues, in the majority of diagnoses on violence and gender policies. In the same report, it is read that apart from Colombia (10 universities), only Argentina (U.N. of Mar de Plata, U.N. of Río Negro and U.N of Córdoba), Bolivia (U. Mayor de San Francisco Xavier and U.T.P. of Santa Cruz), Chile (U. de Chile and U. Academia de Humanismo Cristiano), Ecuador (Central University of Ecuador and Pontifical Catholic University of Ecuador), Mexico (UNAM), Paraguay (Autonomous University of Encarnación), and Peru (PUCP and U.N. del Callao) were the countries in which some of their universities had published their gender policies, which suggests the relevance for the governing bodies of the IES in each country, in whose rectory headquarters for the 200 most important universities in Latin America and the Caribbean, 84% were occupied by men and only 16% by women, in 20 countries of the region (Fuentes, 2016) and the same author points out that adopting these "gender lenses" will allow the examination and understanding of the construction of knowledge in a different way; the identification and prioritization of the problems of the disciplines; and its historical, ethical, political, and social context, among other issues. Including these approaches in the curricular design of the programs will provide the tools to establish inequalities and exclusions in the construction, dissemination, and appropriation of knowledge (p. 71).

Background of Gender and Economy at the Colombian University

The discussion of gender and economy is becoming increasingly relevant, in terms of the role played by HEIs in the exercise of their work and the contribution that they can make in compliance with the SDGs, for more just and equitable societies. In this way, the role that some institutions in Colombia is recognized, by promoting gender equity within their organizations from practice, and not just as part of their administrative structures but also as gender issues that should gain relevance in the development of undergraduate and graduate programs.

The study "University Social Responsibility in the Context of Higher Education in Colombia" highlights the efforts that different Colombian universities have advanced in. It is the case of UNAD – National Open and Distance University – which in order to promote spaces for educational inclusion for students through distance education programs, affiliates companies, unions, and communities. This is how, based on its model, it strengthens its educational project, offering the possibility to its students to advance in their studies without physically attending the institution (Pacheco et al., 2020).

Embracing the principle of gender equality, in terms of equal rights, duties, responsibilities, and opportunities, the universities of Rosario (Bogotá), del Norte (Barranquilla), EAFIT (Medellín), Autónoma de Bucaramanga (UNAB), and Javeriana (Cali), in support of the presidency, UN Women and Oxfam, are developing activities that help to achieve compliance with SDG 5, gender equality, leading the initiative based on the creation of the UNESCO Chair in gender equity, linking activities in undergraduate, postgraduate, extension, and research programs. It is highlighted that these institutions have High-Quality accreditation (Universidad del Rosario, n.d.).

The EAN University, a high-quality institution, in the exercise of supporting compliance with SDG 5, from the area of Organizational Transformation, highlights that 63% of the staff of administrative collaborators and 40% of teachers are made up of women, which is equivalent to a total of 441 employees, 52% are women. At the managerial level, there is parity, 11 women and 11 men. The Institution advances in the creation of "the diversity and inclusion policy" that rejects any form of harassment, mistreatment, and discrimination; it is the first institution of higher education to join the initiative "Gender Parity (IPG) of Colombia" and within the training programs students can take the elective subject Gender and Diversity (EAN University, 2022).

The Pontificia Universidad Javeriana leads the "Gender and Economy" project, which aims to integrate gender issues into economic analysis, which transcend economic and social policies, through the different undergraduate and graduate programs, to promote sustainable development and gender equality. They address issues around unpaid care work, the labor market, inequality, violence against women, and elements of a macroeconomic order (Pontifical Javeriana University).

The Technical Report on Gender Parity in Higher Education in the Colombian Southwest region of the "Corporation for the Integration and Development of Higher Education in the Colombian Southwest" (CIDESCO, 2022), shows quite significant figures in light of equity in this sector, despite the fact that progress has been made in terms of women's participation in higher education, the Gender Gap Index, carried out by the World Economic Fund, indicates that it would take 132 years to achieve gender parity globally. The report shows the data of "The UNESCO International Institute for Higher Education in Latin America and the Caribbean" (UNESCO IESALC, 2021), by 2018 women represented 43% of teachers, a situation that persists according to the information presented by the Observatory of the Colombian University 2022 where female teachers represent 38.67% compared to 61.33% who are men, translated into an increase in the gender gap.

The report presents the population of university students at the national level in 2020, corresponding to 52.97% represented by women, while, at the regional level, it corresponds to 53.19%, which shows the assumption that has been developed that more women study at a higher education level; but it contrasts in the academic and research scenario where efforts to achieve gender equality are scarce.

The profiles held by women in senior management and decision-making positions such as the Boards of Directors or Superiors stand out, but in the case of Javeriana de Cali, 36% of the board members are women and from institutions associated with Cidesco there is no female parity of the 18 rectories. At the vice-rectory level participation is also low, there was barely an increase in rectors going from 18% in 2020 to 21% in 2021, which shows the lack of representation and recognition of women to perform this type of position.

In this way, the progress that the gender and economics conversation has reached the Colombian University is highlighted, as well as the importance that these institutions play in recognizing and promoting different spaces for training, the participation of women and men in terms of equality and in this way, more just societies can be built, with the possibility of providing opportunities and promoting growth and development. This is the effort that Politécnico Grancolombiano and EAFIT Social have been making since 2021, generating spaces for dialogue and proposing debate, around the recognition of the advances that have been made in terms of gender equality in Colombia and Latin America.

In 2021, the conversation revolved around "Gender Equity Within Organizations," a reflection was carried out on gender equity within organizations in Latin America, gender policies, and teaching and productivity in the different sectors of the economy that have applied gender equity policies. Various experiences were collected around the realities of Mexico, Peru, the Dominican Republic, and Colombia approached from the perspective of the public and private sectors. It is possible to recognize the existence of policies and the advances that have been achieved in education, but they are not enough by themselves. Greater efforts are necessary for organizations, and also closer attention to different problems and stereotypes that persist and make these efforts rare.

In 2022, the discussion continues regarding whether organizations promote gender equality, what the guidelines should be, and the policies that should be promoted in Latin America and the Caribbean by the State, and organizations to help reduce the gender gap. In the labor market, in the context of the crisis generated by the COVID-19 pandemic, male participation in the labor force continues to be higher than female participation; women do most of the unpaid work and care work at home, and when they have a paid job, they are presented with barriers to promotion and permanence, a fact that became more acute in the COVID-19 pandemic, strongly impacting women in the region, the unemployment rate for 2020 was 12.4%, maintaining itself until 2021 (International Labor Organization, 2022). As a result of these spaces for dialogue, this book is proposed as a reflection, which includes different experiences and gender perspectives at the Latin American level, and seeks to continue generating dialogue in organizations, through the spaces that can be promoted by universities.

Black-and-White of the Gap, Challenges, and Opportunities

Finally, this black-and-white presentation of gender equality has allowed, beyond recognizing the problems marked over time in terms of gaps, stereotypes, public-private policies, and good practices, to continue with the work of promoting from the institutions of higher education spaces for dialogue that is committed to recognizing and implementing actions that truly contribute to the leadership of women within organizations.

Mónica Colín, an indigenous Mexican with a postdoctorate in Gender and Diversity Studies; PhD in Administration with an emphasis on innovation; senior researcher at Colciencias and current director of Corporate Social Responsibility at Pavimentos Colombia S.A.S., with experience in the development and implementation of gender equality models in Colombia and Mexico, points out the challenges in terms of gender equality: parity in positions of power, understanding that women do not reach high positions, differential research, and evaluation, gender equity programs, non-discrimination policies, having female references, going beyond inclusion (EAN University, 2022).

The challenges that arise go beyond talking about equity. The actions and the exercise that has been carried out throughout this contribution are important so that it can be recognized and put into practice as an instrument for organizations to recognize, within the different experiences and in its performance, the contribution that implies the increase in the participation of women as an agent of change and the contribution that it can make to different fields at the labor level. It should be acknowledged that although the percentage of women who professionalize is higher, let organizations be the space where they can break those glass ceilings, where pay equity is guaranteed, and where they can have participation with parity at the management, administrative, teaching, and research levels, and do not remain only in the fulfillment of requirements.

The issues of inequality, discrimination, and gender violence in higher education are uncomfortable and difficult to handle within the institutions and in the national political context. Despite this, several universities and institutes have recognized and resolutely confronted situations of violence and discrimination. Some institutions have raised gender equity as part of their fundamental principles, established in their statutes and regulations; in addition, they have formulated policies and guidelines to achieve equity, and have created various organizations to develop campaigns, programs, and specific policies for this same purpose. In particular, many universities are beginning to establish protocols and instances to deal with complaints of discrimination, bullying, harassment, and other forms of gender violence (Ordorika, 2015).

The importance of studying the care economy cannot be left aside, since it is women who end up taking on this work and this ends up becoming an obstacle to reconcile the time dedicated to the family and the possibility of participating in the labor market, this is a discussion that needs to be addressed in this context.

There are still many issues to reconcile and deal with, investigate, to declare the Latin American HEIs as having true equality of opportunities in the management bodies of the same universities, the integration of the precept of gender equity in their legislation, the promotion and creation of a plan of equality within each HEI, the reconciliation of professional life and family life through measures such as child development centers in university communities, the increase in the age limits in access to postgraduate scholarships as an opportunity for parity and balance of income, and issues no less urgent, such as the promotion of non-sexist languages in classrooms and university bodies.

References

Arias, G. A. (2021). *Políticas de Género en Educación Superior en América Latina: Una revisión sistemática cualitativa.* UCP.

Arredondo, F. V. (2019). STEM y brecha de género en latinoamérica. Revista de El Colegio de San Luis-Nueva Epoca (pp. 137–158).

Choudhury, N. (2009). How are women fostering home Internet adoption? A study of home-based female Internet users in Bangladesh. *Triple C*, 112–122.

CIDESCO. (2022, August 13). *Paridad de Género en la Educación Superior.* http://cidesco.org.co/wp-content/uploads/sites/4/2022/08/Informe-Tecnico-13-Paridad-de-Genero-VF.pdf

EAN University. (March 29, 2022,). Retos en equidad de género en las instituciones de educación superior. https://universidadean.edu.co/noticias/retos-en-equidad-de-genero-en-las-instituciones-de-educacion-superior

Fuentes, L. (2016). Por qué se requieren políticas de equidad de género en la educación superior? *Nómadas*, *44*, 65–83.

Naciones Unidas. (2015, December 25). *UN.* Retrieved from https://www.un.org/sustainabledevelopment/es/2015/09/la-asamblea-general-adopta-la-agenda-2030-para-el-desarrollo-sostenible/

Ordorika, I. (2015). Equidad de género en la educación superior. *RESU*, 7–17.

Pacheco, C., Rojas, C., Hoyos, L., Niebles, W., & Hernandez, H. (2020). Responsabilidad social universitaria en el contexto de la. *Revista Espacios*, 141–151.

Pavez, I. (2015, December 10). *Unesco. Obtenido de Niñas y mujeres de América Latina en el mapa tecnológico: Una mirada de género en el marco de políticas públicas de inclusión digital.* http://www.tic.siteal.iipe.unesco.org/sites/default/files/stic_publicacion_files/tic_cuaderno_genero_20160210.pdf

Pontificia Universidad Javeriana. (n.d.). *Genero y Economía.* https://generoyeconomia.org/

UNESCO. (2020, December 16). *Hacia el accesso universla a la educación superior: Tendencias Internacionales.* https://www.iesalc.unesco.org/wp-content/uploads/2020/11/acceso-universal-a-la-ES-ESPANOL.pdf

UNESCO. (2021). *Mujeres en la educación superior: ¿La ventaja femenina ha puesto fin a las desigualdades de género?* https://unesdoc.unesco.org/ark:/48223/pf0000377183

United Nations. (09/25/2015). UN. https://www.un.org/sustainabledevelopment/es/2015/09/la-asamblea-general-adopta-la-agenda-2030-para-el-desarrollo-sostenible/

Universidad de Chile. (2020, August 25). Diección de Género. https://direcciondegenero.uchile.cl/project/decreto-que-crea-comision-igualdad/

Universidad del Rosario. (n.d.). *Investigación.* https://www.urosario.edu.co/Investigacion/UCD/Articulos/Cinco-universidades-trabajan-juntas-para-lograr-la/

Universidad EAN. (2022, December 29). *Retos en equidad de género en las instituciones de educación superior.* https://universidadean.edu.co/noticias/retos-en-equidad-de-genero-en-las-instituciones-de-educacion-superior

WEF. (2022). *Global gender gap report.* WEF.

Chapter 9

Academy, Gender, SDG, Equity and Organizations

Gloria Nancy Ríos and Laura Andrea Cristancho

Abstract

Despite the great technological, economic, and social advances and the significant progress achieved by women from the last century until today, there is still a clear division between men and women in the labor market: more women are working, but their salaries are lower, as are their positions and their possibility of full development is reduced.

The gender problem is global, which forces the business sector, as one of the main agents of the market, to build policies around gender equality and the recognition of women as agents who generate growth and economic and business development. In this sense, business projects that seek to reduce gender gaps also impact the achievement of the Sustainable Development Goals (SDGs), because they increase opportunities for equity, freedom, and dignity, for men and women in equal conditions.

What are the challenges and opportunities in gender equity presented by economic analyses in Colombia in a Latin American context?

According to the question, a Latin American economic context of gender gaps is presented, from the perspective of socioeconomic inequality and poverty, sexual division of labor, patriarchal cultural patterns, and concentration of power. Similarly, the effects of the pandemic on women's employment and income are reviewed. When talking about gender gaps and professional contribution to the economy, it is not only a solution to inequalities, it is analytically undoing this cultural conception to give it a new structure of dominance.

There is a lack of conversation about economics and gender because the analysis is found from a macroeconomic perspective when writing that regardless of who performs care work or domestic work can also question

Economy, Gender and Academy: A Pending Conversation, 135–156
Copyright © 2023 by Gloria Nancy Ríos and Laura Andrea Cristancho
Published under exclusive licence by Emerald Publishing Limited
doi:10.1108/978-1-80455-998-720231015

the assumptions of economic science that, by convention, in national accounts, it ignores the value of domestic work and almost always deals with scarcity, selfishness, and competition, and rarely of abundance, altruism, and cooperation.

It must be recognized that the COVID-19 pandemic gave importance to childcare for national economies in general and women's economic participation in particular, which has stimulated a renewed interest in childcare policy in many countries that have implemented lockdowns, as well as women, who provided most of the unpaid care, not only did they lose income due to demands for care but also they struggled to access needs, with some reporting increased personal insecurity.

The economic crises of the last century reflected recessions that had a greater impact on the employment of men since they are usually employed in sectors where employment tends to be unstable or as the economy is called cyclical employment. However, in the crisis unleashed by the COVID-19 pandemic, given their particular conditions, it is women who are mainly affected.

Challenges and opportunities in terms of gender equity present economic analyses in Colombia in a Latin American context, in this context, it is reviewed: the national survey of time use and its findings; the incorporation of the care economy in the measurement of economic growth and poverty indicators by gender and its effects on improvements in the quality of life of the population and its impact on the economy.

Among the advantages of incorporating the gender perspective in the economic analysis, the following perspectives are analyzed:

- The similarities of the experiences of the gender gap and its effect on the economy suggest that the response of public policies of recovery and preparedness with the corresponding recognition, women absorb the costs of care work, with possible long-term negative effects on health, and well-being.
- A greater stimulus to growth, as women bring new skills to work, productivity, and growth gains from greater female participation in the labor force. And, greater productivity and reducing gender barriers.

Keywords: Academy; gender; SDG; equity; organizations; economy

Introduction

Despite the significant progress achieved by the women from the last century to the present, the labor force converges a clear division between men and women, there are a lot of women who work, but their salaries are lower, the same as their occupations and the possibility of their development has been reduced. Women represent more than half of the world's population, and their input to economic activity in terms of direct contribution is well below their potential, which has a negative macroeconomic impact (IMF, 2013).

The political Colombian Constitution establishes in its Article 43 that "women and men have equal rights and opportunities, women could not be subjected to any class of discrimination," and in Article 13 that "the government will promote the conditions of real and effective equality and will adopt measures in favor of discriminated or marginalized groups." Also, in its article 7 "recognizes and protects the ethnic and cultural diversity of the Colombian Nation." Accordingly, to this, the country has ratified several international treaties on human rights, among them, those that guarantee women's rights. It is important to mention the Convention about the elimination of all the discrimination ways against women – CEDAW, which is part of the national laws through the 051 from 1981 law, and the Inter-American Convention to prevent, punish and eradicate violence against women, ratified through the law 248 of 1995.In this context, the National Public Policy of Equity of Gender in Colombia for Women develops from conceptual tools, the equality principle and no discrimination, the gender analysis, the differential approach of the rights and the recognition of the differences and the diversity between them. The gender problem is global, which forces the entrepreneur sector, like one of the market principal agents, to build politics related to gender equality and women's recognition as agents that generate economic and Entrepreneur development. By this side, the entrepreneur projects that follow the gender gap reduction also impact the sustainable development goals, increasing the equity, freedom, and dignity, for men and women in equity conditions.

In the business field, the conditions are difficult, the women have to face marked differences between men and women, the existence of a wage gap related to the Large Integrated Household Survey (GEIH) is 12.9% (DANE, 2022a) and the constant of seeing men in better positions, such as management and a better payment, while the women are concentrated in assistance occupations, that is because the lack of trust or the many conditions that means to hire a woman; this is related to productive aspects like pregnancy, the maternity license, permissions to medical dates, or the child care, among others.

Considering the last mentioned, it works to ask:

Which are the Gender Equality Challenges and opportunities that show the economic analysis in Colombia in a Latin American context?

1. Economic Gender Gaps in the Latin American Context

The world level impact that had the pandemic, and the affectation on the different economic sectors given by the restrictions, qualification, gender, and different occupations, took to the unoccupied reassignment labor force to be slower and had a major impact in Latin America, which is a consequence of the social and economic conditions of the region, the vaccination programs were not fluid, and the inability of stimulate the economy with major resources; as a result, these takes to the region to slow processes and recovery of the labor market (OIT, 2022).

The COVID-19 pandemic resulted in a lower economic development and poverty increase in the Latin American region. It is necessary to make efforts to avoid the multiple crises that are obtained by structural gender inequality and problems in the region in the long and short term. In Table 9.1, the CEPAL (2022) key

Table 9.1.   Key Gender Inequality Elements in the COVID-19 Pandemic From the Economic Perspective. *Source*: Own elaboration Economic Commission for Latin America and the Caribbean (CEPAL).

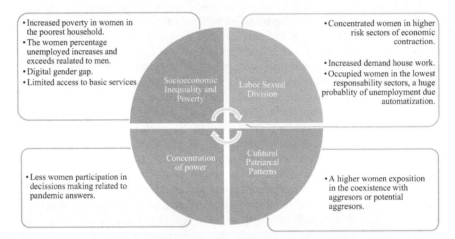

• Increased poverty in women in the poorest household.
• The women percentage unemployed increases and exceeds realated to men.
• Digital gender gap.
• Limited access to basic services

Socioeconomic Inequality and Poverty

Labor Sexual Division

• Concentrated women in higher risk sectors of economic contraction.
• Increased demand house work.
• Occupied women in the lowest responsability sectors, a huge probablity of unemployment due automatization.

Concentration of power

Cuñtural Patriarcal Patterns

• Less women participation in decisions making related to pandemic answers.

• A higher women exposition in the coexistence with aggresors or potential aggresors.

codes identified as the richest basis in the region from the socioeconomic perspective are presented.

Table 9.1 presents the key elements of gender inequality in the COVID-19 pandemic from an economic perspective and proceeds to broadly break down four strands:

• Socioeconomic Inequality and Poverty:

When we talk about poverty, the issue of inequality is reviewed and to rethink if the women's labor input has value and it is visible, also what would happen with this indicator, so we are facing this reality: according to DANE, National Multidimensional Poverty Information in the year 2021 was of 16.0%, 2.1 percentage points (pp) less than 2020 (18.1%) (DANE, 2022b).

However, checking this number with the gender gap we obtain: according to DANE, in October 2022, unemployment by sex increased in terms of the gender gap, this inequality continues, where the unemployment rate by sex was 8.7% for men and women 15.9%, with a gap of 7.2 pp (DANE, 2022c).

According to the World Bank report (2021), Colombia is one of the most inequality countries in the world, and this inequality is transmitted from generation to generation at a higher level than other countries, since education, where parents have primary education, children have few opportunities than in other countries to enter secondary school, and is where, in a partial way, COVID-19 pandemic, the economic perspective presents: whether more equal opportunities are guaranteed in education and health, and also territorial inequalities are attenuated, what would happen?

- Work gender division:

When we talk about work gender division, is the way how society organizes the distribution between men and women, based on the gender roles established by society, also about the culture and the self-tradition of each gender. Many times, this work division is translated in terms of hierarchical power relations and therefore into inequality, this is how domestic and care work is stipulated for women, which has lacked recognition and visibility, and is an unpaid work.

Obtaining the gender equality requires social, economic, and political actions that contribute to eradicate the gender discrimination and the violence against the women and girls. To achieve the aims by these actions, it is necessary to be supported by solid and fairly statistics, as well it must be analyzed and interpreted from a gender perspective. Presented by Juan Daniel Oviedo "División sexual del Trabajo en Colombia – Un análisis desde las estadísticas oficiales" (Women in connection, 2020).

And as has been described throughout this chapter, there is a work devaluation from the women's work, which is settled in the labor market, occupying the most precarious and lower payments. Even joining public activities, women continue to be carrying domestic and care work, which translates into double journeys; Once again, it is important to mention the actions and public policies that must be enrolled to not eternalize these roles and to combat the inequalities that derive from them.

- Cultural Patriarchal Patterns:

Progress has been made with International Human Rights Law to end with the men predominance as a humanity prototype, debating about the patriarchal patterns which grant them prerogatives related to women or populations in conditions of vulnerability, for gender identity reasons, sexual diversity, age, disability, migratory status, among others, created by the called patriarchal pattern.

It can be intuit that all the stereotypes have been circulated from generation to generation, endorsed many times by social sciences, religion, education, among others. Therefore, it remains the inequality power relations that discriminate and violate women, reducing the freedom of decisions of human beings, restricts participation in making decisions, and where forced used it and coercion to submit people, in this case, women.

We hope that these contributions since different approaches and contexts, which are taken by the Revista Latinoamericana de Educación Inclusiva, will help us to deepen into the patriarchal system reflection have been trying to naturalize, showing the impact into the society and the necessity to incorporate a gender perspective in the university studies, to build fair and respectful societies of the human rights, founded by the equality principals, non-discrimination and free human life for all human beings (Jiménez, 2020).

- Power concentration:

The power concentration phenomenon occurs in different areas, and it goes against gender equality because it has been favored the men in the economy, politics, and technology. The main problem derived by the power concentration which are the interests of those who have the power, in this case, men, make it prevail over the general interest and does not permit to proceed with the support of all, for example, in the political class, the main responsible for social change.

When we talk about the power the issue of democracy is touched, which in Colombia has been reduced to a four-year government election, the power is in the hands of few people and democracy becomes an illusion. According to modern constitutions, all votes are equal and worth the same, but the influence of a few, with political and economic power, who stands for the whole country's interests and who can mark out the equity, in this case, gender.

When the impact of COVID-19 on the labor market is analyzed, which is directly related to the economic crisis and what it comes, has taken to the labor world to transform; that is how, the Inter-American Development Bank, IDB, states that labor relations are changing rapidly caused by the COVID-19 health crisis, and the pandemic helps to accelerate an ongoing conversion. There were many cases of unemployment, fewer hours were worked, the income was lower, and that affected the world economy and financial markets. But, also, preexisting problems, such as low productivity, informal labor force, and gender gaps, got deeper (IDB, 2022).

Despite the unemployment, there were some advances like the growth of digital economic activity, remote work and income generation through digital platforms, and the transition to green economies, these are the ideas that are changing the labor markets in Latin America and the Caribbean. According to data from the IDB labor observatory, with a LinkedIn alliance, the technology sector remained without alterations in its recruitment rates from 2022 and 2021, which got easier the transition to remote work and other sectors of telecommuting, which has demanded technological services.

Based on the OIT, the regional participation of women rate that fluctuated at 41% at the beginning of the 1990s had risen steadily to 52.3% in 2019 (average of the first three months). In 2020, in the exact period, the percentage got to 47%, although the regional average became 43%. In 2021, the participation rate registered an insufficient recovery, rising to 49.7%, 2.5 pp below pre-pandemic levels. At the same time, in the third 2021 trimester, the women's unemployment rate is 12.4%, the same as in 2020, which is a sign that does not get any better, and it needs to get low in an important way to get back to the 9.7% of 2019. It is above the general unemployment rate, of 10%, and 8.3% of the rate for men (OIT, 2022).

During the pandemic, women faced the house kipping and unpaid care, besides other feminized occupations: nursing, education, food industry jobs, and domestic service sector, one of the most principals occupations for women in Latin America, this was one of the most pandemic-affected sectors, besides this, the women need to maintain a remote work and the house care, it becomes a requirement factor, that needs to be staked out, brings and it will have productivity consequences like the possibilities to maintain a job or entering to the labor market.

When talking about the gender gaps and the professional input to the economy, it is not a simple inequality solution, it is to analytically undo this cultural conception to give it a new domain structure. It needs to act by the politics and the academia to break those inequalities, and it cannot remain in the research, this is how the author states: the gender-professionalism nexus is the persistent inequality source in our society. Its continued relevance emerges even more from the pandemic crisis as revealing the context of social dynamics, showing a "differential visibility" inside the wellness professionals, associated with gender, status, and power. The attribution of "masculine" and "feminine" connotations (re)produces inequality structures: there are masculine/dominants and feminine/subordinate occupations (Cataldi & Tomatis, 2022).

1.1. Women's Employment and Income Effects From the Pandemic. According to the Economic Commission for Latin America and the Caribbean statements (CEPAL, 2022), the economic contraction source is affecting negatively the occupation and is increasing the lack of labor conditions in the region, which in the women's case represents a setback of more than 10 years in their labor market participation.

It is estimated that female unemployment would reach 22.2% in 2020, representing 12.6 pp of year-on-year variation. The largest drop in the economy occurred in the second quarter of 2020 (ECLAC, 2022), with the unemployment rates and participation impacts shown in Table 9.2, which shows Latin America

Table 9.2. Latin America and the Caribbean (10 Countries): Labor Market General Indicators, By Gender, 2020 Second Trimester (pp).

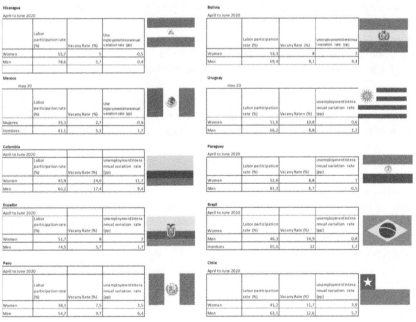

Own elaboration since CEPAL data (2022)

and the Caribbean (10 countries) with general labor market indicators by gender, the second quarter of 2020 (pp).

A GDP drop of 7.7% in Latin America and an unemployment increase of 10.4 pp would have a negative effect on household income (CEPAL, 2022). If the over-representation of women in poor households is considered, around 118 million Latin American women will live in poverty situation.

Still remains a pending Gender Economy conversation, like it is presented by Jennifer Ann Cooper in the economic research journal: Gender economy does not maintain the existence of historical and fundamental differences between men and women, and that is why does not postulate that women need a different economy than men. It does not present, either, those female economists who practice this discipline have a different economic vision from male economists, even more, those female economists have a born intuition and a special behavior to understand women's economic situation. Nevertheless, some of the female economists' concerns and findings can emerge from their own experiences they have had in the academic discrimination and in the job market or motherhood (Cooper, 2021).

A conversation about the economy and gender is missing because the author gives it a macroeconomic look when writing, in spite of who performs care work or domestic work also can question the economic sciences pretensions that, in convention, in the national accounts ignore the value of housekeeping and takes in account almost always with scarcity, selfishness, and competition, and rarely with abundance, altruism, and cooperation. The problem is that the economic theories are sexist, there are not masculine. Sexist is in the sense that there is a slant of gender in theoretical categories used and in the model supposed. The sexist slant emerges also in the thinking like, there is no difference between the economic agents. Men and women are affected in the same way by the implemented economic policies, or the domestic sector is totally flexible and adapts to any macroeconomic change, for example, in inflation or wage levels.

And is also that the economy affects all the economic agents, and is a duty for everyone, from different spheres where they are located to help and to push economic prosperity, some of them with a conscious and realistic look, others from the academic role since the transform of education.

It must be recognized that the COVID-19 pandemic has given real importance to childcare to the national economies in general and women's economic participation, which have stimulated a renewed interest in the childcare policy in many of the countries that have implanted lockdowns, that's why the women, that gave the greatest part of the unpaid care, they lost their jobs because of attention demands, and also the struggled to access to necessities, and some of them reporting increased personal insecurity. Those who tried to work from home also experienced guilty feelings and distress trying to handle the triple occupation (Smith, 2022).

1.2. Colombian Economic Context. The COVID-19 crisis has had main consequences for the population, especially, the mitigation measures that affected the labor force structure stopping a huge quantity of economic activities during the lockdown periods and increasing the unpaid necessities of house care.

In this context, it was an income and human livings contraction; especially for those employees of the intensive economic sectors in physical attendance and for those sectors that could not do telecommuting of the nature of their labor (DANE, 2022d). The last century's economic crises had reflected recessions that impacted at a higher level the men's employment, that is because those are employed by sectors where the jobs are unstable or as the economy calls cyclical employment.

Facing the DANE analysis, in the gender perspective analysis, women are 51% of the working-age population, but in the reality, those are the less-occupied people: before the pandemic 41.4% of the occupied people. At the end of 2020, this percentage became 39.3%. Other indicators shown by the study reveal the gender gap: In 2018, 78.6% of the manufacturing companies were managed by men and 24.1% were managed by women. Wage gap: employed women with labor income received 12.9% less than men in their labor income by 2019 (DANE, 2021).

In the same referent under vertical segregation, where it admits the men and women inequality distribution in the hierarchical scale, concentrating female jobs in lower scales. By 2019, women represented 94% of the working-age population occupied in the domestic service and 76.6% of them were occupied, but they did not have a payment. In the domestic jobs and the unpaid workers are concentrated, respectively, 7.0% and 5.7% occupied women in 2019, and 0.3% and 2.3% are men occupied in this sector.

In Table 9.3, we can see vertical segregation, which shows that women are in some of the activity sectors and in some occupations where the distribution between men and women remains.

According to DANE (2022) and how as shown in Table 9.4, the unemployment rate in 2020 for women was 20.4%; meanwhile, the men's rate was 12.7%, which shows a gap gender of 7.7 pp. Facing 2019, the women's unemployment gap increased by 7.7 pp, and for men by 5.4 pp. This confirms that the pandemic affected in higher level the women jobs offer.

On the other side, how as shown in Table 9.5, the unoccupied population, also was impacted by the COVID-19 pandemic with a strong increase, since in 2019 the unemployment women percentage was 46.9%, and in 2020 was 51.9%. In men's case, the inactive percentage went from 26.1% in 2019 to 29.2% in 2020. So, the direct effect was a setback in gender equality advances, mainly in the employment gap between men and women.

The Colombian argue, starting with the economic context, the gender approach aims to identify and characterize the contextual particularities and

Table 9.3. Women and Men Distribution by Some Occupations and Sectors.

Year	Occupied Women in Commerce, Public Administration, Defense, Education and Health	Occupied Men in Commerce, Public Administration, Defense, Education and Health
2019	53.30%	29.80%
2020	53.00%	29.30%

Source: Own elaboration according to DANE data (2021).

Table 9.4.   Colombia Unemployment Gap in 2020 by Gender.

Tasa de desempleo año 2020, por género

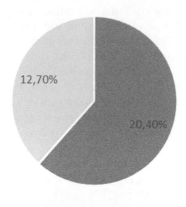

■ Mujeres   ▨ Hombres

Own elaboration according to DANE data (2021).

living situations faced by the people according to their sex and social constructs related to sex, with their implications and economic, political, psychological, cultural and legal differences, identifying discrimination gaps and patterns (DANE, 2022e).

According to what has been presented, in the Colombian economic context, we cannot leave aside the change that has had the care time during the pandemic since the gender gaps, there has been adverse effects on time, meanly in women.

According to the national administrative department of statistics (DANE), the unemployment rate by 2020 is the highest that has been presented in the last decade. For women, this rate was 20.4%, and for men 12.7%, which shows a gender gap of 7.7pp. By 2019, the women's unemployment rate increased 7.7 pp, and for men 5.4, which confirms that the pandemic has impacted a higher level the women employment offers. On the other hand, the number of people outside the labor force, called inactive people, was also seriously impacted by the COVID-19 pandemic. While in 2019, the women percentage outside the labor force was 46.9%, by 2020 was 51.9. A reversal in progress toward gender equality can be observed in labor market indicators, mainly in the employment gap between men and women. This gap has been falling in the last years, however, by 2020 it became at the same level as in 2011 (DANE, 2021).

From the same source or the same context according to the WWB foundation and the Women Equity Observatory (2020), COVID-19 revealed and aggravated the deepest inequality in care work, carried out mainly by women. Above all, because all the pandemic effects had been differentiated. In Colombia, before the pandemic nine of 10 women carried out care work. By June 2020, the number of women carrying out care work increased by 1.6 million compared to 2019, obtaining a total of 7.1 million of seven women compared to only 999.000 men (WWB foundation and the Women Equity Observatory, 2020).

As can be seen, the men and women labor market was highly affected by the COVID-19 pandemic; where the women employment suffered the highest affectation, added to women lost employment because they were in the most affected sectors, like child care, education, it is necessary and urgent to redistributed the home kipping into the different actors that compose the families, the state, the market and inside the society.

In the time care report during the COVID-19 pandemic, how much changed the gender gap, the authors highlight, one of the syntheses where they state, that the figures presented in it, show that care burdens fall on only one sex and are accentuated considering the labor market situation and the geographical region of residence. Therefore, it results very important to create new public policies focused on gender, which reduces the Unpaid Domestic and Care Work (UDCW) of the homes, also it is important to take an account the dynamics and care necessities of each region, after COVID-19. The UDCW job reduction would help women and we would hope to see the positive effects in terms of the recovery of female employment, which has been the highest affected by the COVID-19 health emergency (Tribin, 2021).

According to DANE, since 2018, the gender gap in the labor area has been decreasing, because in that year women obtained an unemployment rate of 14% showing a –6.2 pp gap. By 2019, the gap decreased slightly reaching –5.8 pp, for that time women had unemployment of 13.9% while men were 8.1%.

However, when the pandemic came, the little ground that had gained by the female gender got lost and increased the gender gap. Men reached an unemployment rate of 11.1%, while women 19.6%, which gave a gap of –8.4 for the last 2020 moving trimester.

According to DANE in November 2021–January 2022 moving trimester, the activity areas with the highest number of employed women were Commerce and vehicles repair (1,813,000 of women), Public and defense administration, education and human health care (1,509,000 of women) and artistic activities,

Table 9.5.   Inactive Population Impacted by COVID-19 Pandemic.

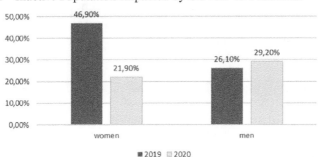

Source: Own elaboration according to DANE data (2021).

entertainment, recreation and other services activities (1,131,000 of women). One of the latest DANE reports assures that by sex, the country reports an increase of 671,000 occupied men and 913,000 occupied women. Thus, the unemployment index stayed at for the first month of the year in 11.2% for men and 19.4% for women (DANE, 2022f).

By August 2022, the total national unemployment gap was 10.6%, by sex and age ranges, the country employment-population increment by the quarter between June and August 2022 was focused on women (+804,000) and men (+329,000) from the 25 to 54 years old. These variations were statistically significant (DANE, 2022).

According to previously given data, inside the Colombian context appears an imbalance when talking about gender, equity, and economy, with the COVID-19 pandemic women in the labor market are the most affected, the unemployment remains deeper in women, a regression in the advances toward gender equality is denoted in the indicators of this market, mainly by the men and women gap. This gap has been decreasing in the last few years, but in 2020 came to the same level as in 2011, and was female employment that suffered the affectations. If it is important to continue approaching ground into this topic and also to stimulate the growth, we need to work on inclusion, women give new aptitudes to the work, the productivity, and the developing advantages. The different women's occupation modalities must be a priority in public policies, these unified relationships between men and women with the productive process participation and organization with the so-called care economy unpaid that increases during the crisis periods, will be a step forward into the crisis to advance in economic and social terms.

2. Challenges and Opportunities in Terms of Gender Equality Presented by Colombian Economic Analysis in a Latin American Context

When talking about challenges and opportunities, it premises that women's entry into the labor market involves a better individual and family situation, however a better economic situation, it begins supposing that men and women participation gaps are generated by the GDP, transforming into an opportunity and a challenge, since it is necessary to think in policies that point to the structure and productive orientation, and that allow demand factors conducting to an equality development, whereby in this point we must take a look to incorporate the care economy into the economic measurement versus what it has found about the time used in the national survey and in the gender poverty indicators and their effects above the population life quality improvements:

• The care economy incorporated into the growing economic measurement.

One variable that must be checked could have an impact on economic growth, like is the care economy, that is how in ILO the care economy is growing in a way that is increasing the child care and the elderly demands from all the regions, so it will be an employment increase in the future years; nevertheless, the care work still remains characterized by the lack of benefits and protections, by low salaries or an un-payment, and for mental and physical risk damages, and in some cases, sexual abuse. It is an obvious requirement for the creation of new solutions for care work on two fronts: in regards to nature and care policies and services facilitation, and in work care conditions terms (International Labor Organization, s.f.)

This is how it is held within the UN political framework, aligned with the SDGs where we have visualized three that point to a horizon in common well-being and growth: SDG5: Gender Equality; SDG8: Decent work and economic growth; SDG10: Inequality reduction; and SDG3: health and wellness.

It has been talked about how to achieve economic growth, and the richness of a country, with the care economy incorporation in the measurement of this growth, it can establish through investment care work policies, which generates employment. In the medium and long term, the care sector's investment will offer positive effects, where these men and women activities generate, without being implicit in the costs or benefits of these activities. About the labor force's educational level, why not think about learning plans, and education for those who work in the care sector and are paid, it will increase their labor capacities, their salaries, and productivity. Shared with the sector regulation and formalization it would have an effect on the system retirement and social protection, thinking about the women's safety and their future.

This is how the women's observatory gives their statement: Investing into the care economy contributes to the productive structure diversification, not damaging the ecological limits of reproduction, which permits a natural heritage efficient management and guarantees sustainable life. The work care conception since a transversal and articulated perspective on modern societies is one of the female greatest givens, reflected by homes and the communities in labor force reproduction, like market activities, employment and public services. This integral approach, which integrates the economic system, and the social organization defines the care economy as a goods space, services, activities, relations, and relative values for the existence and the human being's reproduction. In that order, the care economy contains the whole work that is made by an unpaid way into homes and workplaces that are paid in the labor market (Observatorio de Igualdad de Género, 2020).

When the book *Quién le Hacía la Cena a Adam Smith* is read, the economy's father, shows the life sustainment importance into care, maybe Adam Smith, like everyone considers himself as an economic system externality, making invisible his economy and society input.

The experts affirm that a structural change can be accelerated by equality. And why not with care job equality? It is important to retake Santiago Compromise where reunited governments approved this compromise in XIV Conferencia Regional sobre la Mujer de América Latina y el Caribe, where was situated the governments' importance to do policies, promote normative framework, which energizes the clue economic sectors, included the care economy; counting the multiplier effects that increase the care economy in women labor participation, wellness, redistribution, economic growing and, care economic macroeconomic impact terms; and to design a care integral system, since a gender perspective, intersectionality, and intercultural and, human rights that promote the co-responsibility between women and men, state, market, families, and community, and to include time, resources, benefits and public services in articulated policies, to satisfied different population care necessities, like a social protective system piece (CEPAL, 2021).

Countries like Argentina, the domestic work and non-paid care work distribution is unequal: 9 of 10 women made these duties, which means 6.4 hours per day. They dedicated to this work three times more than men. This contributes to women's labor market occupation being less than men's. Also affects that women have more precarious jobs, which implies a social protection lack; for example, not having access to social work and, in the future, it is difficult to obtain a retirement, because they don't have contributions to have it. The women have a high level of unemployment, they earn less and, consequently, are poorer. In this sense, we need to understand that unpaid work conditions are directly related to how unpaid duties are resolved. In this task, the UDCW participation in the pandemic GDP is 21.8% and shows an increase of 5.9pp respected to the non-time pandemic measurement. The highest UDCW GDP weight is explained by two phenomena: on one side, the scholarship homework and the non-paid care work and, on the other side, a drop of 14 of the 16 remaining activities (such as agriculture, cattle raising, hunting, and forestry) (Mercedes D'Alessandro, 2020).

Checking the care work input, it is important to visualize, give a value and, quantify their input since the hour's quantity demand in care activities, still in post-pandemic, also is not being recognized as a productive area and not integrate analysis models, and not appear their input into the economy, and it must be important to the whole economy operation.

• The National Time Use Survey (NTUS) and its findings.

This part presents the NTUS. It permits to identify the people's duties, counting the minutes and the hours over a period of 24 hours, also this survey permits to identify how much time the people dedicated to care economy work: people care and house kipping, in this writing, the women:

A way to identify how is the Colombian gender gap in the labor market, is to check the NTUS, which is a DANE research developed from September 2021 to August 2021, in comparison to the same period 2016–2017.

Between September 2020 and August 2021, on a national level, women dedicated to unpaid work an average of 7 hours and 46 minutes per day, and men 3 hours and 6 minutes (DANE, 2021).

This survey has its origins in law 1413 of 2010, which establishes the care economy inclusion into the national accounts system in order to obtain the women's contribution measurement into economic and social country development and, also like a definition and an implementation to a public policy tool.

According to this survey by the time September 2020 and August 2021, 53.3% of the men participated in the National Account System work activities, while only 29.9% of the women participated in it.

By the time between September 2020 and August 2021, the paid work time dedicated by men is higher by 1 hour and 20 minutes than women. In exchange, the dedicated one-day time women's unpaid work is higher than men's in 4 hours and 40 minutes. The global duties indicator shows the dedicated time for a person to work activities. It shows that women's home care duties by the time from September 2020 and August 2021, it is almost 3 hours higher than men's. This difference is almost an hour more than found by the ENUT 2016–2017 in the same period (DANE, 2021).

According to Table 9.6, despite domestic duties and housekeeping perception compared to what was found in the ENUT 2016–2017 and September 2020 and August 2021 period, the percentage got down, but the gender gap persists in the unpaid work.

Into the Latin American context by the Colombian equity gender inside the challenges and opportunities economic analysis, the care economy incorporation into the economic measurement and the NTUS was covered in the last paragraphs. Now it will check the poverty indicators by gender and their effects on the population quality of life, if there is an ideal to create a better world, as it was said in the 2030 agenda, about sustainable development, and for Colombian, Latino America, and to the whole world is an opportunity to try to improve the life of all the human beings. The Sustainable Development Objectives are allied to eliminate the poverty, the women inequality, to improve the environmental care, in consequence, to understand the labor market consequences. It is necessary to consider the relations between the two work sectors and, mainly, the work domestic logic.

- The poverty indicators by gender and their life quality population improvement effects.

Before mentioning this idea, it is important to state that, the gender indicators let to measure the projects, programs, and equity gender impacts. And its main function is to show and point out the gender and relationship changes, they measure basically: at which level do women and men participate in projects or programs, and if the gender discrimination had been eliminated, which is the central project purpose.

Table 9.6. Home Duties and House Kipping, ENUT.

ENUT Period		
September 2016 to August 2017		**September 2020 to August 2021**
Men	23.30%	13.20%
Women	10.60%	6%

Source: Own elaboration since DANE Technician Bulletin Data (2021).

This is how it is found a literature quantity indicator with a gender perspective like for example, the worker women percentage in an institution related to the men number in the same place. The monthly expenditure average between men and women; or gender perspective quantity indicators like the women's capacity to manage resources perception (administrative or legal duties; to present and elaborate projects) the condom use in their relationships (Salas, s.f.)

The poverty seen by the gender perspective states that women are poor for discrimination reasons. Women participate in a subordinated character in society, for example, the low access to their economic, social, and political resources management. Their principal economical resource is the work payment, which is obtained in inequality conditions, since the present work gender division where the women take exclusively the domestic care and the child care, and the traditional ways persistence and, the new discrimination to women's entry and permanence into the labor market. Even though the women's conditions are not the same in Latin America in none of the countries, the income between men and women is equal: the existence of a huge occupational segmentation, vertical and horizontal, it makes that women don't get the same positions as men and also the access denied to superior occupations in the same level as men. Into this, it juxtaposes essential visions that located women's characteristics in an inferior situation related to men, leaving their potential in reproduction duties (Arriagada, 2005).

Inside the millennium objectives and the sustainable development objectives, the third objective says: to promote gender equity and women's autonomy, Colombia has defined seven indicators, of which five are selected for this assignment, national goal: to achieve gender equity and women's autonomy, with these indicators: are affirmative actions to increase the women occupation proportion into the executive and legal power in levels 1 and 2, in national territorial level 29; to reduce 3 pp the unemployment gap (to reduce the unemployment at 8.5 and to reduce the informality rate at 45%) and to reduce to 18% the monthly average income gap (Programa de las Naciones Unidas para el Desarrollo, PNUD, 2017).

It is presented some Colombian indicators, from general to extremely monetary poverty by gender, according to the latest data, DANE:

By 2021, the national total monetary poverty was 39.3% and the extremely monetary poverty was 12.2%, by the same way in 2021, the multidimensional poverty was 16.0% 2.1 pp less than in 2020 (18.1%) (DANE, 2022).

The monetary and extremely poverty gender gap related to the household head, sex, and age group has a higher prevalence between 10 and 18 years old, with 27.9 pp and 30.4 pp, respectively. In the gender focus by 2021, the monetary poverty incidences since house care was 37.0% for men and 42.9% for women, showing a difference of 5.9 pp (DANE, 2022).

The foregoing leaves a perspective that checking the Colombian monetary poverty indicator, the highest percentage is located in women, 5.9 pp more than men related to women's quality of life, being part of multidimensional poverty, which has a direct relation to the quality of life, that affects men and women, according to this data.

3. The Economic Analysis Advantages to Incorporate the Gender Perspective

The gap between gender experiences similarities and their economic effect suggests the public politic answers to recuperate and prepare with this knowledge and support, since the women absorb all the care work costs, with possible negative effects on their health and wellness.

The women remain outside the economic opportunities, which is not only unfair, but also it is damage to the growth and everyone's resilience. It is known that in countries where gender inequality is higher, a lower women labor market participation in the gap decrease could be transformed by 35% economic increase. Nevertheless, the process is slow and some of the incidents, like the climate and health disasters, the social disturbs and the war, are worst in gender inequality directly affecting life and the women's subsistence manner or maintaining them apart from the school and work (Kristalina Georgieva, 2022).

How its mentioned in this chapter "Economy and Gender: a pending conversation" the economic, legal, and monetary policies can support the change, for general wellness. Its expressed, by the whole chapter that the gender gap, not only in Colombia, but also at a world level, helps new women's programs and projects policies and also into social safe networks, since the governments have new gender perspective macroeconomic measures, the emphasis must add the presented ideas, as are mentioned by the IMF blog authors:

Increase investment in women's human capital. The benefits that report to women equal access to food, healthcare, and education are especially important to developing and emerging economies. Cash transfer programs like Brazil duplicated the home lending headed by women. The IMF data about technician workers point out that, if by that moment didn't exist the emergency help the poverty rate for these families was passed from 11% to more than 30%, and in exchange, it remains around 8%. Other programs, like online technology, helped to accelerate emergency financial assistance, which supported women mainly.

Another measurement presented by the authors is that women can work outside their homes and become an entrepreneur. The tax reforms, public spending, also about the financial structure and the laws, and market labor can be useful. Give access to accessible and quality kindergarten services, liberate women to the opportunity to work, and, also, create direct jobs. In the developing and emerging economies, the access to mobile telephones and the internet gives economic opportunities. Like, the IMF shows, traditional and digital finances are contributing to finishing the gender gap, in financial services access, like the micro-loans, which converts in a low-income inequality and a higher growth.

In the economic benefits of gender inclusion document: new mechanism new evidence, the authors began with some stylized facts, comparing gender diversity and its effects on production, gender development, also a premise part:

> Probably the participation gap decrease between women and men generates important economic benefits, with two mechanisms that point to larger gains than previously thought. (Ostry, 2018a, p. 4)

In this thinking, they know about gender diversity and sector reassignment. However, when is found a macroeconomic, sectorial, and company analysis that reflects that women and men do production complementary duties, where is important the women role, it presents the advantages to reduce the gender gap:

• A mayor stimulus to the growing: since women give some new work aptitudes, the advantages in growth and productivity with a higher women labor force participation (since the gap reductions that stop the women into work) are higher than those that were thought. In fact, in our measurement exercise, we saw that, in the lower positions about gap gender countries, stopping the gap gender could increase the GDP by 35% on average. Four-fifths are the consequence of the incorporation of workers into the labor force, but the fifth part of the increase would be related to the productivity effect of gender diversification (Christine Lagarde, 2018).

A deepest analysis is presented by the gender inclusion economic benefits document: new mechanism, new evidence, and a developed key outcome, since women give new abilities in their workspace, it is probable that diversification can increase productivity. Therefore, there is beneficial nexus to productivity growth. Hence, exist a connection between the country's productivity growing grade and the country's impulse progress by the FLFP (Ostry, 2018b).

In this same document, to measure the gender diversity importance into the macro data, the economist takes the substitution elasticity concept between women and men (similar, e.g., to the substitution elasticity between capital and work). When the substitution elasticity is too high (technically, when is infinite, the general supposition in macro models), there are no diversity and company benefits that can replace a worker.

• Higher productivity: in the past when data have been interpreted and the gap gender decreased over time contributions to growth from efficiency improvements have been exaggerated (namely, the total factor productivity increases). An increased piece attributed to productivity it is because female participation has increased over time (Christine Lagarde, 2018).

The World Bank stated that, of the 190 surveyed countries, only 12 give women the same legal condition as men. Gender discrimination in social institutions costs the world economy USD 6 billion, since the Cooperation and Economic Development Organization. Nevertheless, in the last few years, the countries have reduced these costs, through social and legal measures, like child marriage restrictions, domestic violence penalties, and elected jobs occupied by women (Kristalina Georgieva, 2022).

• Reducing the gap gender produces the highest advantages at the development level: the peak into the services sector impulse by economic development helps to incorporate more women into the labor force. But our research shows that the female employment gaps stop this process. These barriers vary in the region and the country and are huge in some of the world places: could arise in a tax rate above the women's employment by 50%. And these wellness losses (considered as consumption and hobbies) are important, also if it takes an account the fact that "domestic production" decreases when women enter the labor force (Christine Lagarde, 2018).

Increase the female representation in managing occupations, the IMF analysis shows that, in higher financial institutions women's presence and higher participation in the financial policies is inseparable of high financial resilience, also in the techno financial and the entrepreneur sector, a higher female presence in responsibility occupations its link to better performance and rent profitability, respectively (Kristalina Georgieva, 2022).

This is how the IMF blog (2022) presents that women's obstacles to getting into the labor force are even more expensive, and it is possible that the benefits to close the gender gap are higher than was expected. A data number (macro and micro enological) suggested that women and men complement each other in the production process. The matter is that there is a diversity value: including more women in the labor force should obtain higher benefits than the same increase of masculine workers. This document's results also involve the standard models, which ignore the inclusion of gender in growth and wrongly attribute to technology a part of the growth caused by women's participation (Georgieva, K. El Blog de FMI, 2022).

When are pointed which were the gender equity challenges and opportunities since economic analysis in Colombia in a Latin American context, it has some analysis fronts, for example, the service increase in the developing economies must favor to reduce the gender gap, with a structural transformation; a female work gender gap elimination will create a structural transformation and would lead to a production and wellness increase (not leaving to a side the domestic production as women get into the labor force). The goals would be higher, there are some public policy suggestions that guarantee that women have the same rights to property and credit access, besides others.

Conclusions and Suggestions

- Women offer a double economy input since they study, they get into learning courses, they get into the labor market and still, they don't abandon the house kipping, on the different roles they have, being a mother, a daughter, a sister and, a spouse. The economies move into the labor force market, assuming that socially sustainable reproduction is assured, the care, the food, the clothing organization, cleanness, and, to this is added the gender pay gaps in this competitive market.
- The activities designated linked with the care economy are related to gender inequality and is characterized by having an unfair social organization, where the women do a mayor unpaid duty work of the strongest work sexual division since the economic systems origin or production standards, with the production relations and the labor force; the housework is an underrated work into

an economic model that doesn't recognize it like a value generator, besides it transforms into a non-sustainable model.

- It is imperative to compare and give value, build their work infrastructure, which is part of the care economy, like a sector that produces fundamental goods and services for the social, economic, and productive activity and to answer in a way that contributes to increasing the life quality, also it must be considerate the care as a strategic sector to decrease the gaps and increase the economic growth.
- To approach the IMF support the strategy to incorporate mechanisms that permit to identify, question, and value of women discrimination, inequality, and exclusion, in their countries' members, not only in gender policies development and improvement, but also from the economic figure, with the periodical supervision of each of the countries policies members and also to design and execute programs, fortifying the spending increase, which is destined in programs supported by the IMF, like a mayor preschool employment offer, to give easy commuting; to elaborate gender perspective budgets, in conclusion, to apply economic policies to promote women equality in all the public programs.
- It can be glimpsed that if it is orientating to apply political and financial macroeconomic policies with gender perspective it will be a better increase, higher stability and will permit economic capacities to give resistance and adaptation to the regions, since the change forces, into lower income inequality, to the hole society benefit.
- If after the pandemic, it wanted a long recuperation and to still working on the input that will have the society a participative and thriving economy, it must be taking action through inclusive growth, thinking since social corporative projection where it is important sustainability and perdurability like a prosperity objective, also with a solid growing which is a clue to decrease poverty and to embrace climate change, developing countries must be prepared to affront the most difficult world financial contexts, like those who are living in Ukraine because of the war, economic effects, some countries high rates, which makes future more complex. The law reforms, the innovation, and the investment in people will be a shared higher prosperity.

Economy and gender remain a pending conversation since the world doesn't give women and men inequality conditions importance, which converges into important economic cost and can damage countries' economic health. In the whole chapter can be seen that these costs are even higher than it has been considered and this is now where the arguments are strongly in favor of equality and gender.

References

Arriagada, I. (2005, April). *CEPAL magazine*. Dimensiones de la pobreza. https://repositorio. cepal.org/bitstream/handle/11362/11002/085101113_es.pdf?sequence=1&isAllowed=y
Banco Mundial. (2021, October 27). Hacia la construcción de una sociedad equitativa en Colombia. https://www.bancomundial.org/es/news/infographic/2021/10/27/hacia-la-construccion-de-una-sociedad-equitativa-en-colombia

Cataldi, L., & Tomatis, F. (2022). Gender and professionalism: Still a black box a call for research, debate and action. Suggestions from and beyond the pandemic crisis. *Organization.* https://doi.org/10.1177/13505084221115835

CEPAL. (2022). *La autonomía económica de las mujeres en la recuperación sostenible y con igualdad.* Informe especial COVID-19. https://repositorio.cepal.org/bitstream/handle/11362/46633/5/S2000740_es.pdf

CEPAL, O. M. (2021, February). *Compromiso de Santiago: Un instrumento regional para dar respuesta a la crisis del COVID-19 con igualdad de género.* https://repositorio.cepal.org/bitstream/handle/11362/46658/1/S2100047_es.pdf

Christine Lagarde, J. D. (2018, November 18). Las ventajas económicas de la inclusión de género: Aun mayores de lo que se pensaba. https://www.imf.org/es/Blogs/Articles/2018/11/28/blog-economic-gains-from-gender-inclusion-even-greater-than-you-thought

Cooper, J. A. (2021). *Investigación económica.* https://www.scielo.org.mx/scielo.php?script=sci_arttext&pid=S0185-16672000000400013

DANE. (2021a, August). *Encuesta Nacional de Uso del Tiempo (ENUT).* https://www.dane.gov.co/index.php/estadisticas-por-tema/pobreza-y-condiciones-de-vida/encuesta-nacional-del-uso-del-tiempo-enut

DANE. (2021b, November 18). Technical Bulletin. Encuesta Nacional de Uso del Tiempo (ENUT). https://img.lalr.co/cms/2021/11/18163828/Bolet%C3%ADn-ENUT.pdf

DANE. (2022a, March 8). *Enfoques Género.*

DANE. (2022b). *El tiempo de cuidado durante la pandemia del Covid-19: ¿cuánto han cambiado las brechas de género?* Diciembre de 2022. https://www.dane.gov.co/files/investigaciones/genero/publicaciones/informe-tiempo-de-cuidado-durante-pandemia-COVID-19.pdf

DANE. (2022c, September). *Indicadores de mercado laboral.*

DANE. (2022d, June 2). Pobreza monetaria 2021. https://www.dane.gov.co/files/investigaciones/condiciones_vida/pobreza/2021/CP-pobreza-monetaria-con-enfoque-diferencial.pdf

DANE. (2022e, April 26). Pobreza monetaria y pobreza monetaria extrema. https://www.dane.gov.co/index.php/estadisticas-por-tema/pobreza-y-condiciones-de-vida/pobreza-monetaria

DANE. (2022f, April 28). Pobreza multidimensional. https://www.dane.gov.co/index.php/estadisticas-por-tema/pobreza-y-condiciones-de-vida/pobreza-multidimensional

DANE. (2022g, April 28). Pobreza multidimensional 2021. https://www.dane.gov.co/files/investigaciones/condiciones_vida/pobreza/2021/cp_pobreza_multidimensional_21.pdf

Fondo Monetario Internacional (FMI). (2013). Las mujeres, el trabajo y la economía: Beneficios macroeconómicos de la equidad de género. Estados Unidos. https://www.igualdadenlaempresa.es/recursos/webgrafia/docs/Las_mujeres_el_trabajo_y-FMI.pdf

Georgieva, K. (2022, September 8). Cómo cerrar la brecha de género y hacer crecer la economía mundial. https://www.imf.org/es/News/Articles/2022/09/08/blog-md-how-to-close-gender-gaps-and-grow-economy

Grupo de enfoque Diferencial e Interseccional. (2021a, March 10). *DANE.* https://www.dane.gov.co/files/investigaciones/genero/presentacion-poblacion-fuera-de-la-fuerza-laboral-en-Colombia.pdf

Grupo de Enfoque Diferencial e Interseccional. (2021b, December). *El tiempo de cuidado durante la pandemia del Covid -19.* https://www.dane.gov.co/files/investigaciones/genero/publicaciones/informe-tiempo-de-cuidado-durante-pandemia-COVID-19.pdf

Jiménez, R. (2020). Cambios en los patrones culturales machistas. https://www.scielo.cl/scielo.php?pid=S0718-73782020000200017&script=sci_arttext

156 *Gloria Nancy Ríos and Laura Andrea Cristancho*

OIT. (2022). América Latina y Caribe: Políticas de igualdad de género y mercado de trabajo durante la pandemia. Nota técnica. https://www.ilo.org/wcmsp5/groups/public/--americas/--ro-lima/documents/publication/wcms_838520.pdf

Ostry, J. D. (2018a, November). *Economic benefits of gender inclusion: New mechanisms new evidence*. https://www.imf.org/es/Blogs/Articles/2018/11/28/blog-economic-gains-from-gender-inclusion-even-greater-than-you-thoughthttps://www.uv.es/uvweb/master-politica-economica-economia-publica/es/blog/beneficios-igualdad-genero-economia-1285949223224/GasetaRece

Ostry, J. D. (2018b, October). *Economic gains from gender inclusion*. file:///C:/Users/Usuario/Desktop/provisional/SDN1806.pdf

Smith, J. (2022). From "nobody's clapping for us" to "bad moms": COVID-19 and the circle of childcare in Canada. *Gender, Work and Organization, 29*(1), 353–367. doi:10.1111/gwao.12758

Women in connection. (2020, September). https://womeninconnection.co/biblioteca/presentacion-juan-daniel-oviedo-division-sexual-del-trabajo-en-colombia-un-analisis-desde-las-estadisticas-oficiales/

Index